Ecclesiastical
Embroidery

Beryl Dean

ECCLESIASTICAL EMBROIDERY

B. T. BATSFORD LTD
LONDON

ISBN 0 7134 6252 3

Printed in Great Britain by
The Bath Press, Avon
for the publishers
B. T. Batsford Ltd
4 Fitzhardinge Street
London W1H 0AH

To
M.E.G.T.

Preface to the sixth edition

Thirty-four years, six editions and several books later, I look back to my reaction of incredulous horror on being approached concerning the possibility of writing a book about church embroidery. This is that book, unchanged.

Earlier I had decided to concentrate exclusively upon trying to regenerate ecclesiastical embroidery which had, creatively, degenerated into an entirely atrophied state. I aimed to infuse this aspect of the subject with something of the inspiration found in secular work at the time. But there was nothing up-to-date to base it on – nothing to start from. When struggling with the preparation of this book I well remember searching for modern, well-designed examples. There simply were none in this country. However, interesting work was being done in Europe. I located some pieces and was able to use them as illustrations. For the rest, certain examples which I had been commissioned to carry out for the Needlework Development Scheme (its loss is still lamented) were reproduced, and I depended upon the work done by my students to illustrate points written about in the text.

Our ecclesiastical embroidery course at what was then Hammersmith School of Art (1955) was pioneered by Dorothy Allsopp. With her support, and taught by me, it progressed and many members of those classes are still producing vestments and furnishings, some professionally, some as amateurs.

From those beginnings, it is interesting to compare church embroidery then and now. Large schemes have been designed and carried out for Cathedrals and churches which are recognised as works of art; and there are more modest pieces, well designed and produced, which can be seen everywhere. All are represented in the many exhibitions continually held; this helps to raise the general standard through familiarity. The teaching of the subject is now general and recognised, and there are many lectures. The number of books on all aspects of church embroidery has proliferated. But the most encouraging result of the activity through all those years is found in the setting up of groups of people working under the direction of a trained professional designer, who produce ecclesiastical embroidery of a high standard for their own churches.

Beryl Dean
April 1989

ACKNOWLEDGMENT

To Miss Judith Scott, Secretary of the Central Council for the Care of Churches, I want to acknowledge my indebtedness for reading the manuscript and making many corrections and suggestions. I wish to thank Dr. J. E. Lawe for the care, patience and time he has devoted to photographing the embroidery done by members of my class and myself. Miss D. M. Pattenden has most generously given me advice which is the result of her wide practical experience. To the Benedictines of Prinknash Abbey I am especially grateful for their valuable assistance. Too many to mention individually are those whose kindness and help has made possible this book; to them all and to Miss Dorothy Allsopp, Mrs. Eivor Fisher and Mr. Louis Osman who read through and made suggestions relating to the references to architecture and also supplied fig. V (a), and to Mrs. M. Rice for her contribution to the sections on Lettering and Heraldry, I offer very sincere gratitude.

The Author and Publishers would also like to extend their grateful thanks to L'Art d'Église, Bruges, for fig. VI (d); Casadio, Ravenna, for fig. VII (b); Lionel E. Day, Historic Churches Preservation Trust, for fig. XXIV (b); The Dean and Chapter of Durham Cathedral for figs. III (a) and (b); The Dean and Chapter of Westminster Abbey for fig. III (c); The Embroiderers' Guild Collection for figs. XXV (a), (b) and (c); The Hammersmith L.C.C. College of Art and Building for figs. IX (a), (b), (c), (d), X (a), (b), (c), (d), (e), (f) and XI (a), (b), (c), (d), (e) and (f); Historical Museum, Berne, for figs. XXI (a) and (b); David Holt and Gerald Holtom Ltd. for fig. XXII (a); the Rev. Douglass Hopkins, Rector, Weston Favell, for fig. XXIII (a); Fr. Gertrudis Huber, Freiburg, for fig. XXVI (e); Fr. Lydia Jungmann, Cologne, for fig. XXVII (b), top right-hand corner; Kloster St. Ursula, Augsburg, for figs. XXII (b), XXIII (b) and XXXII; Sister M. Theodata Koch, Kloster Siessen, and Fr. Lisel Lechner, Augsburg, for fig. XXXI (a); Libraria, Stockholm, for figs. VI (a), (b), (c) and XXVIII (c); Museo Nationale, Ravenna, fig. VII (b); Needlework Development Scheme for fig. XXXI (b) and XX (a) and (b); George G. Pace, F.S.A., F.R.I.B.A., for figs. I (b), V (b), XXVIII (a) and XXX (b); Pennsylvania State University for fig. XIX (a); Pontifical Commissione de Archeologia Sacra for fig. VIII (b); Presses Universitaires de France for fig. XV from *Broderies Religieuses de Style Byzantin* by Gabriel Millet; The Rector, Axbridge, for fig. IV (a); Société Immobilière de Notre Dame du Haut for fig. I (a); Schweizer Heimatwerk, Zürich, for fig. XXIII (a); Victoria and Albert Museum, London, for figs. II, VII (a), VIII (a), XIV (c) and XXIV (a); Wilh. Wefers, Cologne, for fig. VI (e); Sofia Widen for figs. XIX (a) and XXVIII (b).

CONTENTS

LIST OF ILLUSTRATIONS

The numerals in parentheses in the text refer to
the *figure and plate numbers* of the illustrations

THE PLATES

LINE DRAWINGS IN THE TEXT

CHAPTER ONE

APPROACH THROUGH THE PAST

In the endeavour to create the perfect setting for corporate worship, there has been in each age a unity of intention expressed through the visual arts. Thus embroidery, by its small but important contribution, becomes one of the subordinate minor arts, to be studied in this context, through its relation to, and interdependence upon, church architecture.

Since the characteristics of the present have evolved out of the past, the following introduction, which must of necessity be brief, may be of interest, if only to explain, in part, some of the causes for the changes which sacred embroidery has undergone.

The secret gatherings of Christians in rooms or chapels were superseded from 312 onwards by public services at which specially enriched versions of the costume of the Roman citizen could be openly worn by the Celebrant at the Eucharist, in 330 Constantine gave a golden cloth cloak to a church in Jerusalem for use at Easter. The conversion of some temples into churches has a parallel in the gradual adaptation and the absorption of the pagan into the early Christian symbols. Likewise, from the dress of the times have derived and developed the shapes of the Eucharistic vestments and also some characteristics of decoration, such as the clavi on the dalmatic and tunicle.

The great Byzantine churches with their magnificently decorated interiors culminating in the richness of the apse, where the translucent mosaics beautify and instruct, prove the fusion of Roman materialism with the spirituality of the Christians, and reflect the awe and passionate sincerity of the early Eastern Church. From the figures and scenes depicted in later extant examples (which are in the tradition of the earlier work) can be recalled the type and shapes and decoration from which later forms of vestment have developed. The grandeur of the architecture is exemplified in the restrained richness of the embroidery; although much of the patterning must have been woven, there is every reason for supposing that a great deal was stitchery with added jewels and couched gold used in various decorative ways.

It seems, from the sparse evidence, that the vigour of the Romanesque style was transmitted to embroidery. In this country it took time, from the sixth century onwards, for churches to become established and for vestments to be required.

Certainly the same spiritual fervour which activated the planners and builders of the great Gothic cathedrals, churches and abbeys also influenced the designers and embroiderers of vestments in Europe and especially in Britain; where the established gold work of the Eastern Church would probably have been known, and where the already existing tradition of fine workmanship had stemmed from the Eastern Church, to be seen, for example, in portions of a stole and maniple from St. Cuthbert's tomb at Durham, worked between A.D. 905–916; also in the vestments of St. Thomas Becket at Sens, and the Worcester fragments, they foreshadow and were prior to the actual **Opus Anglicanum** period (1250–1350), which coincides with the finest architectural and artistic achievements (Canterbury, Lincoln and Salisbury cathedrals were complete). The reputation for perfection attained by this English embroidery caused it to be famed throughout the Continent. There are records showing that successive Popes specifically commissioned and were given copes and vestments of English origin.

1   *The Jesse Cope*

To this great era of church embroidery belong certain essential **characteristics.**

There is a general similarity between **the design** of the embroidery and that of the illuminated manuscripts and missals, for example the Books of Kells, Lindisfarne Gospels and Winchester Bible, St. Mary's Psalter, which indicates, in some instances, a common source; the earlier type of embroidery design (adapted in various ways) shows figures enclosed by foliated scrolls. The Jesse cope, which is mainly gold work on red twill weave fabric, is an example preserved in the Victoria and Albert Museum (1). In the same museum is the blue chasuble, the designs of which exemplify the restraint and spiritual sincerity which was later lost.

At the end of the thirteenth century it is typical for the backgrounds either to be covered with large circles containing groups of figures as in the Ascoli Piceno cope (2), which still has the small triangular hood attached. Or the ground may be divided into quatrefoils, containing the figures of saints with six winged angels (the peacock feathers being prominent symbols) standing on wheels filling the intervening spaces. The Syon cope and the cope in the Vatican Museum (3) which is worked upon red twill in gold and colours resembles the Syon but is in

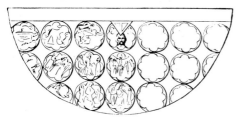

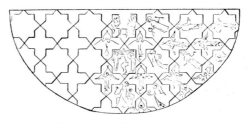

2 *The Ascoli Piceno Cope*   3 *The Cope in the Vatican Museum*

every way finer, both are examples. The Steeple Aston cope, later cut into its present form of dossal and frontal, belongs also to this period.

During the first half of the fourteenth century the design was based upon arcading arranged to radiate from the centre. The close link with the peculiarly English Perpendicular style of architecture is evident. There are meticulously observed birds or figures embroidered in the spandrels, and grouped figures fill

4 *Cope of St. Sylvester*

the spaces depicting incidents in Biblical history or in the life of the Virgin Mary. Typical is the cope (4) formerly in the St. John Lateran and now in the Vatican Museum. It has the orphrey and hood intact and is worked with a patterned gold ground. The Butler-Bowdon cope now in the Victoria and Albert Museum is of similar design, but worked upon crimson velvet. (This entailed first covering the whole with fine material on to which the design had been traced, when the embroidery, which was worked through both layers and the linen backing, was

19

complete, the fine material was cut away close to the embroidery.) As the seed pearls remain in parts it is possible to appreciate something of its original wonderful richness and to visualise it being worn in the setting of soaring Gothic arches contemporary with its creation, remembering always that there was glowing colour on stone (Sainte Chapelle) and wood (some of the churches in East Anglia still retain original painted and gilded woodwork) and glass (Chartres, Fairford, Gloucestershire).

Another remarkable example of about 1300 in the Victoria and Albert Museum is the panel depicting Christ Enthroned, with one hand resting upon an orb, inscribed with the names of the continents then known. The figure, which is one of the largest early embroidered representations, is framed within an arch and surrounded by symbolic emblems.

Also characteristic of the Opus Anglicanum period (1250–1350) was the **method of treating the figures.** The heads were worked in split stitch, with spirals forming the cheeks, with large protruding eyes, high foreheads and unrealistically coloured hair (the same stitch was used for the drapery; this is dealt with in greater detail on p. 144), and the characteristic underside couching of the gold (p. 88).

Contemporary records give an impression of the wealth of vestments produced during this period, and their overwhelming glory, beauty and richness. Interesting as the Pienza cope is (a detail is given on page 145), there are signs foreshadowing the impending decline in design and craftsmanship; which was accelerated by the plague in 1348.

This has been but an outline; to have given more would have been superfluous and an imposition, following the erudition of Mrs. A. H. Christie. Her work *English Medieval Embroidery* covers the period exhaustively.

Many are the remaining examples from the latter part of the fourteenth and the fifteenth centuries. These are mainly the pillar and cross orphreys from chasubles and show how the former delicacy of treatment degenerated into clumsy ill-drawn arcading surrounding squat figures bearing no symbols by which they may be identified. The care and refinement in design and execution have gone; a heavy untwisted floss silk being used for the laid work which replaced the rows of fine split stitch; the heads were carried out in long and short stitch, and the gold, coarser than that used previously, was couched on the surface. This decline was in part due to war in Europe and at home. Materials for embroidery were difficult to obtain and prohibitively expensive, which led to economies in threads and gold by introducing powderings and scattered motifs.

However, with the slightly more general availability of velvets, beautiful brocades and damasks there was a revival and embroidery increased in interest. From the mid-fifteenth century technique developed in new ways. The nature of the materials required that the embroidered units should be worked separately on linen, which when cut out were applied to the background; the result would have been hard, had not delicate rays of gold and spangles been embroidered to break the edges.

A certain poverty of inspiration is observable in the design: the same devices were repeatedly used: the conventional lantern flower, pineapple motif, fleur-de-lis, etc., and odd units in silk appliqué, usually a pun upon the name of the donor, also figures showing the characteristics of the contemporary wood carving and sculpture and worked in laid embroidery (see Chapter X). Then there were six winged angels in abundance, which lacked the elegance of the thirteenth century, but, nevertheless decorative, they display a close parallel with the angel hammer-beams.

Frequently earlier orphreys of poor craftsmanship were applied to grounds embellished with the devices typical of the later fifteenth and early sixteenth centuries. The chasubles were generally of the fiddle-shape, to which form many of the early vestments had been cut down. Wearing apparel was often bequeathed for use in the church.

The City Company palls belong to this period (mid-fifteenth to mid-sixteenth centuries). These include the use of the silk and velvet brocades from Bruges, Ghent and Florence, to which the embroidery was of secondary importance. It shows the same grouping of the figures as can be seen on the monuments of the time (XIII), lettering and heraldry are used for their decorative values. There are examples of all these points in many churches and in the Victoria and Albert Museum, where the Worshipful Company of Saddlers' pall can be seen; it is of particular interest as it exemplifies the fate of other pre-Reformation embroideries. When it was being repaired, one of the small oval panels worked with the I.H.S. was lifted and revealed beneath the embroidered figure of the Virgin Mary, the head having been mutilated. Another example of the same time is the Chipping Campden altar set which also shows traces of a figure which has been removed.

With the Reformation great quantities of vestments were destroyed; some were burnt and the gold reclaimed. The jewels were removed from others. Records show that they were distributed and many vestments were cut up and used as wearing apparel and for furnishings. Examples at Hardwick Hall bear testimony to this. The comparatively few which escaped were further diminished with the rise of Puritanism and another wave of destruction.

Some of the medieval vestments and furnishings which remain were either hidden (e.g. the Abbeydore set) or were sent out of the country, as happened to the Syon cope, which was taken around by the nuns during their wanderings on the Continent.

Some of the embroiderers escaped to Flanders, where they continued to work using similar designs, with the substitution of the saints of the country of their adoption.

In the countries where Gothic architecture had flourished, the embroideries bore the same general characteristics as those described, yet each showed individual modifications of interpretation. The emboidery worked in Germany during this period is of particular interest, strength and variety.

The spirit of the Renaissance permeated embroidery. The intellectual and reasoned clarity shown in the planning of the inlay and applied spiral and strap-work designs carried out in satin and velvet is in direct contrast to the spirituality of the Middle Ages. The figure treatments show the classical influence.

The dependence upon architecture for the form taken by ecclesiastical embroidery is apparent both in Italian and Spanish Baroque (of which there are interesting examples in the cathedral at Palma). The nobility and elegance so easily became the florid vitality to which vestments in almost every museum, especially on the Continent, bear witness. The bountiful swags of flowers, the gold and silver work and the lace, belong to an influence which has degenerated into the meaningless decoration associated with over-high mitres, exaggeratedly large hoods and the over-wide orphreys belonging to stiff and heavy copes. Gorgeous and technically brilliant as the seventeenth- and early eighteenth-century vestments are, their appeal is generally worldly; there are even examples where raised figures were worked in a method not unlike stumpwork; also figure and architectural subjects were carried out in nué to give the maximum effect of realism.

Even the felicity and tenderness of the Rococo had an influence which can be seen in the Roman chasubles and frontals worked with delicate floral subjects intertwined with gold and silver work upon cream satin.

A cope made for the visit of Charles I to Durham in 1633 is of much interest as it shows some of the characteristics of stumpwork adapted for the powdering of embroidered motifs worked upon a dark-red satin ground. Also preserved at the cathedral are four pre-Reformation copes, all having been in use until 1759 when the wearing of the copes was discontinued as it interfered with the set of a full-bottomed wig!

At Westminster Abbey there are the wonderfully preserved copes made for

(a) *Le Corbusier's Chapelle n.-d. du haut, Ronchamp*

(b) *The Chapel of the Resurrection at University College, Ibadan, Nigeria*
(George G. Pace, architect)

The possibilities of a contemporary interior should stimulate and influence the creative embroideress

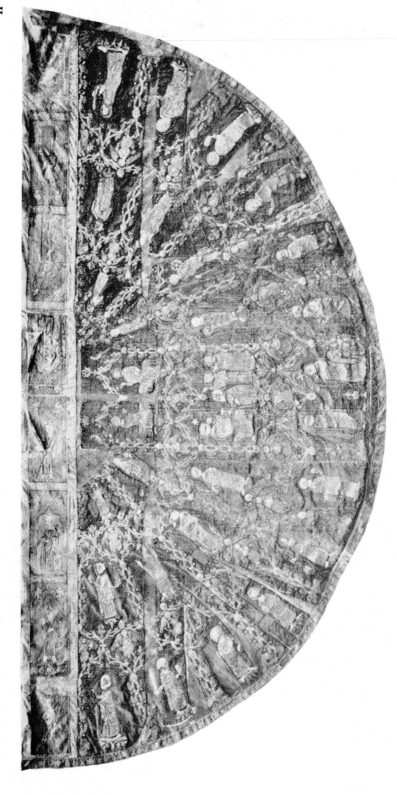

The Butler-Bowdon Cope, circa 1300. An outstanding example of the Opus Anglicanum period, worked in coloured silks, gold, silver gilt and seed pearls upon crimson velvet. Pl. VII shows a detail from the left side of the Orphrey

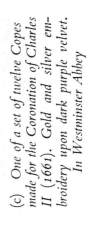

(c) One of a set of twelve Copes made for the Coronation of Charles II (1661). Gold and silver embroidery upon dark purple velvet. In Westminster Abbey

Daisy E. Edis

(a, b) Cope made for a visit of Charles I to Durham in 1633. This is an interesting example of a modified and decorative form of stump work combined with metal threads couched in colour upon the crimson satin ground. In Durham Cathedral

Left: detail of the same Cope

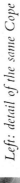

(a) *Altar Frontal at Axbridge Church, Somerset. Begun in 1720, it is worked in cross-stitch and shows an altar of the time. The designs on the top and sides are of equal interest*

(b) *A Dossal worked in silk stitchery, the background sewn with beads, dated 1698. From Weston Favell, Northamptonshire*

the coronation of Charles II. The working of the gold and silver plate over raised shapes makes for rich decoration upon the dark purple and crimson velvets.

The throw-over frontal, pulpit hanging and cushions, made, in part, from a cope belonging to Archbishop Laud, are in Staunton Harold chapel. The sacred monograms within a glory of rays, worked upon velvet, are typical; so too is the architecture of the chapel which is Laudian Gothic. Of similar design is the crimson velvet altar cover and pulpit cloth at Portsmouth Cathedral.

During the seventeenth century, to undertake the embroidering of a frontal was considered a genteel occupation; of those which still exist the one at Axbridge, Somerset, is of particular interest as it depicts a contemporary (1720) altar. Another eighteenth-century pulpit cloth of the same date as the Rococo Gothic church is at Shobdon, Herefordshire. And the frontal at Weston Favell, Northamptonshire, worked in silks and beads is outstanding. These and several other examples are known, but more may have survived the destruction of the Gothic revival; to look out for such pieces, to care and to preserve them would be a real service.

With the Gothic revival, churches, their furnishings and vestments alike, reflected the same derivative style. Although a later and excellent outcome was the effort made to bring back into use the full chasuble. But too often the decoration was imitative, for instance, when lettering was carried out in needlework it still took the form imposed by the quill, and bad variants of Lombardic and Gothic scripts were invented.

Where the direct influence of the Pre-Raphaelites was exercised, religious embroidery of real power resulted, such as the frontal designed by Philip Webb and worked by May Morris for the Deaconesses' House, Clapham Common. In it the ground is entirely covered with leaves and grapes worked in long and short and laid work in silk and crosses in couched gold, spaced at regular intervals.

There are the outstanding designers of the end of the last century onwards into this, those whose work will endure because it reflects that which was best in a great era. Pre-eminently Sir J. N. Comper, W. H. R. Blacking, Sir Walter Tapper and F. C. Eden, all architects and also designers of church embroideries, and whose sphere of activity and influence was and is wide.

Constant repetition and poor imitations of some Victorian design caused it to become outworn through familiarisation. The colours used reflected the range of the newly discovered analine dyes in the middle of the century, but there is now no reason for the liturgic colours to be limited to these particularly harsh variants.

Much religious art has become almost synonymous with the sham Gothic products: to some it seems impious to import new forms into the church, forgetting that each style was modern in its time and as it emerged met with opposition and criticism. The argument that the demand determines the type of goods available can only be met by making people conversant with good examples and to assist choice by guidance and a fuller understanding, so that more adventurous and original church furnishings, vestments and materials may be increasingly sought.

It is of even greater significance that the original concept expressed in the new churches should not be destroyed by the importation of discordant details. It is here that one realises the importance of embroidery: a tawdry desk hanging or a banner of more than the usual congealed conventionalism can shatter the visual unity, which might have been enhanced by well planned vestments and furnishings of design and colour conceived in the same spirit as the whole scheme, so ensuring that the maximum advantage be taken of a great opportunity.

The remarkable post-war renaissance of French sacred art is perhaps typified by the chapel of Notre Dame du Haut, Ronchamp, created by Le Corbusier in the material characteristic of today, reinforced concrete, its use determining the type of plasticity in the structure, massive yet light in impression. Here, with creative vision, every angle, every facet contributes something vital and of inexpressible mystery, which speaks in a living language through shafts of light from strangely shaped windows set in an obliquely sloping wall, or through the figure of the Virgin Mary high up and seen against the sky and fast-moving clouds beyond, or again in the undulating curves of roof and floor; all perfectly adapted to the demands of the liturgy. Yet there, on the well-proportioned altar could be an ill-fitting, tarnished eighteenth-century fringe-bedecked missal stand cover, instead of one embroidered to be in keeping with the spirit evoked.

Complete unity has been attained by Matisse at Vence. The straightforward sincerity of the chapel of St. Trudo Abdij, Male, St. Kruis, Bruges is completed by vestments designed to be in perfect harmony. Also the penetrating brilliance of the mosaic outside, the stained glass, and the depth of the colour illuminated by the light of the concrete-set glass of the baptistery at the church at Audincourt are but a few examples of this vital movement which has its counterpart in England. With Coventry Cathedral, Sir Basil Spence has created a symbol of the living relationship between the artist and the church to which the imagination responds. The Welch Regimental Chapel at Llandaff Cathedral is a perfect entity planned by George G. Pace; it is of particular interest to embroideresses because the frontal and kneelers (in the cathedral) have been designed as an important feature.

Further evidence of the quickening movement stirring the creativity within the sacred arts today is felt through the stained glass for Coventry Cathedral, which testifies to the vitality of the renaissance which this art has undergone. Its impact is a deeply moving and lasting experience. The significance of these and other inspired works for the church may well form an analogy with the twelfth, thirteenth and fourteenth centuries when stained glass, as at Chartres and Sainte Chapelle, and many other creative arts, flourished. With ecclesiastical embroidery the comparison at present almost ceases. There is a real danger that the embroidery may lack the imprint of the vision which has inspired the volition of the present creative movement. For this there are several reasons. The creation of works of real vitality grows out of the somewhat specialised technique and from the use of materials. Few first-rate designers have the time to acquire the skill with which themselves to create in the medium. Workers who possess the technique generally lack the artistic training and imagination to feel and be in sympathy with the intention of the designer, and thereby excitingly unconventional designs lose their spontaneity in the process of conforming to mechanical craftsmanship. Many are the designs prepared by draughtsmen who have little or no real feeling for or affinity with the possibilities of the craft; these result in dull competency. Yet the alternative is perhaps worse—experimentation with insufficient knowledge or experience to achieve a finish up to "professional" standards.

The need for a vigorous approach to ecclesiastical embroidery is acknowledged; the opportunities increase as each new church is completed, or projects are planned for older ones to which comparatively little modernisation has been done, and so much could be done in the future, given courage; which is even more important than funds. (The problem requires to be tackled judiciously, as the limiting factor is usually the existing character of the church interior, which must be acknowledged so that any new scheme accords yet does not imitate.)

Ideals are useless if there is no way of implementing them. The informed amateur can accomplish much if he or she is willing to increase the value of the service rendered to the church by freeing the mind of prejudice, attending classes and studying towards a better understanding and keeping ideas up to date by absorbing the spirit of the age, and by avoiding originality for its own sake, subordinating technique for interpretation, seeking to develop individual artistic impulses and accepting the guidance of those whose opinion is the outcome of specialised study and experience.

Ordinary members of the congregation contribute towards the realisation of an artistic ideal both as executants and, more importantly, by making the effort required to understand and appreciate the new and unfamiliar in art and design, which is never easily acceptable. They will then have a basis of knowledge upon which to form their judgement when and if a forward-looking scheme is proposed; which might otherwise be stifled by conservative prejudice.

It is a tribute to the courage of priests, parochial church councils and congregations when the imagination of creative artists is respected and they are employed to do or to guide work which is essentially their own. In the field of embroidery no less than in the sacred arts as a whole the artist craftsman or woman will have a vision beyond that of his (or her) contemporaries; his interpretation will tend therefore to be startling, and uncomfortable to the ordinary worshipper.

To be taken into account in embroidery is another important factor, that is the preferences of the individual wearer of the vestments; here again, if they have been designed and planned with knowledge, persuasion towards the acceptance of any innovation will be born of conviction.

Artists here and in Europe have been eager to take opportunities of working for the Church, but in this country creativity in the field of embroidery is almost unexplored, although there are signs everywhere of increasing interest and a desire for good design. That there is not more is in part due to the fact that those who commission, donate or receive as gifts are sometimes slow to appreciate the new and different because they have not had the opportunity to see examples nor made the effort of imagination to visualise what could be done, and so the standardised and familiar generally persists. More travelling collections of contemporary vestments, etc., combined with some explanation, might do much to further understanding.

On the Continent really good and interesting vestments have perhaps been more readily accepted. In the following chapter the intention is to try to stimulate the imagination of those who find that their technical skill becomes a handicap, and to help the creatively inclined to realise their ideas by supplying, as far as possible, the technical information required. And for those experienced craftswomen seeking to design, a way of approach is suggested. Then it is hoped that the beginner may be stimulated to develop her interest in embroidery for the church guided by the practical instructions given. Lastly, the traditionally minded who wish to continue along those lines will find that the methods of working are based on the accepted conventions.

CHAPTER TWO

DESIGN AND COLOUR

Embroidery forms an integral part of the applied sacred arts; as such it must be the best of its type obtainable. Having a vital purpose it does not depend upon being kept alive artificially—but is the design worthy? Does it bear comparison with the best architecture, sculpture, stained glass, silver smithing, wood carving, tapestry, etc., of today? Is the meaning expressed through a type of design which is a sincere reflection of the influences which affect and make it contemporary?

Observe the out-worn, out-dated types of embroidered decoration, and the answers are supplied. Reflect upon the characteristics of examples actually being worked today. The majority will still be typical of the imitative, realistic attitude which contributed to the decline in artistic culture in Central Europe in the last quarter of the nineteenth and the beginning of the twentieth centuries. The freedom of approach which was lacking has, in other forms of embroidery, been attained, but ecclesiastical embroidery has been left in its pristine isolation, almost unaffected by changes in style going on around it.

There is in this country a tradition of fine craftsmanship. This absolute technical precision is something which anyone is capable of measuring and evaluating, it is tangible and for this reason embroideries are too often judged on this score alone. The uncomprehending beholder is safe in admiring perfection of stitchery, which is sterile. The work as an artistic entity is, all too often, of secondary importance in this absorption with technical detail, and the germs of a really creative contribution may go altogether unobserved and uncommended.

Yet, if equal consideration and constructive thought were accorded to the design, and the liaison between the designer and the executant were encouraged and strengthened through a greater understanding of the idiom of today, works of real artistic worth would be demanded and created as they were in the Opus Anglicanum period, and they would be worthy of their service to religion and of our heritage.

The fundamental ideal is for the creative artist to possess the requisite skill, knowledge and experience to carry out or direct the fulfilment of her own ideas. In Sweden, Germany and Belgium, for example, there are such workrooms where vestments, altar furnishings and banners of artistic integrity, with a sincere and contemporary approach to the design, embroidery, materials, finish and mounting, are produced, proving that it is possible.

It is still argued that such a practice is not generally economically possible.

31

Because of the resultant saving in time and consequently cost and while there is a demand such commonplace vestments as typified in fig. 13d are condoned and repeated. Though extremes of vulgarity are rare in this country, a poverty of artistic inspiration is fairly general.

A partial but not a perfect solution is to be found in the design prepared either by an established designer or the architect and then professionally executed. This results in a thoroughly competent, liturgical and well-balanced but often very conventional approach; in the end it is a drawing in line and flat colour but substituting outlining cords and pieces of applied material, the whole lacking the inherent qualities peculiar to the craft of embroidery. Another reason why some of the more imaginative and ingenious ideas drawn out on paper fail to materialise is through their impracticability, due to a lack of understanding of the technical processes and limitations of the medium. A further cause of disappointing finished results rests in the executant's inability to visualise or appreciate the designer's intention, so missing the idea in the practical translation. Frequently the time required to think out fully the realisation of an individual commission would be impossible as a commercial proposition.

The amateur (to a great extent relieved of the limitations imposed by the observance of the time factor and profit margin) in her labour of devotion, no less than the professional worker, will gain immeasurably by an appreciation of and an ability to design. Understanding leads to acceptance and ultimately the putting into practice of ideas current at the time. But if only the mannerisms of modern art trends are affected, insincerity and artistic worthlessness result.

It is impossible to give a formula or even "useful tips and hints" as a short cut to designing. All too often a technically proficient adult's critical judgement has progressed beyond her ability to design, and she measures her attainments against highly sophisticated works, without realising the value of attempts which would bear the stamp of her own individuality. Whether latent or active there is some degree of natural artistic activity inherent in everyone; if it can be encouraged and guided a sense of pattern will develop. This might be further activated into a desire to try out some ideas if we discuss a few of the underlying principles.

TO DESIGN

In its most simple form a "figure", shape or unit may be a circle, oval, shell, vase, etc. (5a). Then each can be further developed by its extension vertically or horizontally or in both directions (6b).

First and fundamentally design is an arrangement of **"figures" upon a background** or within a given area; this constitutes the "figure"–ground relationship. Only in their relation to the whole do the parts have structural meaning; so emerges totality of form. This principle put into practice could

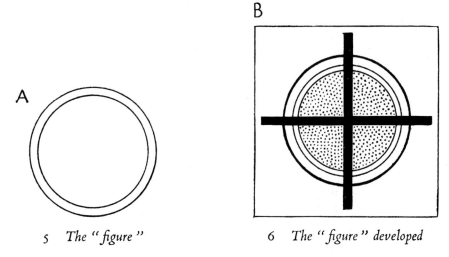

5   The " figure "   6   The " figure " developed

be exemplified in an arrangement of variously sized clavis crosses, well spaced, but not overlapping, within the rectangle constituting the top of a kneeler (7).

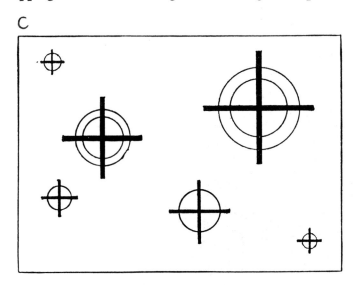

7   " Figures " related to background

(The interconnection between the figure, in its literal sense, and the ground in a more advanced form is illustrated in early memorial brasses and occurs in

33

the planning of a banner. A further development would be the arrangements of several figures in relation to the ground, as for a frontal.)

The second is the principle of **unity**. Here the differentiated parts or forms are related either by similar angles or curves or by a unified direction. For example, the palm leaf can be extended into a tree (*8d*), which in its turn may be further developed by the introduction of variability of direction, provided that it reflects and is related to the angles already included; this adds interest and breaks the monotony (*9e*) which would result from mere repetition.

8   *Unity*   9   *Introduction of variability*

In carrying this principle further, the similarity of angle and line would be stressed and exaggerated in the formalisation of each of the "figures" of which the design is to be composed; it is the factor which determines the placing of each figure in relation to the other and upon the ground.

The third principle is the relationship of direction which produces **rhythm,** and suggests a certain variation within a sequence of movement. An underlying linear rhythm is an integral part of the whole pattern in relation to the ground (*10f*). The forms or "figures" are so conventionalised that a movement common to all is stressed and in their placing one with another and upon the ground, they are so manipulated that the rhythm is preserved.

This is less complicated than at first it may seem, because in design spatial depth need not be considered. When the third dimension is introduced it is purely for its decorative value. There are, however, conventions for representing objects on different planes. In early works figures are organised side by side and above and below one another, on one plane and seldom overlapping, so preserving the re-lationship of direction, for example in Egyptian, Assyrian and Persian art. There are instances where rhythm is retained through the decorative treatment of perspective for its pattern value, as shown in the Gothic use of inverse perspective; here the lines diverge rather than converge.

It follows that if the arrangement upon the ground is flat then it is inconsistent to represent "figures" in the round, and it is not the inten-tion of the designer to attempt realism. It is entirely unsatisfactory to do so, because much which is extraneous to the principles of design gets included instead of being rejected. We all know of banners where the drawing and embroidered line work is naturalistic in intent, yet the colour is conveyed with pieces of flat material (often having an evenly repeated woven pattern upon it). The satisfactory approach is to see the object as pattern and to treat it according to the principles of design.

Fitness for purpose constitutes a principle of great importance when applied to design for the Church. The subject matter and the treat-

10   *Rhythm of line*

ment have to be acceptable as befitting and to conform to certain liturgical requirements. The aesthetic approach needs to be sensitive, indeed it is the inspiration for design of this nature, the "feeling" expressed in a representation of St. Veronica's handkerchief differs from that for a hanging in a children's corner. Considerations of practical fitness are many—for example, a banner is always seen upright and for only a short time on each occasion, whereas a

Gothic chasuble falling in its soft folds and usually seen from the back calls for an entirely different type of ornamentation. The preferences of the individual wearers of the vestments vary greatly and must always be taken into account and respected when preparing designs.

Proportion, being one of the basic factors in design, is important. The ratio of a third to two-thirds is visually more satisfying than half and half. A greater amount of pattern to a lesser area of background or the reverse is preferable to an equal quantity of both. Scale is determined by proportion, so before commencing a design it has to be decided whether one large unit is preferable to a powdering of smaller forms in relation to the whole. The purpose which is to be served will often supply the solution, as for instance an altar frontal in a cathedral will take large bold ornament, which would be overwhelming in a small church. The reverse is a frequent fault; small and detailed patterns are lost when seen from a distance. The importance of proportion cannot be over-emphasised; a design may be recognised as unsatisfactory but the reason is not apparent, until the proportions are investigated, when it may be found that all the component parts of the design are about the same size; by deciding which are important and enlarging them and reducing or cutting out the unessential parts of the design the fault is rectified.

The inspiration for a design may originate in one of the following ways. (But however it starts it is the creative urge, the inner vision, which makes the beginner long to "have a go" and the experienced designer strive to work out and materialise an exciting idea which is in her mind.) Perhaps the most original themes for design are produced by those who have the gift for sketching their ideas as they form, and creating with a line which grows almost instinctively. When interpreted in terms of embroidery there is a personal quality which contributes to the production of work of real artistry.

The subject matter of a design may derive indirectly from some lovely old example, such as a fourteenth-century English alabaster; or a piece of Byzantine embroidery may suggest the idea for some work of today. Deriving inspiration in this creative sense is distinct from merely reproducing or copying, which leads to sterile and unsuitable imitations.

Whatever the creative potentialities of the designer the aim is always to produce formalised decoration which is spontaneous and free and in no way purely an illustration or representational.

In designing for the Church there should be an integration of pattern and subject matter transformed into symbol many of which are in themselves decorative and form an excellent basis for pattern. In this context it may be pointed out that several of the symbols are symmetrical, and this type of pattern has been used so often that much of the impact is lost. As an alternative treatment balanced ornament offers an increase of decorative possibilities. It is therefore suggested that these symbols might be approached as seen from a different viewpoint, perhaps an extension of certain angles on one side to balance a lengthening of lines on the other, and the whole set slightly obliquely. Except where the meaning would be destroyed a certain distortion may lead to a more interesting form.

The actual character of some detail from the surroundings may supply an inspiration; this is an excellent basis from which to think outwards, because it ensures a unity and fitness. The pseudo-Gothic interiors do not inspire, and it is sometimes very difficult to make a design of today which will really take its place in these circumstances, but such limitations have to be accepted and are a challenge to the designer's ability. A design, however good in itself, fails in its purpose if it is utterly out of harmony with its surroundings.

Another source of inspiration may come from the actual materials used for embroidery, the design growing out of and around the use of a woven or printed pattern.

The ultimate application of the design is discussed in the appropriate sections (see also Chapters III, XI and XIV). The importance of **the chasuble** justifies additional consideration. The placing of the ornament gains much from a more original arrangement in place of the familiar round or oval vestment motifs placed at the junction of the Y-shaped orphrey of the Gothic chasuble, although the maquettes designed by Matisse for use in the chapel at Vence are remarkable. A few alternative schemes such as filling the yoke formed by the Y shape with an all-over repeating pattern which is rich in effect and well within the capabilities of the experienced designer are indicated (without detail) in fig. *11b*. A fresh approach may stimulate ideas, the rough sketches (*11f*) indicate something of the possibilities which might be the outcome of developing the pattern outwards from the centre back. There are more interesting variations upon the theme of cross or column for the decoration of the Roman shape, for instance the substitution of one large symbol.

The very nature of **the cope** gives scope for large-scale and dramatic treatment, where this is applicable. A handsome contemporary example from the Continent has a triangular shape over the shoulders filled with intersections of solid embroidery; the outlines extend over the whole cope to form a large-scale diamond pattern in line.

With the shaped cope the decoration is generally concentrated in the

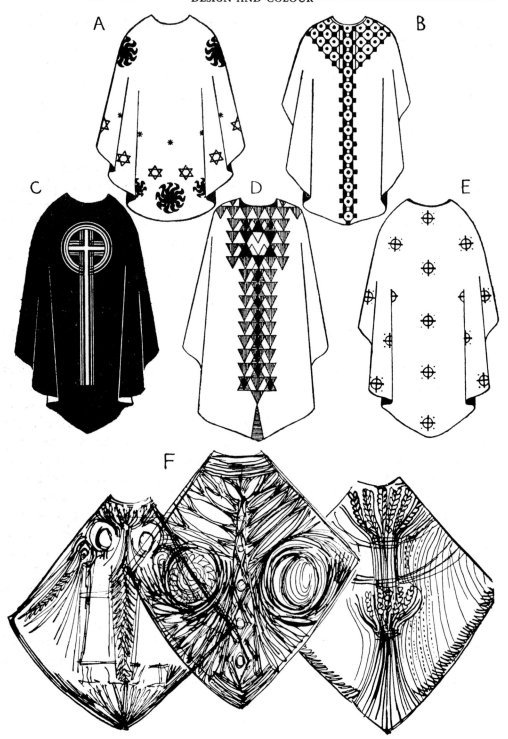

11 *Types of decoration for Gothic Chasubles*

enrichment of the hood, which becomes unified with the construction. If there is an orphrey it may also be decorated.

Where a woven pattern in the fabric can be "used" a simple all-over decoration might be evolved by developing isolated units (with embroidery) at regular intervals, or stressing and repeating lines down the centre back of the cope and filling the remaining areas with spaced geometrical units. Another suggestion for a cope with no orphrey might be the concentration of decoration down either side of the front.

Stoles need not be decorated with crosses though some users may like a small cross to mark the centre back of stole and the centre of the **maniple**. The use of one cross is required in the Roman rite. The early examples of stoles were usually narrow and the same width throughout and were entirely embroidered with repeating geometrical pattern. Modified by terminating the ornamentation about 10 inches from the bottom these examples, which can be seen on effigies and brasses, etc., are an inspiration for design. In complete contrast, and often preferred is a very simple well-proportioned unit or symbol at each end.

The limitations attaching to the designs for the **burse and veil** are discussed in Chapter III and **altar linen** in Chapter XI.

The frontal is more interesting to design than might at first appear as there is no valid reason for limiting the decoration to a series of divided panels, nor must there be a super-frontal, or the one large isolated central motif. Where an all-over simple geometrical pattern is carried out it has a close affinity with the character of the contemporary architecture. As an alternative the rectangle may be conceived as a whole and the larger than usual symbolic decoration planned to fill it. Straightforward decorative figures and symbols, large enough to fill the space, yet making flat patterns are more likely to take their place amongst other decorations in a new church than would small and ineffective groups. Full advantage should be taken of the sheer beauty of the materials available, many of these call for a simple direct design treatment. When planning a frontal, space should be left at the top if there is to be a super-frontal (see also Chapter VI).

Hearse cloth or palls need not lack interest, provided that the design is suitable; white, purple, blue, red or gold are generally used.

Banners (see Chapters X and XII also) give real scope to the designer, who must first ascertain whether it is to stand in the chancel, if so it must be planned as a part of the whole scheme. Whether the subject be a figure or an emblem the composition in relation to the ground and lettering is important.

Colour

An architect, envisaging the scene as a whole, has pointed out that the colours used both in the decorations of the very early Church and in the wearing apparel were, in general, soft and limited; but that the Byzantine churches were gorgeous and the congregation equally lavishly adorned, then later, the Gothic cathedrals and churches were richly ornamented but that the colours worn by the congregation would have been less brilliant. The classical architecture became a background to the rich vestments and sumptuous wearing apparel of the worshippers. Whereas today the colours worn by the congregation are mainly neutral and are seen against a setting of plain white walls, the colour being concentrated upon the altar and the vestments.

The **liturgical colours**, white or gold, red, green, rose pink and black or purple, are not any special tints or shades, that they are was a Victorian idea and completely false, and one which we want to get away from. All greens (for instance) are liturgically "green". An exception is white which (if intended to be festive) is interpreted as gold or a mixture of gold and white; in this case, it is the use of plain unrelieved white that is Victorian and decadent! Passiontide red, always a deep and sombre shade, is perhaps another exception.

Whether the requirements imposed by the liturgy are accepted as a stimulus or a limitation they have to be adhered to. Much variation can be contrived, provided that the colours are recognisably those prescribed. Some of the colour combinations present a problem which cannot be solved merely with a separating black outline. An understanding of tone value will help. The colours of light in the spectrum are in their natural sequence (a rainbow): yellow, yellow-green and yellow-orange are the lightest. Green, blue, orange and red are medium in tone. And purple, blue-purple and red-purple the darkest. When hues are lightened with white they become tints and when darkened with black they are shades.

Of the neutrals, white, pale stone and pale-blue grey are the lightest in tone. Fawn and grey are medium. Black, brownish grey and gunmetal or slate-grey are the darkest tones.

Whilst yellow, red and blue are the primary and green, orange and purple the secondary, russet, olive and citrine are the tertiary colours.

The use of colour is essentially spontaneous, the application of theory tends to an uninteresting result. There are, however, certain points which, if observed, help in determining a scheme, and rectifying mistakes.

When equal areas of two or more colours of the same tone are put together, each fights the other for dominance and a dazzling effect results in which neither colour can properly be seen: for instance a very pale blue and equally pale yellow. This can be rectified by introducing contrast: (1) by reducing the area of one and increasing the other, and (2) darkening the blue.

A satisfactory colour scheme includes contrast of tone, i.e. both shades and tints; also one or more of the primary colours if required, in varying proportions.

The introduction of neutrals and subtle colours will enhance the beauty of rich bright ones.

When a scheme is mainly composed of warm colours and neutrals (those with even a little red in them) a small amount of cool colour (the blues, pale yellow, greys and white) will usually help. And the reverse, a little warmth to an otherwise cold scheme.

A series of colours in their natural order, perhaps purple, red-purple, red and pink, will produce harmony. A touch of discordant colour livens up a scheme; a very little dark old gold would add interest to this harmonious range.

ENLARGING AND REDUCING

Beginners can gain confidence by "doodling". Many delightful ideas are formed in this way, and they can be arranged to make patterns which if suitable can be utilised for the decoration of vestments, etc. This simple approach is infinitely preferable to the over-ambitious attempts at realism. However, as many of the most promising sketches are too small, the following method is a straightforward way to enlarge them (*12*).

Enclose the sketch within a rectangle or a square.

Decide the measurement required for the enlarged vertical (or the enlarged horizontal).

Extend the vertical line A–B in the diagram by this measurement—to C.

Draw a line diagonally from corner to corner D–B in the sketch, and extend it indefinitely.

Run a line at right angles from C until it meets the diagonal at E.

Complete the rectangle by extending a line at right angles from C–E until it meets an extended horizontal from B.

Thus the width is enlarged in proportion to the length.

Make a grid over the sketch, and divide the enlargement with the same number of lines. Mark in the relative positions and connect up with a continuous line.

In order to reduce in size, the method is reversed.

12 Enlarging or Reducing

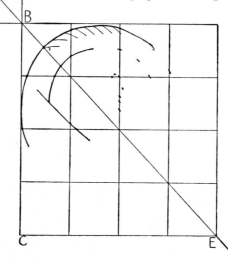
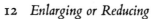

(a) *Altar, Cross, Candlesticks and Frontal for the fourteenth-century church of Shere, Surrey; designed by Louis Osman. White horsehair, with white horsehair fringes and gold and silver "Lurex" raised settings of natural crystals of twelve precious and semi-precious stones. Embroidered by Thea Sommerlatte. Motifs and sculpture by Geoffrey Clarke*
(Detail, below right)

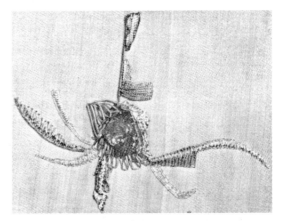

(b) (below)   *Frontal for the Welch Regimental Chapel, Llandaff Cathedral, designed as a part of the whole by George G. Pace. Light old gold cords on very dark blue velvet, details embroidered in white with a touch of red. Executed at the Royal School of Needlework*
(Detail, above left)

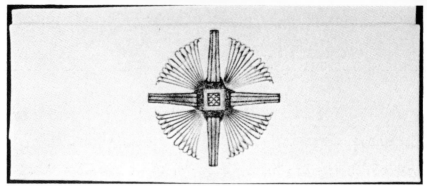

(a)   *Burse and Veil of cream gros-grain, raised couched gold. Rays and arms of cross terminating in seed pearls. Designed and worked by Beryl Dean for the Needlework Development Scheme*

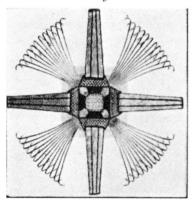

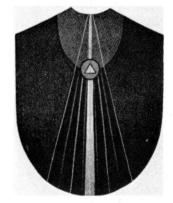

(b)   *Burse*

(c)   *Chasuble, by Anna-Lisa Odelquist-Ekström, of Libraria, Stockholm*

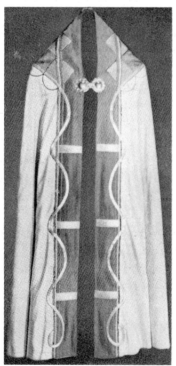

(d)   *Cope, by the Bénédictines de St. Godelieve, Bruges*

(e)   *Chasuble, worked for Wilhelm Wefers, Cologne*

CHAPTER THREE

THE LITURGY

"The practice of defining the Church's seasons and feasts and saints' days by the use of special colours only became systematised at a comparatively late date in the Middle Ages. (The Lichfield Cathedral Use of *c.* 1240 is the oldest we now know.) Before that, even the great cathedrals were content to use their best and newest sets of vestments for festivals, and the older and shabbier things for lesser feasts and ferial days. Even after the cathedrals had developed a distinctive Use, it is doubtful if any but the greatest and richest parish churches followed their lead. Abroad, Spain and France developed probably the most elaborate colour sequences of all and these were generally followed by the diocesan clergy until the modern Roman sequence displaced them."

At the time of the Reformation here, and therefore at the period to which the Ornaments Rubric in the Prayer Book refers, the most general rules, though only very loosely applied, were probably unbleached linen for the first four weeks of Lent, and a deep red for the last two weeks: white from Whitsun to Easter, and for the Sundays following. Red was used for apostles, martyrs and evangelists, white for the Madonna and for virgins; blue for Advent and Septuagesima; a mixture or blue, green or even yellow for confessors. There was no universal ferial colour in England—generally a second best of any colour would be used for Sundays outside the main sequence, or possibly a green, or a mixture.

The most widely adopted use in the Church of England today (although there is no officially prescribed use, except in the diocese of Truro) is:

White, and/or gold for All Saints' Day, Baptisms, Confirmations (or red), Weddings, Dedication of Churches, Christmas, Feast of the Epiphany, Easter, Ascension, Trinity Sunday, Feasts of Our Lady, Feasts of Virgins (if not martyrs) and in the Roman Church—Feasts of Confessors.

Red, Feasts of the Martyrs, Whitsuntide or Pentecost, Feasts of the Apostles (if martyrs), Holy Innocents. And in the Roman Church, Holy Innocents when falling on Sunday. The Third Sunday in Advent, the Exaltation of the Cross, Feast of the most precious Blood.

Blue or Violet used in the Church of England for Advent, Lent, first four weeks (or Lenten white), Rogation Days, Vigils, Ember Days (if desired).

Purple used in the Roman Church for Holy Innocents, Vigils, Advent, Lent, first four weeks, Passiontide, Rogation, All Soul's Day.

Passiontide red used in the Church of England for remaining Sundays in Lent and
for Good Friday (but altars bare).

Green for usage in the Church of England, Epiphany-tide, Season of Trinity to
Advent, Feasts of the Confessors (with blue) and in the Roman Church,
Epiphany-tide, Trinity to Advent.

Black for Funerals, All Souls' Day (or blue or violet) in the Church of England,
and in the Roman Church, Good Friday.

Rose pink in the Church of England can be used after Trinity and as a general
ferial colour and in the Roman Church for the Fourth Sunday in Advent
and Mid Lent Sunday.

Yellow in the Church of England, Feast of Confessors.

Lenten Array, "off white". Used throughout Lent, or for the first four Sundays
only. Design on frontals stencilled or appliquéd in red or blue. Church of
England and Roman Church.

Passiontide red is a deep, sombre colour, generally trimmed with black
orphreys or embroidery, whilst for Whitsun and feasts of martyrs, etc., it is the
noble bright red with characteristically exultant design.

But it must still be the practice for most of the poorer parish churches to
simplify this use, and for them perhaps the best and soundest tradition is to adopt
a sequence of three frontals only, a best "white", a ferial of mixed colour, and a
Lenten frontal, either (preferably) the unbleached linen as it is the greater
contrast and therefore has the most forceful teaching effect, or a blue or violet if
preferred.

We are so familiar with the very ordinary types of these colours almost
always used that a more artistically beautiful variation is sometimes neglected.
Conformity to liturgical usage is stressed, but, whilst it is adhered to it is still
possible to add interest by selecting, for instance, a green with a touch of blue and
grey in it, or an olive green is lovely with gold. And a lighter yellowish-green
makes a wonderful foil to a darker green—a touch of green lurex might be added.
Think, for example, about red as a colour, imagine the wonderful range of reds
which exist, refer to the medieval paintings to see its luminous beauty when used
in conjunction with dark greyish "inky" blues.

Purples can be crude, harsh and "acid" and violet often insipid. It is more
difficult to find satisfactory purples, but it is not impossible. It is a colour which
changes with the light, and may appear almost black in some lights.

The prevalent colours of the carpet must be taken into consideration when
planning a scheme or adding to one. Often beauty which has been built up with

care is almost totally destroyed visually by the carpet being either too strident in colour or wrong in character, sometimes too recognisably domestic in origin.

It is essential to select colours for the altar hangings which harmonise with each change. Much has to be taken into consideration when adding some new vestments or furnishing; it is so important to review the surroundings and existing hangings, etc., before making a choice, and, rather than introducing some entirely new note of colour, selecting, perhaps, a darker or lighter tone of one of those already in use. This preserves the unity. Various aspects of day and artificial light can make a great difference to colours; it is always wise to "try out" colours in the surroundings and the existing light before making a decision. Some fluorescent lighting causes unpredictable changes.

Because, in daylight, the colours of stained glass are so strong they too must be taken into account, and also the general colour of the stonework or wood. In planning the restoration of St. James's, Piccadilly, Sir Albert Richardson has created great beauty by the choice of the two tones of the particular light blue with the dark wood and carvings, against which, when in use, the acid yellow of the embroidered hanging behind the altar is perfect.

It is important that the colour scheme as a whole should be planned from the beginning, especially in a new church, so that as each vestment or furnishing is added it may conform to the unified whole. It is wise to seek the guidance of an artist with an informed opinion and whose vocation it is to visualise and plan such schemes of decoration.

Tone value has been mentioned; the proper understanding may help to solve the problems of many a colour scheme. This subject is more fully discussed in relation to design in Chapter II.

Reference should also be made to the appropriate chapters for further information concerning all the foregoing subjects.

THE ALTAR-FRONTAL AND SUPER-FRONTAL OR FRONTLET

The significance attached to the altar makes it the most important focal point of each church. Therefore there is a certain amount of ritual to be observed, especially in relation to the preparation of the linen; this is given in Chapter XI and the measurements and methods of mounting are dealt with in Chapter XIV.

The frontal or antependium either hangs, or is fixed to a stretcher, or is clipped into place in front of the altar. The colour is in accordance with the season. Here there is scope for really interesting decorative effects with embroidery; the type of design and workmanship is, to a great extent, determined by the distance from which it will be viewed. All too often a stereotyped arrangement of panels and orphreys is used.

Another reason for the prevalence of frontals with the monotonous arrangement of divisions made by the use of orphreys is in order to cut up the width, as the average altar is wide in relation to its height. There are, however, other and more original ways of rectifying this (artistically the gain is immeasurable when there is no super-frontal). The same applies to the use of fringes and braids which are so mechanically used for edgings and finishings. Yet with a little more imagination and time alternatives can be devised, such as faced points and scollops, or embroidered patterns and decoratively couched cords.

Over the frontal is usually placed a super-frontal or frontlet; this is a strip the same width as the frontal, but only 6 or 7 inches deep. Sometimes it is worked in one with the frontal and appears as a border. Frequently one separate frontlet is used with several frontals; this requires forethought in its planning both in colour and design.

The Roman rite suggests that the frontlet should be some 6 inches deep and sometimes fringed: although usually the same colour as the frontal it can be neutral or contrasting.

In the Church of England the Laudian, draped or throw-over frontal is generally used where the architecture of the church is classical or classical in style, or for a nave altar, where it is seen from all angles by those walking around. This type of frontal is formed from a rectangle of some suitable fabric and completely covers the altar. In another form it may be shaped at the corners, by inserting gathered fullness. If there is decoration, one large-scale unit in the centre front looks well, but usually it is the dignity and restraint and the fall of the material which is so right with this style of architecture.

THE RIDDELS

The primitive Christian altar stood beneath a canopy supported on four columns, with curtains between them which were drawn together during the most solemn part of the liturgy. Some altars still retain the dossal and riddel curtains at sides and back, either hung from posts set in the floor, or with the riddel curtains hung from hinged arms secured to the wall or to a support at the back of the altar. These curtains are generally, but not always, attached to the rods, by laced cords. The curtains must be sufficiently full; they are generally plain, but an all-over pattern of small scattered units of embroidery can look excellent and is preferable to an arrangement of embroidered orphreys. Unless they are changed with the season there is no stipulated colour, for these or any of the other curtains in the church, but where the back is visible they should be lined.

THE DOSSAL

This is the hanging behind the altar. It usually matches and is fastened to the rod in the same way as the riddels, or it can be mounted on a stretcher. The Steeple Aston dossal and frontal were made from a cope of the Opus Anglicanum period and are on loan to the Victoria and Albert Museum. The Chipping Campden set is the earliest extant in this country; it is typical of fifteenth-century design and workmanship.

THE BURSE OR CORPORAL CASE

The burse is the case formed from two 9-inch (or 8-inch–10-inch) stiffened squares, joined with a hinge, in which is kept the folded corporal, when not in use. The front of one square is embroidered and two short pieces of cord, narrow ribbon or an inset gusset are sewn at the sides. The burse generally (but not always) stands with the hinge side uppermost when it is not placed over the chalice veil upon the chalice. The embroidery can be very rich, and there are no particular limitations attaching to the design except that it should match the chalice veil and go with the vestments of the day.

THE CHALICE VEIL

This is a square of 20 to 24 inches, though now more often the smaller size; it varies according to the height of the chalice. It is made of silk and lined with silk or some softly falling fabric, whereas the burse is lined with linen, well washed and ironed. The embroidery is usually placed in the centre of one of the sides of the veil; it should not be so stiff that it prevents it from hanging freely when covering the chalice and the 6-inch square pall upon it. When designing it must be borne in mind that the decoration will be seen as it falls down from the chalice; therefore figures should stand when the veil is in position. The centre is usually left plain, but in most sixteenth- and seventeenth-century veils there is an elaborate all-over pattern. A second linen chalice veil is sometimes used.

In the Roman Church the veil can be larger, about 2 feet 6 inches square; there is often a border design all round, but it can have more decoration.

THE AUMBRY VEIL

This veil covers the aumbry only when the Sacrament is there. It can be embroidered. There is no rule or custom for the colour.

49

THE TABERNACLE VEIL

The rules of the Roman rite require that the tabernacle should be "decently covered with a canopy". This veil, which covers it completely, should fall gracefully and be divided down the centre. Where there is a detachable top to the tabernacle it is placed over the veil. Where the shape allows, the curtains should be full, supple and rich; if there is embroidery it is restrained. The veils are changed with the vestments, but purple is used in place of black. In some churches white is in use continually. The veil may be made of any material that is not transparent.

THE VEILS OF CIBORIUM AND MONSTRANCE

The ciborium, or alternatively the pyx, in which the Blessed Sacrament is reserved inside the Tabernacle, is covered with a white veil; it is usually cut circular with a small round hole in the middle for the cross or knob on top of the lid. If the material is soft and light it drapes gracefully when there is embroidery upon it this is of gold or silver but light and pliant, but the inevitable fringe round the bottom is uninteresting. Whatever is chosen the same should finish the small circle.

The monstrance veil is usually a length of silky white material nearly twice the height of the monstrance, which hangs softly and, preferably, unlined and undecorated. It should not be shaped like a stiff, four-sectioned tea-cosy.

THE HUMERAL VEIL

Another "veil" which can be decorated with embroidery is the Humeral Veil; this is lined (shantung is suitable) and is about 3 yards long by 24 to 26 inches wide. The embroidery should not prevent it from draping, as it is worn over the shoulders when the priest carries the Sacrament in procession or moves it from the tabernacle; it is also worn by the sub-deacon during part of the High Mass, when holding sacred vessels.

The valances which are a part of the baldaquin, the tester and the portable or flexible canopies (though sometimes over-elaborately embroidered) do give scope for really interesting decoration. Silk, velvet or other suitable materials can be used.

THE VESTMENTS

THE COPE

The cope is derived from the "lacerna", which was a semicircular mantle wrapped around the shoulders. Originally introduced for the use of officers in the

Roman army, it was fastened with a clasp, which later became the morse. Due to the persecution of the Christians it was not until about the seventh century that it developed as an ecclesiastical vestment. It was at first an outdoor garment, and liturgically was used especially for processions. Silk coppae are first mentioned in a Spanish inventory of the eighth century showing that it had come to be made of richer materials, the border or orphrey along the straight edge being embroidered, and often the whole surface. During the Renaissance the orphrey became 8 or more inches wide and very stiff, and the hood, from being a small token triangle, got larger and larger, outlined with fringe and attached to the lower edge of the orphrey it reached halfway down the back of the wearer, an exceedingly ugly and ungainly proportion. In Northern European countries, including Great Britain, it is usually attached to the top edge of the orphrey and in the South to the lower edge. The hood has undergone various changes, latterly its true function is being revived; it hangs in its natural folds, this is more graceful and still allows it to be enriched with embroidery. The shape of the cope too is returning to that which was customary from the fourteenth to the seventeenth centuries, having the narrower orphrey shaped to fit the wearer's neck.

THE MITRE

The official dress of bishops and archbishops includes the mitre. In the early extant examples such as that which is attributed to Saint Thomas of Canterbury (from the Treasury of Sens Cathedral and now lent to the Victoria and Albert Museum) the triangular form was smaller and of a better proportion than those used in the present day. The mitre has evolved from a round cap, until in the twelfth and thirteenth centuries the two peaks were right-angled and united by a piece of material to cover the head. Later the angle became acute, until the mitre became larger and higher, losing its gracious proportions; the lappets have persisted and are embroidered and attached on either side of the centre back.

When designing a mitre the band around the lower edge befits the shape and form, but the vertical band (*Titulus*) is not necessary, it limits and restricts the design.

THE PALLIUM

The pallium was originally formed from a wide strip of folded cloth worn over the shoulder; it can be seen worn by bishops and archbishops in early representations. Later the pallium, made of wool, changed in form until it became narrower, hanging down the centre front and centre back in the form of a Y-shape. The pallium is not now worn in the Church of England.

THE EUCHARISTIC VESTMENTS

The Mass vestments are symbols of virtues and duties laid upon Christians. They are also intended to remind us of certain events and aspects of the life of our Lord.

In vesting for Mass the priest puts **the Amice** on his head, takes the strings round his neck (front to back) crosses them there, brings them back to the front, across the chest to the back, crosses them again and brings them forward, round his waist to lie in the front. Then he puts on the alb, and maniple, stole and chasuble and then drops the amice down so that it falls in a gracefully draped hood on the neck of the chasuble. This is done in the Church of England, where the amice has the apparel to slightly stiffen it. It is a rectangle of approximately 25 by 36 inches and is of linen, attached along one side is the embroidered apparel; this is removed when the linen is laundered. Each tape is at least 5 feet long.

He then puts on **the Alb**, a long white linen garment. There can be apparels on the cuffs of the alb and towards the hem can be placed one or more embroidered apparels.

The priest then girds himself with the cincture or **girdle** which is a thick cord of silk, linen or cotton with tassel ends; it is the symbol of holy purity and was originally used to tie back the alb when working or walking.

The Maniple is placed upon the left forearm. In colour, shape and design it is like the stole. Originally it was a small towel for wiping away dust and perspiration in the hot climate, and its folds served as a purse. It signifies the sheaves of good works.

Next is worn **the Stole**; it is put around the neck, crossed over the chest and held in place by the ends of the girdle. It is the special symbol of the dignity and reminds us of the yoke. The stole is a long strip of cloth matching the chasuble in colour and design. The Eucharistic Stole can be longer than the pastoral or preaching stole and is the one worn with the vestments; it usually shows below the chasuble.

The last vestment to be assumed is **the Chasuble**. Originally it was worn over the toga and was circular with a central opening for the head; its use was retained for church services. Saint Apollinaris in the mosaic from the Church of S. Apollinare in Classe is depicted in the attitude of prayer wearing a circular paenula (chasuble) *(13a)* over a long tunic with clavi; over the shoulders is thrown a pallium. Gradually the materials from which it was made became richer; the shape, still ample, was slightly modified. The seam down the centre front and back called for decoration. This was usually a narrow strip of material applied in the form of a Y-shaped cross with the addition of embroidery. The chasuble

(a) *Detail from the Orphrey of the Butler-Bowdon Cope (Plate II), showing design and technique characteristic of the Opus Anglicanum period (pp. 2–4). The vestments worn include: a mitre (the lappets can be seen); the amice with an embroidered apparel; the alb, also with an apparel; the stole, showing beneath the dalmatic; from under the full chasuble shows the sleeve of the tunicle; and there are also gloves and buskins*

(b) *St. Apollinare, from the mosaic in St. Apollinare in Classe, Ravenna. It shows the cone-shaped chasuble worn during the sixth century*

(a)   *Burse, embroidered with silks in cross and tent stitch, English, fourteenth century. Many are the symbols incorporated in the design (see pp. 37–44)*

(b)   (left)   *The Symbol of the Anchor and Fish, third century, from the catacombs of St. Priscilla, Rome*

of Saint Thomas of Canterbury (preserved in the Treasury of Sens Cathedral) is typical (*13b*). Later the chasuble was further modified, material being cut away to give greater freedom for the arms (*13c*). Still more was cut until the fiddle-shape or Spanish and other variations of the form known as Roman were established. On the back was the large cross, or the "column" or letter "I" which stands for Jesus with "I" for "J" according to the Latin spelling. Many vestments of an earlier

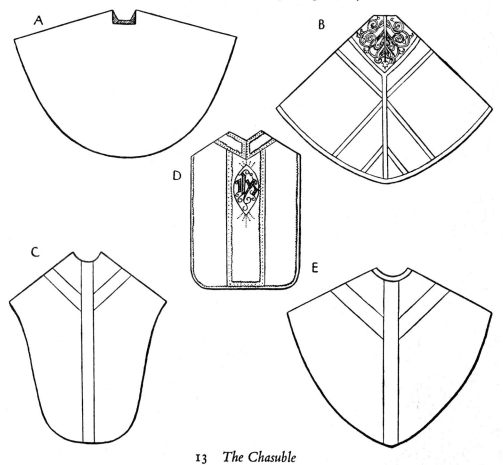

13   *The Chasuble*

date were mutilated when cut into these shapes; one instance is the Clare or blue chasuble in the Victoria and Albert Museum. There are also many examples of the embroidered orphreys referred to. In fig. *13d* an example of the stiffened board-like Roman type of chasuble is shown, with some feeble, ill-proportioned decoration; it is meant to show the tawdry use of gimp and embroidery. The front is always cut away to a greater extent than the back.

55

The larger, ample form of chasuble was retained until the early sixteenth century, then in Italy first they were cut down and the fashion later became widespread. But the Gothic form of chasuble never went entirely out of use and is that generally worn in the Church of England; in the Roman Catholic Church it is being revived both on the Continent and here. Its dignity is more widely recognised today as a result of the revival of the shape, but with a seam on the shoulders for economy of material, which as the symbol of the seamless garment causes it to lose something of the symbolism. In fig. *13e* can be seen the modified form of the full chasuble now generally in use. This shape has no interlining, and the colour of the lining is a contrast to that of the vestment itself.

THE DALMATIC AND TUNICLE

The **Dalmatic is worn by the deacon** or Gospeller, and the **Tunicle by the sub-deacon** or Epistoller; both vestments follow the colour of the chasuble. They are of simple shape, either seamed or laced together only under the arms. They can have two stripes (*clavi*) which run down from the shoulders, and there are two apparels, front and back, one towards the neck and the other towards the hem of the dalmatic; the top ones are about 4 inches wide and the lower are more. On the tunicle there are generally only the apparels near the neck. In both garments the fronts and backs are alike. On either side of the neck at the shoulder there are cords with rich tassels. In the Roman Church a part of the seam is left open and is laced together.

There are excellent recent examples where the clavi are applied in plain material, in place of the usual braid or gimp bought by the yard; and instead of stitched-on apparels, there are wide borders of simple but effective large-scale embroidered and applied decoration, being in the traditional positions on the garments the form is preserved but it is expressed in a more interesting way. The shape is ample and the sleeves and sides are usually seamed for the whole length, although they may not be joined at the bottom.

Just as the Gothic chasuble is more graceful than the Latin shape so too are the dalmatic and tunicle. The deacon wears the stole, but placed over the left shoulder and not about the neck.

As a bishop wears the dalmatic over the tunic, his are generally made of a thinner material. This is the reason for the sleeves of the tunic being narrower and longer. His vestments also include the amice, alb, girdle, stole, maniple, chasuble and kid or silk gloves (which if embroidered should not be over-ornate).

CHAPTER FOUR

SYMBOLISM

Symbols have survived from the earliest times; their significance lies in the higher beliefs and meanings given to visual forms. Symbolism is a picture language which appeals to the mind through the eye. Attributed to the circle are but slight variants of a universally accepted meaning. As the sun, to the prehistoric sun-worshippers it represented their God. To the Egyptians, the circle having no beginning and no end, symbolised life and eternity. The circular arrangement of the great stones at Avebury and Stonehenge, and the monoliths and round towers so widely distributed testify to the symbolism attached to its use; later incorporated into Christian art the circle continues to convey its meaning of eternity.

Existing pagan symbols and decorations were adapted to the new belief; one such example is to be found in Coptic tapestry weaving where the winged victories flying with a wreath over the head of an emperor or other personage were developed into Christian angels, bearing a wreath encircling a symbol.

To avoid persecution the early Christians adopted some of the outward signs but invested them with an added significance (the pagan symbol of life was a fish, to which there was the further significance. The initial letters of the Greek words for Jesus Christ, Son of God, Saviour, form together the Greek word for a fish). Alternatively they employed symbols whose meaning was known only to those of like faith or incorporated them with other ornament to escape notice, for instance the cross disguised to form the mast and rigging upon a ship. Others can be discovered on the Coptic tunics and fragments from the wrappings preserved from the burying grounds of Egypt.

The main sources of knowledge concerning early Christian symbolism are from the catacombs, and Byzantine sculpture and mosaics, also pottery found in tombs. The Anglo-Saxon carved figure subjects and later the interlacing ornament on the Celtic carved crosses and illuminations, the alabasters, ivory carvings, enamels and sculpture of the Romanesque art provide examples, and the medieval manuscripts and stained glass were also rich in symbolism.

Pictorial art combined with symbolism was used for a definite programme of teaching. Mosaics, of which those at Ravenna attained perhaps the greatest beauty, large connected schemes of stained glass surviving still at York, Fairford and elsewhere, all served a practical purpose. So too the mural paintings at

Kempley, Gloucestershire, or Hardham, Sussex, to mention only one or two English examples in which we can still see the design as a whole.

In the present day certain emblems are repeated frequently whilst others are seldom seen; some of these latter have greater **value as decoration** and because they are less familiar arouse more response in the beholder. A little research will be amply repaid by the wealth of ideas obtained: the earliest examples are full of vitality and variety and many can be adapted for embroidery.

The origin of many symbols is lost in the remote past; sometimes their interpretation has been changed in the course of time. There are many books on the saints and their emblems and on the heraldry and symbolism of the Church, the following are only a few common examples and suggestions for their interpretation and use.

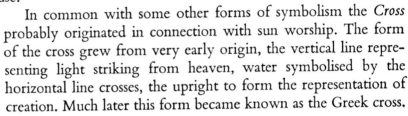

In common with some other forms of symbolism the *Cross* probably originated in connection with sun worship. The form of the cross grew from very early origin, the vertical line representing light striking from heaven, water symbolised by the horizontal line crosses, the upright to form the representation of creation. Much later this form became known as the Greek cross.

The *Swastika* or *Fylfot*, a cross with flames streaming from its ends, believed from prehistoric times to bring well-being, is thought to be the oldest Aryan symbol; it is attributed with but slightly different meanings in its widespread use.

The *Tau* or *Tat Cross*. In common with other forms its symbolism originated in connection with sun worship. Later it was used as one of the emblems of St. Anthony.

The *Ankh* also symbolised creation and is frequently found from earliest times in Egyptian art.

The *Latin, Calvary* or *Passion Cross* was not generally used as a symbol in Christianity until the fifth century; until this time the *Chi Rho* was used.

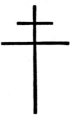

Later known as the *Cross of Lorraine*, it is to be found in early Greek and Byzantine art; it is formed by the addition of the scroll bearing an inscription nailed to the cross of Calvary.

The *Greek Cross*. At first the Latin cross and Greek cross were used indiscriminately.

Clavis, a cross within a circle. This was widely used in its slightly varied forms, and can be seen repeated many times upon the Charlemagne dalmatic.

The numerous variations of crosses with arms of equal length were adopted by the Crusaders; the shape fitted the shield; they became the crosses of heraldry.

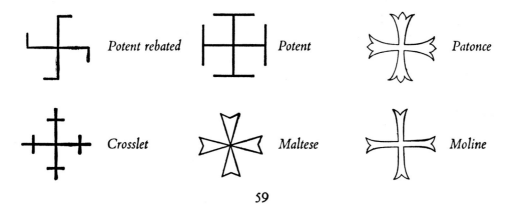

Potent rebated   Potent   Patonce

Crosslet   Maltese   Moline

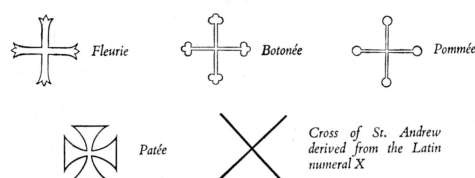

Fleurie *Botonée* *Pommée*

Patée Cross of St. Andrew derived from the Latin numeral X

SYMBOLS OF THE TRINITY

The *Equilateral Triangle* had a significance long before it was used in the Christian Church as a symbol of the Trinity.

The three hares or rabbits.

Three circles interlaced the emblem of the Trinity, the three eternal beings in unity; this is of later origin.

The *Double Triangle,* the seal of Solomon. The perfect God and perfect man. The lower horizontal represents the spirit, the sides the soul and the body meeting at the apex and pointing upwards. With the apex of the second triangle pointing down the Deity descends into matter.

The anthropomorphic trio, the Father crowned and enthroned, the son crucified between his knees, the Dove descending above the Father's head.

THE PERSONS OF THE TRINITY

The symbols of God the Father

For several centuries *the hand, the arm* and *the eye of God* were the only symbols employed for the first person of the Trinity. There are many examples of the hand and arm of God emerging from formalised clouds with or without rays. These can be seen in the decorations and illustrations of manuscripts, alabasters, ivory carvings, etc.

THE SYMBOLS OF CHRIST

The *Chi Rho* is the earliest monogram of Christ both in the Eastern and Western Churches. It was adopted as a sign by Constantine in A.D. 313. (An early example can be seen at Lullingstone, Kent.)

The IHS or IHC gradually replaced the Chi Rho.

The monogram XRISTOS NOSTER (Our Lord Jesus Christ) is less frequently seen.

INRI, Jesus of Nazareth, King of the Jews.

The *Lamb* with the standard, the "Agnus Dei", signifies the Risen Lord. The Lamb of God, an early symbol. Also the *Sword, Rainbow* or *Book with Seven Seals*, symbolise Christ as the spotless sacrifice for sin. The *Good Shepherd* carrying the Lamb is another symbol of Christ.

The *Fish* was used as early as the second century and was one of the secret symbols. Frequently found in the catacombs.

The *Vine*, a symbol of the Redeemer.

The *Pelican* feeding her young, with her own blood by tearing open her own breast, represents Our Lord feeding the faithful with His Body and Blood. Also Mother Church giving life to the faithful. The symbol of Corpus Christi.

The *Passion Symbols* owe their existence to their association with Christ.

THE SYMBOLS OF THE HOLY GHOST

From earliest times in Christian symbolism the Holy Spirit has been represented by the *Dove*, sometimes with a halo. There are many decorative and simple renderings from early sources which are an inspiration to the embroideress when designing. The later realistic approach limits the stitchery methods which can be used.

Tongues or *Flames of Fire* represent the coming of the Holy Ghost.

SYMBOLS OF THE PASSION

The *Chalice* and *Crown of Thorns*, with or without the nails, are often used exclusively. The following are the other symbols of the Passion:

ladder	pincers
the dice	hammer
seamless robe	pillar
the cock	scourge
spear	reed and sponge
sword	nails
sponge	**rope**

thirty pieces of silver and the crown of thorns.

OTHER SYMBOLS

A.M. Ave Maria, Hail Mary and A.M.R. Ave Maria Regina, Hail **Mary** Queen.

These are purely modern, Continental and of Roman Catholic usage.

 Alpha and Omega—the beginning and the end. The first **and** last letters of the Greek alphabet.

The Crowned M or the Lily Pot, these are the English symbols of the Madonna.

 The Pentalpha, five-pointed star, *The Star of Bethlehem*. It stands for the descent into matter and for man as the Son of God. It was the attitude of prayer and still is in the Eastern Church.

 The Star of Jacob, with eight points.

 The Ship riding amidst storms represents the image of the Church, particularly in the early days of Christianity.

The *Sun*, the source of light and heat, has been accepted as a symbol of the "Sun of righteousness" and comes down from the early Egyptian usage, when it had attached to it large outspreading wings.

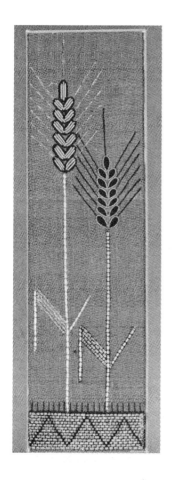

(a–d) *Symbols, embroidered in the methods described in Chapter 7. Designed and executed as an exercise by members of a class for church embroidery at Hammersmith School of Art and Building*

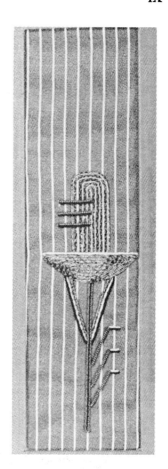

(a) *By Sister Kathleen Snelus*
(b) *By Sister M. Raymond*

(c) *By Ethel B. Stevens*

(d) *By Constance Beacham*

Symbols, designed and executed by Winifred Whenman (a), Harrie Nimmo (b), Mary Bates (c), Sister M. Emmanuel (d), Muriel Dale (e), and Walter W. Mitchell (f)

The *Crescent Moon*, the symbol of Byzantium. It also represents the feminine principle; the Virgin is sometimes shown standing upon a crescent moon. The sun and moon together symbolise the male and female, birth and death. They can be seen on the John of Thanet embroidered panel depicting the Christ enthroned, in the Victoria and Albert Museum. The sun and moon are also used as attributes of the Virgin Mary—Rev. 12.

Stars, when worked, had a meaning apart from mere decoration which was that of a watching, guiding Providence.

Eschallop Shell, usually associated with St. James the Greater, was a sign of pilgrimage, to the city of Compostella where, according to legend, laid the body of St. James.

The *Anchor*, and anchor terminating in a cross, meant steadfastness and hope; when shown with fish it expressed the hope to be in Christ; this was a very early symbol, examples can be seen in the Lateran Museum, Rome, and one *in situ* at the catacombs of St. Priscilla.

Water, represented by wavy or pointed horizontal lines were the feminine principle.

Animals used in symbolism

Many remarkable examples can be found in the Opus Anglicanum embroideries. The twelfth-century bestiaries should be referred to as the contemporary sources of much earlier animal drawing. They will be found as an inspiration to the designer of today.

The *Lion* symbolises St. Mark, it is usually winged; when a book is included it is as one of the gospels. It means strength and in the Jewish faith stands for the tribe of Judah.

The *Bull*, usually winged and with a book, represents St. Luke.

The *Eagle* is recognised as the symbol of St. John; usually winged and includes book. (There are beautiful representations of the Evangelists amongst the Limoges and the English enamels of the twelfth and thirteenth centuries.) It also symbolises triumph over death, and in Christian art the Ascension. Also represents the Resurrection.

Twelve Sheep with the Shepherd in the centre symbolises Christ with the apostles; there are many interesting examples, for instance in the carving at Chartres, and others in mediums which include mosaics in Santa Maria, Maggiore and San Clemente in Rome, where the Lamb of God is represented as a sheep with human head.

The mythical *Unicorn* is regarded as signifying virginity. Mrs. Jameson

65

(*Sacred and Legendary Art*, Vol. I, p. 33) says that it is appropriate only to the Virgin Mary and St. Justine.

The Hart or Hind has a double significance: (1) The type of solitude and purity of Life. (2) The type of piety and religious aspiration. (Ps. 42, verse 1, "Like as the hart desireth the water brooks, so longeth my soul after Thee, O God".)

The *Serpent* or *Dragon* represents evil; it also has another meaning which is that of healing.

Three Fish symbolise baptism.

The Fish, Basket and *Five Loaves* are often used as symbols with reference to the miracle of the feeding of the five thousand.

The Peacock signified in pagan times, the apotheosis of an empress. The early Christians exchanged this for a general emblem of the mortal exchanged for the immortal.

The *Cock* was the symbol of St. Peter and of repentance.

The mythical Phoenix symbolised resurrection, immortality, eternity.

The Dove with the olive branch symbolises Peace.

A *Dove or Doves drinking at the Fount* signified eternal life. A fountain has the same meaning.

Symbolism of Plants

The *Fleur-de-Lis* was the earlier form and later the Lily or Annunciation lily associated with the Virgin Mother; they symbolise purity and innocence. In Roman Catholic countries the snowdrop is also sometimes dedicated to the Virgin Mary.

The *Rose* is consecrated to the Virgin.

The *Crown Imperial* symbolises sovereignty.

The *Columbine* is emblematic of the Dove, the Holy Spirit.

The *Palm*, one of the earliest symbols, is of victory, and adapted to Christian usage through triumph in the race of life. There are delightfully decorative renderings in the catacombs. The tree is that upon which the tree of life is based. The palm tree was an emblem used in the Middle Ages as triumph over adversity.

Passion Flowers symbolise the Passion of our Lord. The ten petals represent the apostles without the one who betrayed and the one who denied his Lord, the other parts all having their respective meanings.

The *Olive* stands for peace and goodwill.

The *Pomegranate* symbolises the tree of life, and is usually shown with the seeds revealed, each being a potential tree, it is therefore an emblem of future life. (Also symbolises the Church because of the inner unity of countless seeds in one fruit.)

The *Tulip* symbolises the emblem of the chalice. The Holy Grail and the women.

Love-in-the-mist represents the soul almost hidden in green, the emblem of the earth, and therefore incarnation.

With *Honeysuckle* these flowers were used in the sixteenth century and onwards for Church embroidery, especially in Italy.

Bay, Laurel, Ivy, Myrtle, were originally pagan and came to mean destruction and death.

The *Thorn* symbolises tribulation.

Corn, being the source of the staff of life, symbolises material and temporal prosperity. Wheat has a similar meaning. It is also a symbol of the Eucharist.

Symbolism of Colour

The attributions of characteristics to colour are traditions which vary from time to time, country to country, East to West.

White, being the greatest heat of metal, symbolises God. Also the innocence of the soul, purity of thought and holiness of life.

Gold or *yellow* which it represents, symbolises sovereignty, the sun, love, constancy, dignity and wisdom. Also used for confessors.

Red (1) The colour of blood—appropriate to Feasts of Martyrs. (2) The colour of fire—appropriate to Whitsun.

Green represents the earth, and gives promise of future fruitfulness, birth, and therefore symbolises hope.

Blue signifies eternity, faith, truth and the feminine principle.

Purple for royal majesty. Ecclesiastically purple and violet are variants of the same colour. The distinctive use of a special shade of purple belongs to the Use formerly distinctive of the City of Rome itself.

Ash-colour often in pre-Reformation inventories called white, was and is still generally interpreted as unbleached linen, sometimes holland. It was the invariable Lent Use in England before the Reformation, and is widely used (in most of the Cathedrals for example) today.

Black is symbolic of material and spiritual darkness, and the evil principle.

Rose Pink signifies Divine love.

Dark Red symbolises destruction and is the colour for martyrs.

See also Chapter III.

Symbolism of Numbers

Three symbolises the Trinity.

Four, the evangelists.

Six, the attributes of the Deity, power, majesty, wisdom, love, mercy and justice.

Seven symbolises perfection and completion. The golden candlestick of the Jewish Temple was seven-branched. Or seven gifts of the Holy Spirit. Also the seven deadly sins.

The *Octagon* signifies regeneration.

There are *Nine* orders of angels in the celestial hierarchy.

Seraphim—six-winged, feathered body, swinging a censer.

Cherubim—six-winged, feathered body marked with eyes. The hands are uplifted in adoration.

Thrones—six-winged and holding a pair of golden scales.

Dominions—four-winged and wearing a triple crown and chasuble.

Virtues—four-winged, the body being covered with blue feathers, holding a sceptre.

Powers—holding a scourge and leading a devil tied by a chain.

Principalities—four-winged holding a palm-branch in one hand and a glass vial in the other.

Archangels—two-winged, in armour, standing within a fortress and holding a sword.

Angels—wearing an alb and holding a spear. Nearby two naked souls kneel in supplication.

The Symbolism of the Nimbus

Nimbus or *Aureole* surrounds the head only. The Christian nimbus was not met with until the sixth century. The early form was circular for Saints; a cross within it is sometimes given to God the Son. The square nimbus was of a later origin and signified a living person. Hexagonal for allegorical persons (Giotto's frescoes at Assisi).

The *vesica piscis* or mandorla was confined to figures of Christ or the Virgin Mary or Saints who are in the act of ascending into heaven. This is the glory surrounding the whole person, elliptical in shape.

The Emblems associated with Saints

Necessarily only a few of the Saints and their emblems can be mentioned here, but there are many excellent books of reference; some are given in the bibliography.

The Saint and the emblem only are given.

Andrew: The cross saltire.

Anne: Depicted teaching the Virgin as a child to read.

Anthony: Usually depicted as a venerable, bearded figure, holding a Tau-shaped staff.

Barbara: The patron against lightning, fire and thunder; she holds her tower; Patron Saint of architects, builders and firework makers.

Catherine of Alexandria, holds the barbed wheel of her torture and sometimes a sword.

Catherine of Siena: She wears a crown of thorns and holds a burning heart.

Cecilia: Sometimes holds organ, pipes or a harp.

Christopher: Represented as a giant holding a staff and wading through a river carrying the Christ child on his shoulder.

Edmund: King of East Anglia holds one or more arrows.

Gabriel, the archangel: Sometimes wears a coronet, or is dressed in white, holding a lily. He usually has a shield with Ave Maria upon it.

George: Clad in armour slashing the dragon with a sword or piercing it with a lance.

James the Great: Is represented as a pilgrim with staff, wallet, a scallop-shell on his hat.

James the Less: A fuller's club.

Jerome: One of the four Doctors of the Western Church; he wears a cardinal's hat, holds a book and ink-horn. A lion also.

John the Apostle: Represented as a younger man; his emblem is a chalice with a snake or dragon emerging from it, with the eagle and book of the Gospel.

John the Baptist: He is represented clothed with camel's hair, leather girdle and holds a lamb.

Jude the Apostle: Holds a club, an axe or a saw, or else a book or the scroll of his epistle.

Lawrence: He wears vestments of a deacon and holds a gridiron.

Luke: Ox, usually winged. With or without book.

Mark: Lion, also winged. With or without book.

Mary the Virgin: Usual emblem the lily, also an M surmounted by a crown.

Mary Magdalene: Shown as a Christian penitent with flowing hair and holding an ointment-pot.

Matthew: Represented as the Angel, he may hold a sword or money-box, even a carpenter's square. With book or scroll, and angel, with sword and fish, with money or money-bags underfoot.

Michael, the archangel: Sometimes clad in armour, sometimes in alb and strikes down the dragon. He is also shown with scales of justice.

Patrick: Snakes.

Paul the Apostle: Bears a sword.

Peter the Apostle: A key or keys on a chain. Also with fishing-net, with a cock, or crucified upside down.

Philip the Apostle: A basket containing loaves or a long cross.

Simon the Apostle: Holds a fish, an oar, an axe or a saw, or a book.

Ursula, crowned as a princess, holds or is transfixed by arrows. She is also shown sheltering her companion virgins under her cloak.

Veronica: She bears a handkerchief with the imprint of the face of Christ upon it.

CHAPTER FIVE

MATERIALS

We have seen how, throughout the centuries, background materials have been inter-related with the type of embroidery worked upon them. Until the present era there have been four main basic materials, linen, silk, wool and cotton. In the weaving these have sometimes been mixed and metal threads inserted; alternatively there were the processes producing velvet and the mercerising of threads, but there has never before been the immense variety of fabrics now obtainable through the introduction of the innumerable man-made fibres spun and woven into many interesting materials.

But have the people concerned with Church embroidery kept pace with all these developments or taken full advantage of them? Not at present in this country. Where the new synthetic metal thread has been used it is sometimes to weave designs of sixteenth-century Italian origin! (On the Continent more inventiveness has been shown.) But first there must be a demand for new materials produced for ecclesiastical purposes, and this will only come about when an increased understanding and appreciation of the results gained by experimentation with materials in other fields of embroidery are applied to needlework for the Church.

Until the usual suppliers feel justified in stocking the type of fabrics needed for a less rigid approach to Church embroidery the designer craftswoman will have to seek amongst furnishing and dress materials or handwoven fabrics for what she requires.

Even one experienced in their use will find difficulty in deciding the suitability of some textiles produced for a purpose other than for the Church. But if certain principles are applied it will be easier to arrive at a decision. First, is the material under review really suited for a sacred purpose or is it too undeniably associated with domestic furnishing or dress? Secondly, does it fulfil the requirements which will be made of it when in use, for instance, will it withstand the wear? The rub upon a chasuble is greater than the wear which a chalice veil will receive. Thirdly, is the fabric suited to the proposed use; if it is to hang or be draped will it be pliant enough to fall in graceful folds as required for one type of frontal, riddels, copes and Gothic chasubles? Fourthly, is the weight and thickness right (if too light it can be remedied with an interlining)?—but when too thick for the scale of the article, bulky corners and turnings may make it impracticable. Lastly, if the material to be selected is intended as a background, make sure that it is neither too strident in colour nor so complete in itself that it would dominate any applied decoration, rendering it superfluous.

Generally the character of woven or printed patterns is too closely linked with prevailing fashions in furnishing and dress for these fabrics to be satisfactorily used for the Church. But there are the rare and rewarding exceptions which are well worth the seeking as these provide the inspiration for delightful embroidered decoration, by "using" the woven or printed motif or pattern as a basis upon which to build simple units of design. Examples of this method of creating without previous experience or drawing can be discovered from an examination of some of the illustrations. When the colours or the woven pattern form a reversible fabric, another source of inspiration is provided; for example, imagine a heavy rayon dress material with tiny green crosses on a dark-green ground, with the same thing in reverse on the back. A larger cross of similar shape could be cut out, turned over and replaced as an inlaid counter-change, which with the right outline and the addition of some little crosses in the form of gold studs might be developed into an interesting idea for decoration which could be adapted in many different ways.

An appreciation of the nature and characteristics of fabrics will lead to a feeling of affinity, from which can grow the inspiration that will become a complete idea. To give an actual instance: the background texture for a banner was envisaged, but could only be obtained by hand-weaving natural raw silk with a twisted one and adding some gold thread; after this had been applied to the backing, parts were covered with layers of light blue and black tarletan. To obtain the texture a large meshed net was put over the whole, upon this was placed some dark grey, rough and slightly metallic fabric which acted as a foil to the bright red and gold Indian silk, gold kid and square meshed black net. This amalgamation of textures was carefully planned; the subject depicted was a saint, the method being appliqué. This is typical of the approach to the experimentation in which new and old materials combine in a juxtaposition of textures. Alternatively a motif can be repeated several times; it may be composed of two or more textures used together with restraint, which is effective. Two concentric circles, one of bouclé and the other velvet might be applied to a ground of fine wool, with a superimposed cross couched in Japanese gold.

The surfaces resulting from the use of materials and threads should be recognised for their textural value, whether they be smooth or knobbly, bright, mat, ridged, soft, striped, transparent or rough: then their aesthetic potentialities can be discovered, bearing in mind that the material should be in scale with the design; and above all consider them in relation to metal threads; a smooth shiny

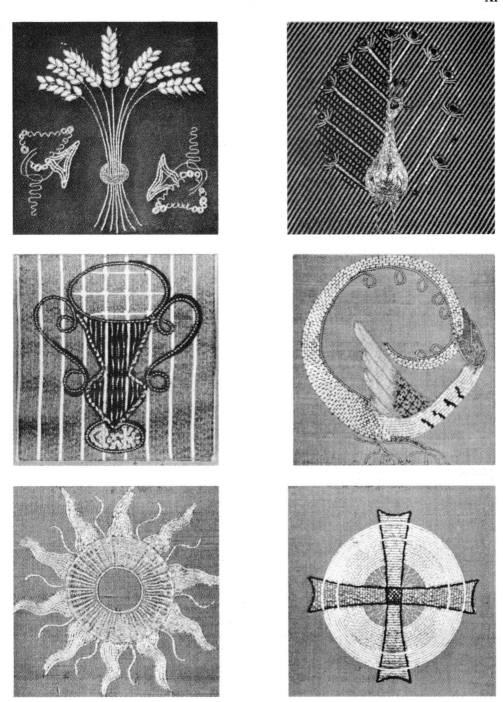

Symbols, designed and executed by Marjorie Lawe (a, b), Doris Ambridge (c, d), Lucy G. Polman (e), and Sister Kathleen Snelus (f)

Contemporary fabrics showing contrasting qualities of texture, interesting either as backgrounds or for appliqué. Included are silks, satin, linen, wools, mixtures of cotton and wool, rayon, nylon, velvet, and mixtures containing "Lurex" metallic yarn

surface will conflict whilst a dull silk and wool mixture will enhance. The use of textured materials, such as cotton with a slub and wool, will produce a problem in transferring the design, calling for ingenuity to overcome the difficulties. A suggestion might be to trace the design on to tissue paper and tack through before tearing it away.

No purpose would be served by listing the novelty fabrics; they are developed and become very popular for a few seasons to be replaced by others. Some of the delightful woven patterns are obtainable in soft-furnishing materials of rayon and cotton. There are crease-resisting nylon-velvets and needle cords. Rayon, grosgrain, faille, slipper and duchess satins are obtainable in many lovely colours and are reasonably priced. When its inclusion is justified the surface of crystal nylon is unique. The many lovely mixtures which include a little wool make excellent background materials.

The conventional textiles change little; they have withstood the test of time and their reaction to the technical processes involved in embroidery can be anticipated. These points in their favour have to be weighed against an often restricted colour range and lack of originality.

Such basic materials as corded silk, faille, satin, velvet and fine ribbed silk are supplied in the liturgical colours. Banner silk primarily for Masonic use is obtainable in a range of good colours. There is cloth of gold, also variously coloured golds and silver woven with untarnishable Lurex thread. Polanaise, glazed cotton and taffeta (when suitable) are conventionally used for linings.

It is rewarding to hunt for the more subtle variations of colour and texture amongst furnishing and dress textiles where a wider range of the basic materials already mentioned can be found, and in addition grosgrain, Italian and Swiss wild silk, silk dupion, even silk waste is excellent (but not easy to find) and many more beautiful silks. Millinery velvets have a short pile and being firmly woven are good to use and the colours interesting. Shantung and other similar materials provide linings; the introduction of some unexpected touch of colour is often an advantage. The lovely bloom upon a really heavy pure silk and the depth of the shadow between the folds is unsurpassed. Yet, as we have seen, the characteristic qualities of other less orthodox materials make them desirable.

Judged aesthetically there seems absolutely no reason for selecting either brocades or damasks as backgrounds for embroidery, because these materials are complete in themselves. The woven pattern, which is usually fifteenth- or sixteenth-century Florentine in derivation, should render it unsuitable for superimposed ornament, except perhaps when this is of similar style. Yet one frequently sees formal heraldry or naturalistic drapery carried out in appliqué cut from damask with a large-scale design of flowing foliation, this and other pieces may be applied to a background of still another sumptuous damask. Added to this embroidered design may be unrelated in line and subject to the background: any unity in the total effect is lost.

These points apply to braids also. These are often charming in themselves but misused when applied indiscriminately and mechanically in conjunction with patterned materials of a totally different character. Gimps seldom present a satisfactory finish; sometimes they seem lacking in character and finicking for otherwise magnificent vestments. Some more inventive edgings can be evolved with cords and narrow ribbons, etc., which form a part of the general scheme instead of introducing an entirely new note and drawing attention to outlines which should be unnoticeable. In Sweden braids and plain ribbons are combined and developed into designs which are the sole embellishments on vestments; the restraint and perfect proportions possess an unsurpassed dignity.

Some of the so-called liturgical fabrics are harsh in colour and shoddy in appearance. When selecting it is essential to recognise and reject those materials which simply imitate the more expensive real goods, as they have little beauty of their own and there is nothing to recommend them except cheapness. If this is an important factor it is infinitely preferable to choose a good, dignified and unpretentious material with its own intrinsic charm, such as fine wool, rayon or cotton mixtures, linen or some of the fabrics woven from the man-made fibres, where these are acceptable.

It seems that there is some reaction against silk and towards heavier fabrics woven with a mixture of cotton slub and wool, specially for the white or cream vestments, it certainly makes an excellent basis for the sparing use of strident colour and the shine of metal threads. Many recently made vestments and furnishings show an imaginative choice of fabrics in suitable and subtle variants of the liturgical colours. At Shere, Mr. Louis Osman has selected a soft, shimmering silvery green for a frontal of outstandingly original symbolic design, for another the interest is centred on the lumps of precious and semi-precious stone which seem to "grow" out of the gold-work surrounds and white cloth of woven horsehair. The symbolic significance refers to Exodus, Chapter 39, and Revelations, Chapter 21. These striking examples are in perfect accord with his whole concept, which includes the altar, cross, candlesticks, ambry and floor tiles.

Emerging from the unconventional use of materials are practical considerations, such as the position of joins due to differences in the relative widths available. This should be anticipated prior to purchasing, because, together with matching up the pattern, it can alter the total amount required.

Dress fabrics are usually 36 inches wide, woollen cloth 52–54 inches, furnishing 48 inches and the hand-woven silk for vestments is 60 inches. White linen is procurable in several widths, fair linen in few (this is very closely woven). When linens are to be used for vestments to be worn in the tropics it should be chosen for its suitability, as they have to be washed often, and be light for travelling, any decoration must be washable too.

There is so much prejudice to overcome in this matter of textiles that the whole subject requires individual and independent thought. The guiding factors must remain the fitness for the purpose, so that when the whole is complete the work will contribute to the surroundings against which it is to be seen.

14   *Byzantine silk cloth, with a red ground and woven pattern in gold with a blue outline—Tenth Century*

CHAPTER SIX

EQUIPMENT—FRAMING-UP— TRANSFERRING

The equipment needed for ecclesiastical embroidery is simple. This will be seen from the illustration (*XIV*).

The first essential is a good strong frame (known as a slate, four piece or rectangular frame) large enough to take the work. (The size is determined by the measurement of the webbing attached to the crossbars or rollers, i.e., 18 inches, 20 inches, 22 inches, etc.)

Next, a pair of trestles made so that the top bar can be adjusted to support the frame by means of the pegs which are moved either up or down as required. These trestles or stands are not necessary and many substitutes can be improvised.

On the half-imperial drawing-board are shown a 12-inch ruler, set-square, pair of compasses, one HB and H pencil, indiarubber, drawing-pins, all used during the process of the work to ensure accuracy.

For transferring designs a strip of felt or soft cloth is used, also a pin-vice (or the needle can be held in a little holder made of folded paper); a tin of black pounce, which is powdered charcoal, and another of white pounce, which is powdered cuttlefish, to both of which a little magnesia is added to give weight; a pouncer which is made from a roll of felt or soft cloth; and a clean duster or cloth with which to flick away surplus pounce after painting on, and another kept for cleaning up prickings after use.

For painting on a No. 0 or No. 1 sable water-colour brush is necessary and tubes of white, black and blue water-colour; also some small weights with which to keep the tracing in position on the material.

During the process of framing-up, steel pins are needed; also a packing needle large enough to take string, a ball of very strong string (not too thick), a reel of strong thread and a tape measure.

Have a pair of small scissors with good, sharp, firm points (because the wire threads need to be cut). A larger pair of scissors is essential for cutting out. Also necessary are two thimbles and packets of crewel needles of good make (Nos. 8 and 9 are useful sizes) and some sharps for making up and tacking. Also chenille needles Nos. 18, 20, 22, with which to take ends through, and tapestry Nos. 18, 20 or 22. Though ideal for the purpose, the flat-ended type of stiletto shown is not now obtainable (the round end of a nail-file is sometimes useful in its place); a good ordinary stiletto is essential. For use when cutting up purl a little board should be made by sticking felt to a piece of cardboard. A piece of beeswax through which to pass the sewing thread, also a skein of Japanese gold are shown, and the hammer and nails used for stretching.

FRAMING-UP OR DRESSING THE FRAME

When couching down Japanese gold and metal threads, both hands are required for the manipulation, and it is therefore essential to use an embroidery frame. By doing so puckering is avoided; another advantage is that it is possible to view the embroidery as a whole, which enables the balance, colour and emphasis to be considered as the work progresses.

It is usual to have a backing. This can be of evenly woven white or unbleached linen or holland. It should be coarse or fine according to the nature of the work, and is generally thoroughly washed and shrunk before use.

METHOD

1. Cut the backing to the thread at least 1 inch larger than the material to be embroidered. All materials must be cut with the selvedge way running down. This is most important to the finished result, the only exception is when it is artistically justified by the advantage gained in having a pattern or stripe running in the opposite direction.

2. At the top and bottom fold down $\frac{1}{2}$ inch on to the wrong side, hem down if likely to fray.

3. At both sides fold back a good $\frac{1}{2}$ inch, insert string at edge, pin in place. Stab stitch with a strong thread, using a back stitch at intervals, see diagram (15a).

4. Measure the exact centre of the webbing attached to the rollers or cross-bars of the frame; mark this permanently (X in 15).

5. Put a tack down the centre of the backing, place this to the centre of the webbing, when in position pin with the pins at right angles to the edge, work outwards. Using very strong thread, overcast, starting at the centre each time and stitching towards the ends. Repeat for the second roller. This is shown in the diagram (15). (If the work is large a ridge can be avoided by placing the right side of the backing to the right side of the webbing, pinning and doing the overcasting on the wrong side.)

6. Slip the two side pieces or slats through the slots in the rollers of the frame. (These flat laths have holes pierced at intervals along their length.)

7. Extend so that the backing is almost taut and insert the four pegs or split pins into the appropriate holes. Measure for accuracy.

8. Take very strong string of sufficient length and thread this into a packing needle. Lace through the sides of the backing and over the side pieces at about 1 inch apart, as in the diagram. Leave about 18 inches (more when some of the material is rolled in), wind round the ends of the frame and tie off (1 in 15).

9. Cut by the thread the piece of material to be used (selvedge running down), tack down the centre using a fine silk thread. (When the whole area is to be embroidered, a fine linen is used.)

10. Place the fabric with the centre directly over the centre line on the backing.

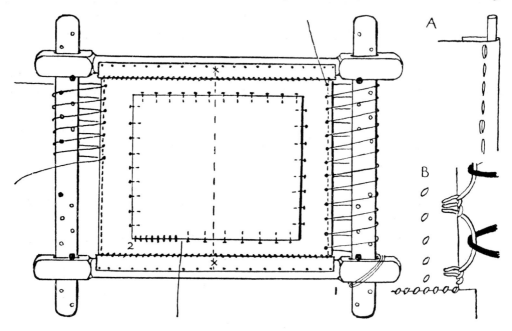

15   *An embroidery frame*

11. Working out from the centre, pin with the head of the pin outside and pointing inwards.

12. Stitch with fairly long straight stitches as at 2 in the diagram, or the piece can be herringbone stitched. Complete the top and bottom, then the two sides.

13. Tighten up the frame and brace up the sides so that it is absolutely taut. It should always be tightened up when it becomes at all slack.

Alternatively for embroideries which will take a long time to execute, instead of folding the side edges of the backing over string (as at A) they are hemmed down (as at B), then with a fine string groups of three buttonhole stitches are worked at 1-inch intervals, leaving a loop between each group. The stronger string is then laced through this loop and over the side pieces of the frame, as at B in the diagram.

TRANSFERRING THE DESIGN

The pricking and pouncing method is most suitable for this type of embroidery because accuracy is essential. Care must be taken to "keep the drawing" and the construction of the design throughout. If the design is mechanically traced round in outline without thought, the finer points and subtleties will be lost.

For the more spontaneous worker this method has the disadvantage of putting a permanent line upon the material. But by planning ahead these limitations can be overcome. If the embroidery is to be built up with the materials, then the main lines (which are unlikely to be altered) can be traced, pricked and painted, the more tentative lines traced, pricked and tacked following the pouncing. Where a hard line would be a drawback spaced dots and key points can be painted in or tacked before removing the pounce.

METHOD

1. Trace design to tracing paper, cut larger than the design (this protects the edges from surplus pounce).

2. Mark in centre line and cross line at right angles if applicable. Do not prick.

3. Mark corners or the edge of the article with spaced perforations, later tack in before removing pounce; never paint. As after embroidering the outline shape is seldom unchanged.

4. Taking the felt or soft material, fold and cover with tissue paper; this shows up the lines of the design. Put the tracing on this and with a fine needle (No. 9 or 10) set in a pin-vice or held in several folds of paper prick little holes close together following all the lines. Hold up to the light to see that none have been missed.

Some workers prick from the front and some from the back of the tracing; the result is the same.

To pounce and paint:

1. With the frame on a table, build up with books under the area to be transferred so that it is firm.

2. Place the pricking upon the material, check the centre lines to see that they correspond; keep in position with weights.

3. Take the black pounce for medium light materials, white for dark, or a mixture of both for very light fabrics.

Dip the pouncer into the powder, shake off surplus. With a small circular movement rub the pounce through the perforations, gradually covering the whole design, replenishing the pouncer as required but taking care not to put on too much, nor going over the same piece more than once.

4. Lift the tracing away carefully.

5. Paint in the lines of pounce, with a very fine brush, using water-colour; if found necessary a little gum arabic can be added. For woollen materials use oil colour diluted with turpentine.

6. Commence at the nearest part and cover with paper as completed. Care must be taken to avoid jolting the frame until finished. This painting must be done with a feeling for the design, watching that lines "run through" and are accurate.

7. When finished flick away the pounce with a clean duster or cloth making sure that all is removed.

ALTERNATIVE METHODS

1st. Keep perforated tracing in position with weights, dampen a pad with petrol or benzene, rub on to a cobblers' heel ball, then with a circular movement rub over all the lines.

2nd. Spray fabric with methylated, petrol or benzene, rub French chalk or pounce powder through perforated tracing, remove carefully and again spray.

If the embroidery, when it is in the frame, seems too large to reach comfortably it must be rolled in, but before doing this put running stitches round some of the lines of the design, with tiny stitches on the right side and larger ones on the wrong; this is to keep the two fabrics together. Then slacken the frame, withdrawing the pegs and the side-pieces from the end to be rolled (both if necessary). Insert a piece of soft fabric cut to the width of the backing, attach to the webbing. Roll round one (or both rollers) leaving the part to be worked exposed (as the work progresses it will be unrolled). Replace side-pieces, tighten up and put in the pegs, then tighten up the stringing. It is then ready for use.

If the embroidery does not cover the whole area, for example a wide orphrey down the centre back of a chasuble, then backing linen large enough to take the embroidery is framed up, and that portion of the chasuble mounted on it and

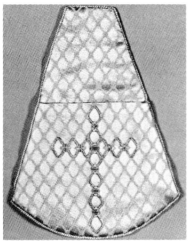

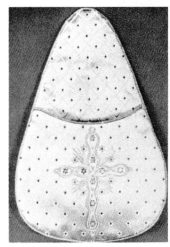

(b–d) Designs for Alms-bags evolved (b, top right) from the use of contrasting metal threads, by Ivy Lawrence, and (c, d) from the development of patterned material, by Dorothy Hobhouse and Muriel Dale

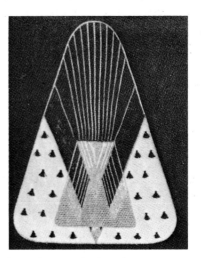

(e, f) The Alms-bag of dark blue and white has a dove worked in aluminium. The cover for a Bride's Prayer Book (a) is of gros-grain embroidered in silver of different thicknesses. Both by Beryl Dean for the Needlework Development Scheme

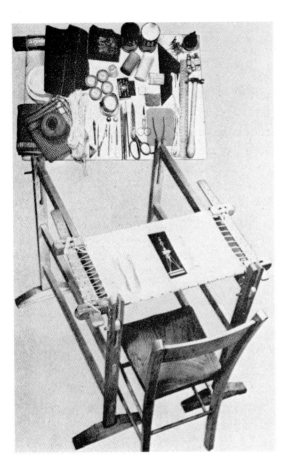

(a)   *An embroidery frame set up ready for working. It rests upon a pair of trestles, the top bars being adjustable. Behind is a drawing-board upon which are the various items of equipment required for embroidery*

(c)   *The Saddlers' Company Pall, early sixteenth century, possesses features typical of the time (page 21). The brocade is approximately contemporary with the origin of the design of the present-day damask (b) and of many others still being copied and used (unsuitably) as backgrounds for embroideries of totally different character*

tacked out. The material on either side being folded up and covered so that it causes the minimum inconvenience during the working.

Couched gold and raised work cannot be rolled in, consequently it is often necessary to complete every stage of each section before unrolling, as it may be impossible to reach it again. This imposes upon the creative executant an almost insuperable difficulty as it calls for a perfectly clear mental picture of the whole right from the commencement.

When embroideries are large, and the design is arranged in scattered units, the material is pinned out, care being taken that the grain of the fabric down and across is straight and at true right angles. The design is then painted on before framing. Enough, or as much as possible, of the backing required for the embroidered areas is then mounted in the frame, and a section at a time pinned on to it (if fine needles are used on delicate fabrics no mark remains). Then it is zig-zag tacked to the backing and the frame is tightened up for the completion of the embroidery. A fresh section of the backing will be used each time the material is moved, the remainder of the stuff being rolled to the side of the frame and covered.

For a frontal unless the fabric is used running along the width (if it is wide enough) the joins must be seamed, first matching up the pattern, using overcasting, back-stitching or machine-stitching; the selvedges should be snipped and then opened out and well pressed on the back. This is then applied to the framed-up backing linen, the design traced on, then worked.

But when the frame is not large enough to work all of it at once, each section is embroidered and joined together afterwards, loose lengths of threads being left where lines run over the joins, these are completed after the seaming. The unimaginative and stereotyped arrangement of panels and orphreys is used partly for the sake of expediency, as several people can work separate pieces, and these can then be assembled and mounted upon a backing in one long embroidery frame; as it is impossible to work comfortably from further away than about 14 inches, all the pieces should be pinned and tacked into position upon the backing whilst it is out flatly; afterwards it can be rolled in for the working and unrolled as it proceeds.

When units have been embroidered separately upon linen, they are applied to the background material which has been mounted in the frame, or it may have been stitched on to a framed-up backing linen.

The necessity for such careful preparation may be found irksome, but it is really worth doing. Something of real value could be marred by a pucker which catches the light and becomes conspicuous, or a line may be distorted. Careless

85

painting-on can cause the subtility of a shape to be lost or an inaccurately drawn cross to look amateurish, whatever the workmanship.

If the embroidress is inexperienced in the use of a frame, it is essential to practise from the very beginning, keeping one hand above (usually the right) and the other below, wearing a thimble on the centre finger of both hands. It takes time to attain the perfect control which produces a rhythm in passing the needle through with the upper hand to its return by the lower. It will be apparent that both hands have to be free for holding and stitching not only the threads but cords, spangles and applied fabrics. Ordinary stitchery (such as long and short) must be mastered before attempting the greater difficulty of manipulating the gold, for, whereas silk will stand up to repeated unpicking, the gold covering will wear away and reveal the bright orange core of the Japanese gold.

CHAPTER SEVEN

GOLD WORK

HISTORY

Gold, being the most precious metal, has from pagan times symbolised life-giving power. Decoration, as associated with religion, was probably embroidered and included golden discs and studs, as can be deduced from more durable evidence. The development in the production of metal threads has subsequently influenced the methods of work.

In the East the thread used was made from very narrow strips of gilded or silvered paper wound round a silk core; this was, and still is, couched down with a finer silk thread. (Although Japanese gold as we know it was not introduced into England until about 1860.) Narrow flat strips of gold couched down seem to have been an early method, which was also later used in the West and can be seen on the remarkable medieval horse trapper, which, made into a chasuble, is now in the Cluny Museum in Paris.

Very fine gold, silver gilt and silver twisted round a fine core of silk was the thread most generally used; it was known to medieval Western Europe as Cyprus gold. In Tudor inventories there are references to Venice and to Damascus gold. Its manufacture was further developed in Nuremberg, and in England by the Guild of the "Gold and Silver Wyre Drawers".

The high percentage of gold in the thread used for working the wonderfully preserved tenth-century stole and maniple from the tomb of St. Cuthbert (on view in the Library at Durham Cathedral) made possible a unique technique. The linen couching thread was taken through the loops on the back formed by the previous row of gold and although the material has perished, the gold stitchery is linked together, and the silk embroidery holds the remainder.

The method of underside couching characteristic of the Opus Anglicanum period (1250–1350) was rediscovered by Louis de Farcy. It was worked by bringing the linen couching thread up through the linen and silk background materials: it was then taken over the fine gold thread and returned in the same hole, pulling a little loop of gold down and through on to the back (*16a*), the then couching thread would be brought up to the surface again in preparation for the next stitch. By planning the spacing a pattern (usually a chevron) was formed: the front and back are shown at B and C in fig. *16*. When used as a filling the direction taken for the lines of gold was generally straight through the shape or followed the grain of the fabric. Time has proved this to have been a durable and very pliable technique. There is a predominance of gold work on all the wonderful Opus Anglicanum specimens. On one of those in the Victoria and Albert Museum can be found an early example of padding. It is on the Lamb which formed the morse of the cope from Steeple Aston, which was made into a dossal and frontal.

Surface couching had continued to be extensively practised elsewhere, and in England by the middle of the fourteenth century it was superseding the underside couching and contributed to the decline in the standard of workmanship; another cause was the prohibitive cost of materials due to the war. However, in the early fifteenth century, technique developed in new ways due to the introduction of fabrics requiring different embroidery methods. The applied units called for the introduction of couched rays of gold and many little spangles. Where the background was entirely covered solid areas consisting of rows of gold were couched down in an immense variety of diaper patterns. The subjects included architectural and other details which were emphasised by a padding of string, this combined with silk embroidery formed the hoods, and orphreys on copes and chasubles of the fifteenth and sixteenth centuries in Europe and can be seen in many museums. There are the earlier Byzantine examples, where such a padding under the gold has been used with the beauty of decorative restraint. This applies also when similar methods were incorporated into the embroidery upon the funeral palls belonging to the City Companies and Guilds.

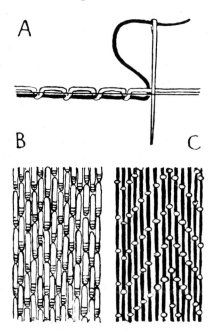

16 *Underside couching*

This chapter concentrates upon the techniques found in gold work. To study a truly delightful artistic application of many of these look carefully into the sixteenth-century altar frontal which depicts in the centre the crucified Christ, on the left kneels Ralph, fourth Earl of Westmorland, and his sons, and on the right his wife and daughters. It is in the Victoria and Albert; there, and in the British and Ashmolean Museums, are embroidered bookbindings showing the use of the purls. Silver plate has been worked into the decoration upon the beautiful copes made for the coronation of Charles II and preserved in West-minster Abbey. Gold plate taken across vases in high relief forming part of arabesque decoration upon the orphreys of two copes of the present day in Westminster Cathedral is, in a different way, no less beautiful.

A fine gold or silver thread passed backwards and forwards across a template cut in parchment or vellum has been used in conjunction with basket stitch and open fillings for interpreting designs of Italian origin. Examples of embroideries for Jewish ritual show the same methods, though richer and heavier in appearance. The same basic stitches, but often without the parchment foundation, have been selected for the working of the most interesting Byzantine and Greek embroideries for ecclesiastical purposes.

The older methods of couching having been superseded in the second half of the seventeenth century by the method now used, with the introduction of Japanese (and Chinese) gold into the West, the scale and method underwent a further slight change. The increased thickness of the threads led to more outlining and larger areas of surface couching which could be worked directly upon the background fabric. Effects obtained by the spacing of stitches and gradation of colours produced an appearance of modelling in the folds of drapery and called for great technical skill.

METAL THREADS

The amateur worker experiences difficulty in identifying and knowing what metal threads are obtainable. The photograph (*XVI*) shows some of the standard and most useful threads. The *appendix* at the back of the book gives a list of a few of the firms from whom they can be obtained, though they may not continue to be made or supplied. The following notes will help the embroideress who is not conversant with the threads. One of the inherent difficulties in procuring most of the items listed lies in the fact that very small quantities cannot be obtained; in nearly every instance the minimum amount is usually in excess of the requirements of the amateur; but where the subject is taught stocks of gold are sometimes kept for the students to use. Prices vary too much to be included. It is always worth getting the best quality; it is so disappointing to see the beauty and result of long labours spoilt by tarnishing, though nothing can prevent this happening to certain kinds of thread; to keep the work and thread well covered, and airtight (when possible), will help. Never wrap in tissue paper unless it is acid-free, nor handle the gold unnecessarily; those who suffer with "clammy" hands must be specially careful in this respect.

Japanese gold is the basic and most widely used thread for Church embroidery. It is satisfactory because it is untarnishable, being made from narrow strips of gilded paper wound round a core of orange silk. It is sold by the hank of ten skeins and sometimes by the single skein, each of which comprises about $14\frac{1}{2}$ yards.

In plate XVI the various threads shown are somewhat smaller than their actual size.

1. Japanese gold, size K.1.
2. Japanese gold, size K.2. There is also a K.$2\frac{1}{2}$.

These are suitable for large-scale work, and require expert manipulation.

3. Japanese gold, size K.3.
4. Japanese gold, size K.4. These are the sizes needed for smaller embroideries such as a burse and veil.
5. Japanese gold, size K.5, which is finer again and is useful for details.
6. Japanese silver, size S.2.
7. Japanese silver, size S.5.
8. Japanese silver, size S.7.

Japanese gold and silver, though by no means cheap, cannot be too strongly recommended. The same applies to the cords made from Japanese gold, they are pliable and easy to sew. It is not possible to purchase short lengths of these cords. Four yards is about the minimum.

9. Japanese gold cord No. 3. There is also a $3\frac{1}{2}$.
10. Japanese gold cord No. 4. These would be used for large-scale work.
11. Japanese gold cord No. 5 might form the edging for a burse.
12. Japanese gold cord No. 6.
13. Japanese cord No. 7. These are suitable for outlining parts of the embroidery.
14. Maltese silk or horsetail, supplied in a few shades of yellow also grey and white; it is used for couching down the gold and silver and is sold by the skein.

The metal threads are usually sold by weight, those containing gold and silver by troy, and aluminium and all imitations by avoirdupois.

The gold and silver threads are made in three qualities. The most expensive and least likely to tarnish (being the purest) is Admiralty or Government standard and identified as $2\frac{1}{2}$/90. The normal quality called gold $1\frac{1}{2}$/50 and the cheaper known as gilt; it is preferable to avoid this if possible, because in common with tinsel discoloration takes place in time. Most of the following items are made in all qualities.

As firms have their own methods of identifying sizes, those given on these pages may not be applied in all instances. The purls, or bullions are known by the manufacturer's needle sizes. No. 7 is an average size, Nos. 8 and 9 finer, and suitable for smaller pieces of work. The very large ones (not often required) are called bullion, these are not shown.

15. Passing thread No. 3. It is made from a narrow metal strip wound round a core of silk. It is usually couched, double or singly and is used mainly for ceremonial embroidery.

16. Passing thread No. 6. Even in the gold quality both will tarnish in time. These threads are smooth. The passing and tambours can be threaded into the needle for stitching and are excellent for open laid fillings. They are not inexpensive but are of good quality: $\frac{1}{2}$ oz. is the minimum supplied. Larger sizes are made.

17. This is called Imitation Jap. No. 2, it is similar to tambour; it is made from a very narrow synthetic metal strip spun round a rayon core; it is flexible and works easily, but is too fine for general purposes. It comes in a rather warm pinkish gold. As it weighs light it is very inexpensive and is untarnishable; 1 oz. is the minimum supplied.

18. Aluminium, a smooth Tambour No. 5 is untarnishable, has a dull surface and is slightly darker; it contrasts in an interesting way with the shine of silver.

19. Aluminium, smooth Tambour No. 15.

20. Aluminium, smooth Tambour No. 16.

21. Aluminium, smooth Tambour No. 16a. These are brighter and lighter and all will thread into the needle for stitchery. Not less than one ounce can be purchased, but it weighs very light and is most inexpensive.

22. Fine cord, gold is not untarnishable; it gives a precise line which is sometimes required but is somewhat hard and stiff. It is sold by the yard.

23. Crimped gimp; this is decorative and gives an interesting texture when couched down with a very fine thread, but its application is restricted. Gold, size F.1, is shown; there is also No. 1 which is coarser: these are not cheap, $\frac{1}{2}$ oz. minimum.

24. The three-ply thread shown is gold 137/4, super.

25. Three-ply silver, F.1, 50%. These give a pleasing texture quality when couched down, and a $\frac{1}{2}$ oz. of either the gold or silver can be procured.

26. Known simply as "Grecian" it should be referred to as such. The size shown being large and is gold.

27. Grecian, medium.

28. Grecian, small. These are supple and attractive but would not be "in character" with all schemes.

29. Plate is a narrow flat strip of gold-covered metal; at present there is only the one width. The quality shown is gold $1\frac{1}{2}$/50%—$\frac{1}{2}$ oz. can be purchased.

There are several kinds of Purl. These are made from fine gold or silver-covered wire twisted spiral-wise like a spring; being hollow some are used by cutting into short lengths and sewn like beads. Ceremonial and badge work is done almost exclusively with these threads. It is always advisable to have the Admiralty quality if possible. Though not shown all are made in silver too, but this is apt to turn very dark in time. All are sold by weight, and 1 oz. of each is the minimum supplied, but $\frac{1}{2}$ oz. of Admiralty quality is possible.

30. Rough purl, No. 7. It has a characteristically dull surface.

31. Smooth purl, as its name implies, is smooth and shiny. Size No. 7 is shown.

32. Bright check purl (No. 7 is shown), when cut into small bead-like pieces, produces a rough sparkling texture.

The bead or pearl purls are made from coarser wires and are sewn over for edgings in continuous lengths.

33. Bead purl, size Very Fine.

34. Bead purl, size super.

35. Bead purl, No. 1.

36. Bead purl, No. $1\frac{1}{2}$.

37. Bead purl, No. 2.

38. Bead purl, No. 3.

39. Yellow raising thread for padding. $\frac{1}{4}$ lb. is the smallest quantity obtainable, but coton à broder, star silko or linen embroidery thread of similar size can be used in most instances. Padding is not often done with thread now; more frequently yellow (or for silver, white) felt is used and this can be purchased from almost any embroidery department or shop.

40. This thread, which is in the nature of a Passing, is known as check on silk (quality gold); it is attractive when couched down. The thick size is 16×3.

41. The finer size of the above and known as 8×2. $\frac{1}{2}$ oz. is the least that can be bought of either.

42. Concave spangles in 3 sizes: minimum quantity sold $\frac{1}{4}$ oz. of each. They are not always in stock.

43. L.B., F.B. and No. I Spangles, flat gold: $\frac{1}{4}$ oz. smallest amount sold.

44. It is now more difficult to procure pearls in different sizes. Some types have a rough edge to the hole and this cuts through the thread. The stud shown is but one of many sewn-on or clamp-on varieties to be found; as they change according to fashions it is pointless to show examples. When used with ingenuity, suitable studs can enhance many schemes of decoration.

The jewel shown is of the sewn-on type. These are flatter and therefore better

BYZANTINE EMBROIDERY
FROM ROUMANIA

(a) (above)   *A cuff, dated 1586*

(b) (right)   *A Stole End (1586)*

(c) (below)   *A Eucharistic Veil (1493)*

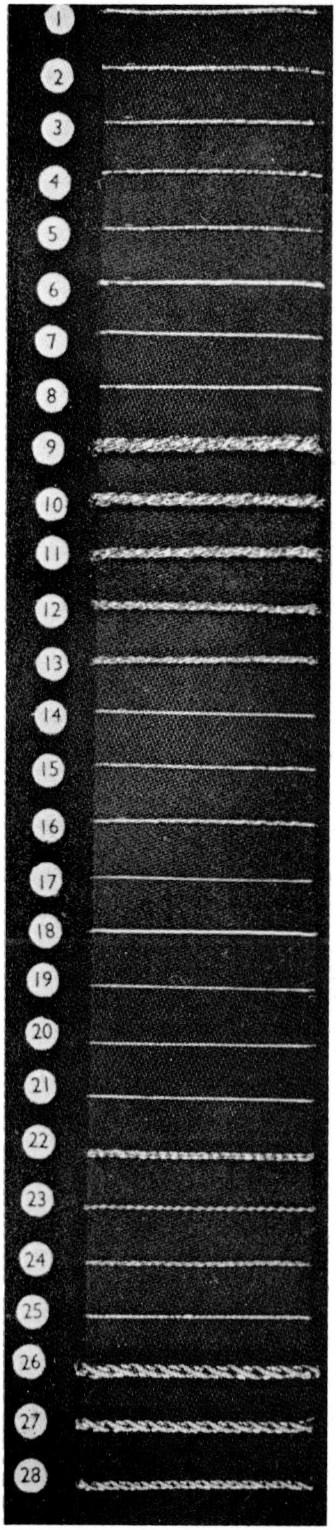

1–13 *Japanese Threads and Cords*

14 *Maltese Silk*

15–21 *Passing and Tambour Threads*

22–28 *Cords and Twists*

29 *Plate*

30–38 *Wire Purls*

39 *Raising Thread*

40–44 *Fancy Threads and Spangles*

45 *Flat "Lurex"*

46–47 *Twists*

48–51 *"Lurex"-covered Passing Thread*

52 *Russia Braid*

53 *Fringe*

The Threads, etc., which are here shown (rather smaller than the actual size) are described on pp. 90–95 and in the Appendix

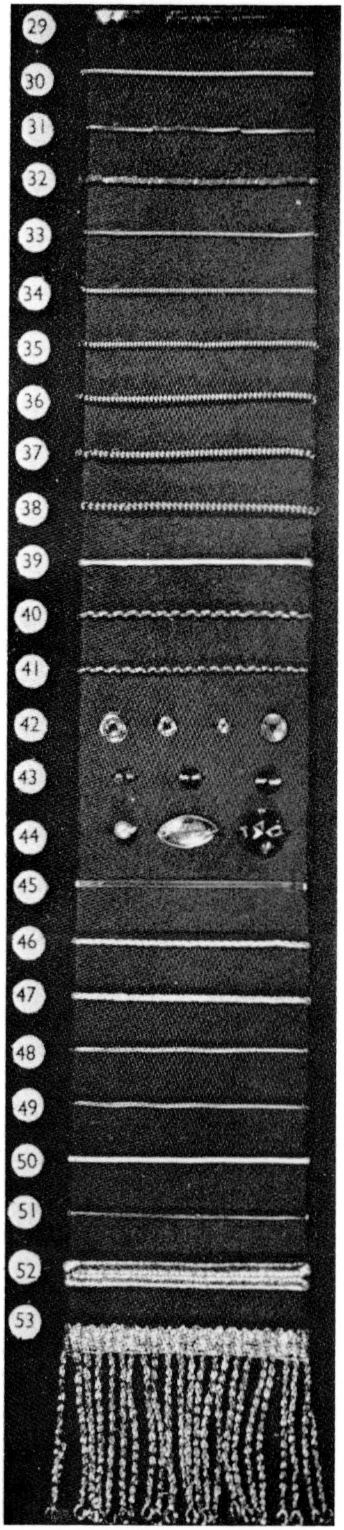

than the ones set in a mount. The clamp-on variety, being associated with dress, are apt to look a little cheap, as indeed are many of the jewels supplied. So they should be selected with great care, and the bright mirror-like ones rejected. Old sewn-on jewels are to be found in more sizes and a richer quality than the ones now made.

45. Lurex is obtainable on reels in gold and silver and many colours; the one shown is the continuous flat strip type. It is untarnishable and washable and very inexpensive, and is obtainable at most stores in the embroidery or knitting departments.

46. Aluminium Twist, two-ply: a fine flexible cord; it is attractive when combined or used as an edging with silver.

47. Aluminium Twist, three-ply: this is more useful as it can also be stitched as a cord. 2 oz. of either is the smallest amount which can be bought; it is inexpensive and weighs fairly light.

48. Lurex-covered passing thread, No. 13, the narrow strip of Lurex is wound round a nylon core. It is flexible and should be couched down double or singly. It is not intended to be threaded into the needle. This thread will not tarnish and is inexpensive; it is procurable in 1-oz. and $\frac{1}{2}$-oz. reels. This example is a pale, cool white-gold, which can be used as an interesting contrast to the usual gold threads.

49. The same thread in copper.

50. Lurex in porcelain white covers the core of nylon. It is original and particularly effective when used on dark backgrounds. Being metallic it does not become grubby with wear.

51. The same thread covered in gunmetal Lurex; this adds interest by introducing a darker tone, yet retaining the metallic shine, it is useful for outlining in addition to the purposes which Passing threads are usually put. Threads of this nature will be further developed and the range of colour and size extended. They should be watched, as the up-to-date designer will need the greater choice when it becomes available, for the expression of contemporary ideas.

52. 5/32 inch Russia, this has many uses when a wider flat gold is needed both as an edging or for line work; this size is usually obtainable in smaller quantities. (Several other widths are made from $\frac{1}{8}$ to $\frac{1}{4}$ inch, but are not generally procurable, when specially produced it is in lengths of 36 yards. If smaller quantities are required it is advisable first to enquire whether the size and length can be provided.)

53. Thread fringe, $1\frac{1}{8}$ inch: this is usually obtainable and sold by the yard. Obtainable from trimming departments in the larger stores are a variety of

synthetic gold braids and covered cords (not shown here) excellent for an experimental approach but which are not very hard-wearing.

Gold work is characteristic of ecclesiastical embroidery. The nature of Japanese gold and the metal and wire threads must be fully appreciated and their application understood, as each has its own particular technique. Having considered the influence of the surroundings, practicability and background materials upon design, we can now contemplate the inclusion of these specialised methods which develop from the threads, and affect the approach to designing for the medium.

When embarking upon a frontal, banner, chasuble or burse, etc., the embroideress may have a preconceived mental picture which she aims to interpret in flat pattern, selecting the methods most suited to carrying out the plan envisaged; or the idea may evolve from an ability to think and create in terms of dull, bright, rough and smooth, threads, this being the very essence of the imaginative approach which leads to intuitive design. The chance juxtaposition of some textured fabrics may be the inspiration for a whole design. As an example, try for yourself. Take a skein of Japanese gold, look at it afresh and watch the gleam change with every movement; get the feel of it; try it against white kid or scarlet poult, some ice-blue woollen material or with charcoal grey velvet; add a tiny pearl. Experiment with all sorts of lovely bits and pieces. Surely the thrill will set the imagination visualising possible ways of combining other exciting textures, and from this, tentatively at first, will emerge in the mind some shapes which might form the theme, when developed, for a design or form of decoration. Maybe it would need enlarging, or the addition of other rhythmic lines and shapes, but there is the nucleus of an original design which has grown out of an appreciation for the beauty inherent in the thread.

EFFECT OF DIRECTION

This leads to more advanced and conscious planning. If the designer feels an affinity with the gold she will be able to think ahead and take into consideration the play of light upon the direction taken by the gold so that it becomes an integral part of the whole. A solid golden spiral, such as a halo, is most effective, or a curved shape stitched with rows running parallel with the general direction. This would be in direct contrast to taking the gold straight through or across or with the grain of the material. A repetition of wavy lines will give an unexpected play of light. Another example can be found at the turn of an angle, similar to a mitred corner, and can be used to decorative advantage. It is only with experience that the results of a change of the direction in the laying of the gold threads can be foreseen: sometimes the light will catch and emphasise an unimportant or ugly feature, therefore the direction should always be carefully planned before beginning to stitch, in order that the flow of the threads may enhance or make more understandable the subject of the design. A direct and straightforward approach to filling a shape is invariably the most satisfactory. All the foregoing points should be searched for and studied in the illustrations.

TEXTURE

There are many methods of treating the gold in order to produce textures which can break up the surface. Basket stitch is but one example; the gold or silk is taken over a foundation of string, and so catches the light (*23b*). Padding of various kinds produces many different textures, some of which are shown in working diagrams (*22, 26, 29*). There are crinkled or check threads which, when couched down, contribute another type of texture effective when contrasted with the smooth gleam of Japanese gold. And further, by knowing something of the potentialities of the wire purls and other threads, the field of possibilities is extended, though these include some which are not conventionally associated with church work. If interest is added and they are durable, surely there is no logical reason for disdaining their inclusion? Many are the advantages to be derived from using traditional materials in a fresh way or by working old methods with new products. This applies to texture and will be found illustrated and explained further in relation to the diagrams dealing with the subject of texture (*23, 24, 25*).

TONE

Another characteristic of gold work, which can be developed by the designer and executant, is the ability to change the tone value and the appearance of the gold by couching it down with threads of different hues; it will be made to seem warm if hot colour, or cool if a cold one, is used for the working. By regulating the space between each stitch a graduated effect can be introduced, and by definite grouping and spacing of the stitchery, isolated or all-over patterns are possible, using one or more colours.

By this stage it has become apparent that schemes of interesting complexity are attainable by working the whole design with gold and metal threads exclusively; contrasting the richness obtained by raised gold against one of the numerous lace-like open fillings, adding perhaps the shine of a little golden plate. How wonderful this could be! But—it must always be borne in mind that unless the strictest discretion is exercised the result may be appallingly common and vulgar.

If there be the slightest doubt it is infinitely preferable to choose to keep the introduction of glitter to a minimum, thus adding extra value to the gold by the restraint imposed. There is an individuality and beauty gained only by this approach, which cannot be too strongly advocated. It is preferred by many as being more suitable for adornment with religious significance.

PROPORTION

In the early stages of planning a piece of embroidery, which includes some gold work, consideration must be given to the important question of the proportion of metals to colour. It is usually more satisfactory to make either one or the other predominate. If the interest is to lie in the colour, then some of the less brilliant metal threads might be selected. But if the supporting colours are kept fairly neutral or restrained they will not detract from the subtlety of the variegated golds. The proportion of background to pattern, if greater, can be assessed as a positive factor, acting as a foil to the smaller amount of richness. If the reverse is chosen, then the background is of secondary importance. It is seldom satisfactory to have an almost equal quantity of brilliant colour and of gold, as they fight for dominance and the beauty of each is thus diminished.

TONE VALUE

The actual tone value of the gold must be weighed up. It usually appears in the middle range, being medium, unless made darker or lighter by the colour with which it is stitched down. There it will not show up fully unless the background is definitely lighter or darker than itself, regardless of the colour. We have all seen examples, such as gold devices embroidered upon grass-green fabric. Then, because they tended to sink into the background, a remedy for the defect was sought by putting a dark line all round the gold parts, so that from a distance the outline assumes undue importance, upsetting the balance intended: whereas the choice of dark olive or light grey-green as the background would have given the necessary contrast and subsequent visual repose.

A straightforward linear approach with gold couched down is frequently fitting for its purpose and has the advantage of retaining the niceties of the drawing. There is a trend towards introducing gold only as line work, though this is admirable because it is simple and allows for a spontaneity of approach, it may in time become monotonous, especially if this restriction is the outcome of ignorance or lack of skill in the wider application of metal threads.

In outlining with gold threads the basic points in the technique of gold work are encountered; these will be explained with the aid of diagrams. The importance

98

of practice cannot be over-stressed, as the manipulation of the gold needs a dexterity quite apart from the experience of ordinary embroidery. Each stage should be mastered before passing on to techniques beyond the capabilities of the worker, otherwise the result will appear laboured.

Having selected the correct size of Japanese gold the beginner will avoid damaging the skein by carefully winding two threads together on to a roll of soft material about $1\frac{1}{2}$ inches in diameter.

Japanese gold is usually laid two threads at a time. They remain on the surface and are couched down with small stitches taken across at right angles and should be the exact width of the two strands of gold; if they are insufficiently wide the gold is nipped into a waist. Horsetail or Maltese silk is used for the couching; it is made for the purpose, but can only be obtained in a few colours. For stitching the finer sizes of Japanese gold and other metal threads, also for articles which will not have very hard wear, sewing silk is excellent because of the infinite range of colours. (There is a slightly greenish-yellow which, when used for pale gold, contrasts beautifully with the warmer ones.)

To commence couching make a knot and a tiny back stitch on the outline with the sewing thread and bring the needle up at the start of the line, bend the gold back to form a loop, and take the needle down into it. The next stitch will be taken over the two gold threads fairly close to the first; subsequent stitches should be evenly spaced and not too far apart (as in fig. 17a). Some workers slightly twist up the gold between each stitch, but usually this need only be done where a loosely twisted length is encountered. At the end of the row, and wherever necessary, the gold is cut to within about $\frac{1}{2}$ inch and is taken through to the back either by threading into a chenille needle or by means of a strong silk "sling" in a chenille needle (as shown in the fig. 17b). When possible it is generally preferable to work the silk stitchery first, then after doing the gold work to take the ends through when the particular shape has been completed (although not usually necessary until the end they can be cut down to about $\frac{1}{2}$ inch and pasted back); they then become "worked in" as the embroidery proceeds. These orange ends are one of the troubles encountered in gold work, as they are apt to catch in the working thread and get pulled through to the right side; when this happens the stitch must be pulled out, withdrawing to the back the orange end.

Good sharp corners are most important; the couching stitches must remain regularly spaced, so that, if a stitch comes close to the corner to be turned (as at the top, fig. 17c), it is necessary to put a stitch over the outside gold thread only, followed by another spaced symmetrically with that on the other side of the corner. In the lower one in the same diagram the spacing is such that a stitch is needed over each gold thread separately, so that the shape is kept rigid.

To deal with a more acute angle, as at D: having taken the last stitch before turning the corner, bring the needle out a little beyond the point (a point should always be accented) and stitch over the outside gold thread (some people keep this tight by making a tiny back stitch into the material where it will be covered). Now bend the gold at an angle, twisting it up slightly so that no orange will show. Bring the needle up on the outside and make a stitch across both. Next

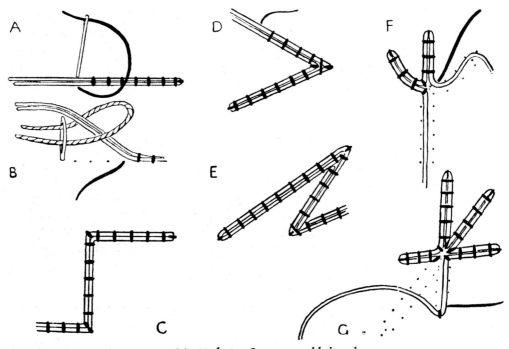

17   *Manipulating Japanese gold threads*

form a stitch at right angles over the inside gold thread at the corner and bend it, stitching over outer and inner gold strands. This must alternate with the opposite couching.

When working a very sharp point the method is different. At the top corner of fig. *17e*, after working the last couching-stitch before the turn over both gold threads, the inside one is cut, leaving about ½ inch. Then the outside gold is taken well beyond the point, stitched and bent sharply round, and is kept in place by another couching-stitch a little lower, and alternating with the one opposite. Now bring the needle up in position for the next stitch, but before completing it place a new gold thread in position and continue the couching. The two Japanese gold ends can then be taken through. In the second corner it will be noticed that in order to maintain the spacing, the stitch directly after the one taken over the single gold at the tip of the point is made across the corner of the outer thread of gold. Except for this difference the method is a repetition of the former one.

In fig. *17f* and *g* the same principle is shown applied to two different examples. By planning ahead many linear patterns can be executed by manipulating one continuous single metal thread. It will be seen from the diagram that for the start the metal thread is sewn down at the centre; having secured it the couching thread is carried across on the back to be brought up at the point in the outline, and a stitch is taken over the gold, which is then bent round to form a double row. These are couched down together until the centre is again reached. The

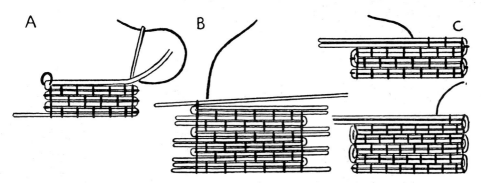

18   *Turning the threads at the end of a row*

process is repeated for each point until joining up with the commencement, when both ends can be taken through.

When there is more than one row, or a block of metal threads to couch down, the stitches are arranged in a brick pattern. For the commencement the gold is usually bent to form a double thread (though when applicable two separate threads are sometimes preferred, the ends being taken through before starting the couching). Of the various ways of turning gold at the end of the row, fig. *18a* shows that most suitable for smaller shapes. It will be seen that at the end of the first line of gold a small couching-stitch is taken over the single thread which is bent round, whilst the sewing silk is passed underneath to be brought up at the opposite outline. Here it is taken over the single gold one again, which is bent round and the two are couched double. When the outline is again reached the process is repeated. The advantage of this method is that it is decorative, especially for tapering shapes, and an outline is unnecessary. It is not practicable for large areas as the tension would vary from row to row.

The method shown in fig. *18b* is the most generally employed. The way of commencing is, however, different. Having couched the gold double along to the end of the row, the first thread is cut and the second turned, a new thread is placed by its side, and both are couched, as shown in the diagram. The original gold being cut, the other is bent round and another new one inserted; this is repeated and the ends taken down.

Alternatively, using the Japanese gold double, both can be turned together at the end of the line, using either of the methods illustrated in fig. *18c*. But it

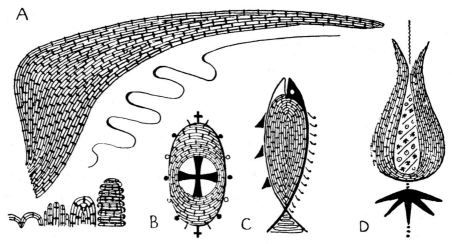

19   *The direction of the gold threads*

must be done very evenly and on large-scale work. The disadvantage is that it does need some type of neatening to cover the edge. Another method of dealing with the turn is by cutting off the gold sheer with the background. This cannot be recommended in any circumstances, as it requires a fairly broad outline to neaten and strengthen the edge.

Blocks of solid gold couched in straight horizontal or vertical lines having been considered, the treatment for irregular shapes, curves and circles will now be undertaken. Much thought should be given to planning the best possible way of laying the gold in relation to the shape to be filled. A beginner will be tempted to couch round the outline, then, as the lines converge towards the centre, the light will catch the turns in the gold which will develop into veins with the most unforeseen consequences. To keep the unbroken sheen of the gold when dealing with some difficult irregular shapes, it is usual to take one or two rows round the outline. Then, as in fig. *19a* when there is an outward curve in the wing, to insert a single or two short lengths of gold (taking the ends down afterwards); the next pair will probably be shorter. After this another longer row is put in, followed by two short ones; this is continued until the shape is completed. To ensure that the beginning and ending of all the rows shall be inconspicuous, they all vary according to the requirements. The regular bricking of the sewing will be upset by the inclusion of the short inserts of gold, consequently the spacing will need constant readjustment. This method is difficult and calls for experience, but the result, especially when raised with padding, is very rich, though this can be misused in an effort for greater realism.

The direction and the method of laying the metal thread will depend upon the form to be filled, but in general the rhythm will be echoed. Fig. *19b, c* and *d* are further examples. In the fish the turn of the gold forms a vein which is used decoratively. It will be noticed that the first line of gold is taken right through the centre of the pair of shapes which symbolise a pomegranate; other rows run parallel with the first and are taken through to the edge. Every shape must be considered individually. These general principles may assist in deciding which treatment to adopt. The examples of embroidery reproduced here should be examined and illustrations of the points discussed should be carefully studied.

To fill solid pointed shapes and those with corners the method will obviously be a repetition of those used for outline work, though even these must be adjusted to the particular purpose: for instance, when filling in a cross, instead of following round the outline, then couching the inside space with gold. It is preferable, as in fig. *20*, to commence with a double strand of gold couched down the middle of the top arm of the cross. When the centre is reached one strand is turned to the right and stitched across diagonally at the corner of the centre. The other is turned to the left and stitched in the same way. The gold thread is taken to the end of the arm, stitched and bent round to return, whilst a new length of single gold thread is laid by its side; they are then couched down together until the centre is reached; then each is stitched singly, the double gold is couched up to the top of the first arm, as shown in the diagram (*20*), and the process is repeated until it is filled in to the outline. For the bottom arm of the cross a new double thread is started and worked in the same way, being divided on reaching the centre.

A circle couched spirally is one of the most effective uses for any metal thread. In fig. *21a* each of the Japanese gold threads is started separately on the outline, leaving a short space between. The stitches in the first row are as far apart as practicable. They are evenly bricked until in the fourth row the spacing is changed to anticipate leaving out about one in every four stitches in the fifth row: with each subsequent row fewer stitches are retained. By planning ahead the spacing must be kept as even as possible and no two stitches should be directly under each other. The overcrowding of stitches as they converge must be avoided; this applies to all curved shapes.

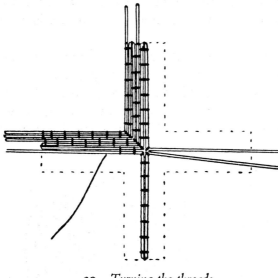

20   *Turning the threads*

The smaller circles (*21b* and *c*) show two of many decorative methods of stitching. Haloes are frequently stitched in a similar way; if the gold used is too coarse a ridge will be formed and it will be very difficult to embroider the face and hair right up to it. If the halo is put in afterwards it is apt to spoil the line unless it is in scale with the working of the flesh.

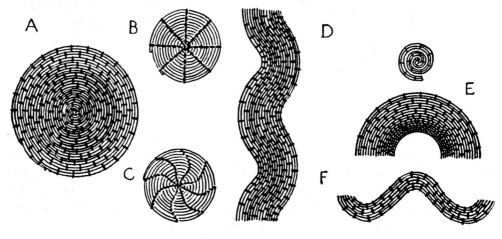

21   *Stitch spacing*

Fig. *21f* is a simplified approach to fig. *21d*. The couching stitches are further apart on the convex edge of the curve, and closer together on the concave, and are evenly spaced in the centre. When the row of gold is sewn in the same way on the other side the bricking is retained.

When sewing with a coloured thread, advantage may be taken of the density of the converging stitches on curves and circles; sometimes the number will even be increased as shown in fig. *21e*.

It is also possible to introduce variation into the spacing of the couching-stitches in order to heighten the effect of interlacing, as for example in the crown of thorns (*22*). Supposing that one band is gold interwoven with another of silver, take gold threads of sufficient length and commence by stitching down (in a darker colour) all the strands composing that which is underneath, until the

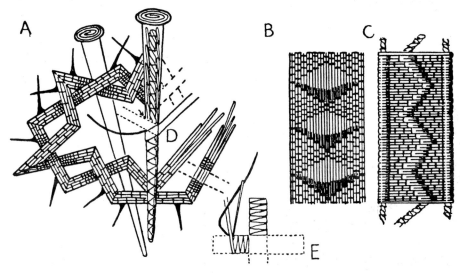

22 *Sewing down metal threads*

point is reached where it becomes the upper one; then turn the whole bunch of threads aside out of the way. Start stitching the silver ones; these will be taken over the gold, with stitches of a lighter colour placed further apart. But as they start to get closer together again and the colour darkens to form the shadow, then a few more openly spaced lighter stitches are worked before the silver threads are put aside and the gold ones put over the silver and stitched with the lighter colour. This procedure is repeated as shown in the diagram. The thorns would be worked in long and short stitch.

Another method of treating the sewing down of metal threads is to brick-stitch the background areas leaving the gold unstitched as it passes over the pattern; this is, of course, worked a row at a time, and gives a raised effect when completed. A very simple example of this Italian method of couching gold is given in fig. *22b*. Many more intricate patterns could be developed on the same lines.

In the example in fig. *22c* a tightly twisted string of the macrame type has been laid along the lines to be raised. It has not been turned but cut at the points and sewn over with a waxed thread. The double row of gold has been secured at the edge and passed over the string and the background couching—bricked. A stitch would have to be worked on either side of the raised line to define it. Many are the patterns which could be worked out in this method.

As a contrast, plate can be introduced to give a smooth shining surface. If it is to be raised, string should be sewn down and if necessary lines of stem stitch added to complete the padding. The waxed thread, being brought out in position for the first stitch, is taken through the little hook formed by folding back the end of the strip of plate, and it returns through the material to come up on the opposite side. A stitch is taken across the plate, as shown in fig. *22d*. The plate is then bent over on itself and again stitched across on the opposite outline. The flat Lurex thread is treated in the same way (*22e*).

Another variation of sewing string as a raising medium is illustrated at A in fig. *23*. Here it is in diagonal or oblique lines across the space; the gold is treated singly, though it can be double: in either instance the stitches sewing down the gold must be at right angles to it, and there should be one stitch on either side of the raised bar. Other patterns can be built up by placing the string in different ways, not necessarily in continuous lines, but as isolated units.

Basketwork is seen frequently and many variants can be devised. All have a foundation consisting of bars of string stitched down with waxed thread. It is important to cut each bar a fraction inside the outline; it will be found easier to manage if the first stitch is taken over the string a short distance from the end; this keeps it tethered and makes it possible to secure the cut end more firmly and neatly. Double threads of gold are taken over two bars of string; if Japanese, it should be slightly twisted up between each of the stitches, which are taken across the gold and sewn with a strong thread; a tiny back stitch worked after the couching-stitch will enable the gold to be bent back on itself and replaced in preparation for the next stitch. In the pattern shown in fig. *23b* two rows of double gold are taken over two bars of string and the next two rows alternate. On larger areas varied spacing can form more intricate patterns; on smaller ones it is suitable to take the gold over the same two bars of string in each subsequent row (as illustrated at C). Pliable threads give the best results, such as Japanese, plate, Tambour, Lurex-covered Tambour, stout or untwisted floss. A limitation of basketwork which has to be accepted lies in its sheer thickness: in consequence a rather heavy outline is the only means of finishing the necessarily rough edges.

Again there are many ways of introducing small shapes padded with felt, parchment, leather or cord. One example is shown at D. The little squares of felt are sewn down alternately, then the metal thread or silk is taken across the padding and stitched in the alternating squares. The effect is accentuated if a darker thread is used.

This leads to a method much favoured in the sixteenth and seventeenth

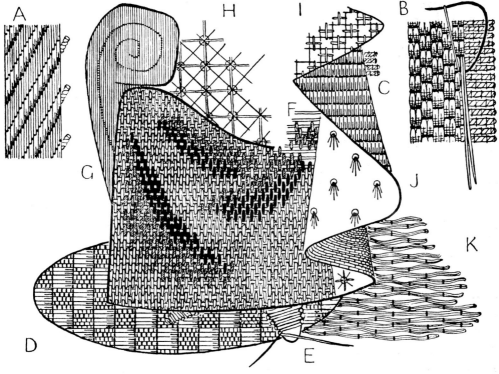

23   *Contrasting textures*

centuries, especially on the Continent. The shape to be worked is cut slightly smaller in parchment, leather or cord and stitched in place. Then the Tambour, passing, narrow plate or any other suitable thread is taken backwards and forwards, close together, across the template, a fine sewing thread stitches it either side of the bend, then it is taken underneath to the opposite side where the process is repeated. The foot in the diagram (*23e*) is worked in this way.

Fig. *23* shows the lower part of a seated figure in diagrammatic form. It is devised to illustrate the value of placing together textures of different types worked in opposing directions, each filling being selected to fulfil the decorative requirements and to be suitable in scale for the area to be covered. For this reason short stitch or "burden stitch" worked in silk has been chosen as the best method for conveying the rhythm of the folds in the drapery of the garment (at F). It will be seen that spaced lines of single or double gold are laid horizontally; they can be kept in position with small, self-coloured couching-stitches, far apart. Filo floss, filoselle or anything suitable can be used for making the short vertical stitches which go over alternate rows of the gold. This is one of the few methods by which graduation of colour can be introduced.

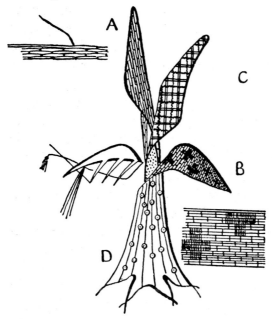

24 *Decorative treatments*

In the remaining solid filling (*23g*) the background metal threads are placed vertically for contrast. The spiral is executed with stitches of colour taken over single strands of the metal thread. It will be noticed that some of these are too long to be left unattached. If they were couched down with tiny stitches in self colour it would not detract from the main line.

The open laid fillings (H, I and J), and also many more which can be invented, are all worked with Tambour or passing threads in a variety of thicknesses and metals and are threaded into the needle; they also include little flat spangles.

The areas of plain background material become an asset, adding something positive to the composition, because they bring in alternative proportions. These in turn are set off by the irregularity achieved by laying and couching the metal threads loosely in the method referred to as waved gold (*23k*).

The diagram should not be taken too literally; it is intended to convey the interest to be gained from the contrast of the various techniques, and to stimulate the imagination into finding new ways of planning embroidery for the adornment of the church. If the whole figure were to be completed in a like manner, there would be a resultant surfeit of pattern; though the points discussed could be applied and developed when planning any type of decoration.

The solid filling covering the topmost leaf (*24a*) in the little tree of life is most effective when a single soft flexible thread, such as Lurex-covered Tambour is used. It should lie along the material and be couched with widely spaced stitches of a darker tone; these are bricked with those of the previous row. Another solid filling, which is one of the many little patterns formed by sewing with colour over a double or single metal thread, is given in the diagram at B; whilst at C just one example of many forms of tartan is shown. Work the first crossing, stitching down the lines where they intersect, then complete the next, etc. If threads of different types and colour are used the result is decorative and quick to achieve. The trunk of the tree (D) is worked by laying converging strands of some metal thread and sewing on to it little concave spangles at intervals. The rays so often depicted in medieval paintings can be interpreted in this method. The remaining leaf might be applied with embroidered lines.

In contrast to the more formal fillings used in gold work, there are many open, free-hand decorations which can be devised by couching single metal threads in the pattern called, in terms of machine embroidery, "vermicelli". It is invaluable for presenting a "broken" or soft edge, being light and delicate. This is shown at A and B in fig. *25*. The angel is adapted from one upon an early sixteenth-century chasuble in the museum at Prague, it is worked mainly in appliqué. In the wings the scale and zig-zag patterns F and G break up the surface, as they too are worked freely; these and many other patterns of a similar nature can, if required, be worked right over an outline or applied area, introducing an accidental note.

The play of light as the metal thread is turned at the corners of the wing of the dove (C) and the way in which the radiating string padding of the halo causes a shine upon the gold (H) add interest when introduced in conjunction with the free-hand and the more formal fillings, one of which is given at (I). This pattern possesses an invaluable feature in its adaptability, as one side of a shape can be made to fade into the background. The little crossbars can either be worked in silk or with short lengths of check, rough or smooth purl.

Very simple lines repeated in graduated thicknesses of couched metal thread are always attractive. This is shown at D, also in fig. *25*. At E one of many little freely worked pieces of ornamentation is given; more difficult but very rewarding are similar designs interlaced; these require two or more threads or cords and much forethought.

The main influences which affect the visual arts in each age are also observed in the trend of design for crafts such as embroidery. When applied to gold work this means that each worker should select the right method with which to capture and retain the spirit of the design.

The following diagrams will illustrate this point. In the first chalice (A in fig. *26*) the precision and regular interplay of wide and narrow lines will call for a method capable of expressing these characteristics. It could be achieved by using varying sizes or altering the number of Japanese gold threads, adding little jewels or pearls. If the addition of rays surrounding the Host would be an advantage, then lengths of crinkled plate could be used. This is done by holding it along

25   *Solid and open fillings*

the length of a screw or a comb and indenting it with the thumb nail. It is then sewn down as shown in the diagram at B.

The chalice (C) which was taken from an eighth-century Byzantine carving has a character all its own, and this must be retained if it is to be expressed in terms of embroidery. Should an outline method be chosen then a stitch such as heavy chain (D) is suitable as it is capable of variations in its width. A smooth Tambour or passing threaded into the needle could be used for the working. (Fig. *26e* shows how the metal should be unwound from the core, which is threaded into the eye, then the point of the needle is drawn right through the core; this prevents it from becoming unthreaded and if the metal went through the needle it would wear away and cause damage to the material.) If this chalice is to be treated as a solid entity a thin padding put under the metal threads would be an advantage; the background portions could be stitched as suggested in the diagram (F) and an outline attached when needed.

The drawing at G is of a chalice in the modern idiom and was taken from an embroidery of German origin; it requires a completely different treatment.

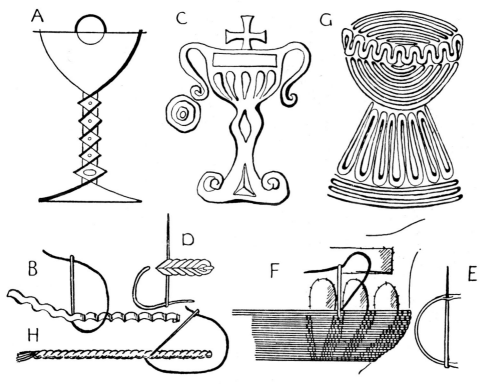

26   *Contrasting characteristics*

The freedom can best be preserved by sewing down cords of the required widths. **To sew the cord** use a waxed thread; the stitch should be taken at the same slant as the twist, the needle going down through the cord between the twists at H (never right over it). To turn a corner take stitches into both sides of the cord and pinch it into a good point. If the angle is very sharp then it is better to cut it, leaving a half-inch end, and start again slightly below leaving another end, both of which would be taken through to the back of the work, first piercing a little hole with a stiletto. The advice concerning the turning of corners will not apply to this chalice, but, in common with attaching wide cords, the stitches might well be taken alternately into either side to facilitate the turning.

Each of the crosses given in fig. *27* requires individual interpretation. For the cross of Lorraine (A), use any kind of round thread stitched down invisibly; a dark metal on a light background or a light one on a dark ground with little spangles in the spaces formed by the crossing threads would keep the simplicity. Endless are the ideas which could be devised on similar lines.

The little cross of contemporary shape might be filled solidly with single or double metal threads stitched down in diagonal lines with colour. These are

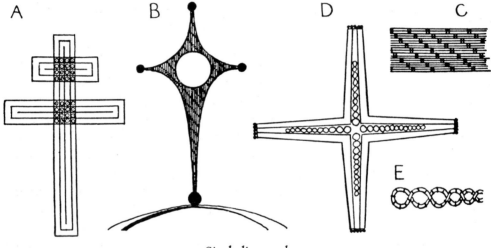

27   *Single lines and mass*

taken at right angles to the metal thread (diagrams B and C). And the padded satin-stitched circles at the terminals would complete the work.

At D the cross could have a couched metal outline, or be padded and covered with rows of Japanese gold. The little wavy pattern in the centre (E) might appear fine and delicate like filigree.

The object of including figs. *26* and *27* is to point out that the nature of the design and the method selected for working it out are interdependent, as one grows out of the other. The wider implication lies in the ideas which these simple suggestions may ingenerate. So often embroiderers of great skill are content to continue to work the Gothic-style sacred monogram and the Latin cross alike with basketwork. If these little examples have awakened the ingenuity so that even one interesting use of metal threads is evolved, then the aim has indeed been achieved.

D'Or nué is the method whereby coloured threads are sewn over gold to give a gradated and luminous effect. It is the quintessence of all that is lovely in gold work. Colour and gold merge into each other with a unique richness. Unfortunately this technique is seldom practised now, partly because it is not only one of the most difficult, but the slowest of all methods; also its uses are limited and it calls for an exceptional creative and artistic understanding in the execution.

The historical examples will not help to inspire the embroiderer of today, as they are the very negation of the contemporary approach, being entirely representational. This method of shaded gold was found to be the ideal means of expressing the exuberance of the Baroque; it seems to have been established first in Flanders. There are both Flemish and Florentine fifteenth- and seventeenth-century examples in the Victoria and Albert Museum. These later copes have hoods and orphreys which show the typically realistic interpretation of the modelling and high relief of the Baroque architectural background to the figures, which usually have the separately embroidered and applied head and nimbus (occasionally they are painted). Another treatment was to work the gold up to the outlines of the flesh, then to embroider the faces and hands in brick or short stitch directly on to the background material. Some of the Golden Fleece vestments are outstandingly rich examples of this shaded gold method.

A technical masterpiece, influenced from Italy, is the panel depicting the "Adoration of the Shepherds" and worked in 1637 by Edmund Harrison, who was a professional embroiderer to James I and Charles I and later to Charles II. It will be observed that some of the draperies are worked in this way, but over silver or silver gilt. Many examples can be found where smaller areas have been introduced into embroideries composed mainly of some other stitchery.

The late Monsieur A. Pirson, who was an authority on *Or nué* as a technique, carried out the restoration of many historic examples. A modern panel worked by him is full of interest, as it combined other decorative stitching in filo floss for the wings of the angel. For the face the gold was stitched down flatly, and it was then entirely covered with long and short stitch on which the features were outlined. The method advocated by M. Pirson for working shaded gold is given in the diagram (*28b*).

It is essential to prepare a coloured working drawing before starting upon *Or nué*. Frame up the backing. Choose and apply the linen upon which to work. If this is not too fine the threads can be followed and will serve as a guide for keeping the rows straight. (A yellow or white linen dyed has the advantage of making any gaps less conspicuous.) Paint on the design. Select the size of Japanese gold which is suitable in scale. One or more threads of filoselle or filo floss silk are best for the stitching; for gradation have only three or four sharply defined tones.

In *Or nué* the gold covers the whole surface, and the pattern is oversewn in coloured threads. By means of spacing, gradation of the amount of gold allowed to show, and of the colour, is obtained. Sometimes the reverse arrangement is more effective, to leave the pattern in gold by stitching over the background; in the diagram the scroll is treated in this way. Two methods of working are given. The first is perhaps more straightforward for a beginner.

METHOD A (*28*)

Take a double row of gold, have a needle threaded with waxed Maltese silk, bring it up on the right-hand bottom outside edge, and sew into the loop of the

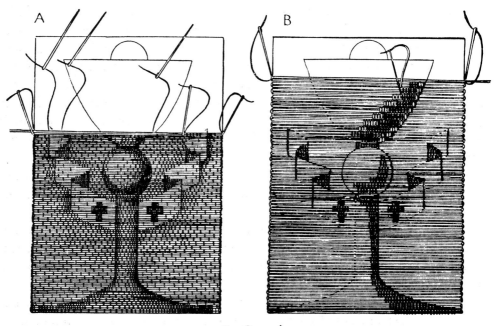

28   *Or nué*

gold. Thread up another needle with Maltese silk, stretch the gold right across and with it stitch the gold on the left-hand outside edge.

To work the chalice design: the first stitch or two will be taken over the gold and will be in the background colour; it will be brought up in preparation for the second row and laid aside in readiness. Then another fine needle threaded with the darkest chalice colour will make several stitches over the gold close together. When the highlight is reached the lightest chalice colour is introduced. These stitches are further apart, and are followed by a medium one, and so on until the end of the row is reached. The gold is turned, stitched, and stretched right across and secured on the right-hand side again. Then each needle in turn is picked up for the working of the stitches, which should be bricked as far as possible. In a more complicated design there will be many colours each with its needle. It should be realised that the diagram can only show the stitch spacing and not the colour changes.

The preparation for the method (28b) is the same, except that a single thread of Japanese is taken across and back, being stitched at each bend at the outside edges, until the whole area has been covered (it has not been completed in top in the diagram). The strands must not be too close together or it will be impossible to see the design, nor should gaps appear.

Over double gold take stitches following all the outlines, which would be in the darkest colour. With a thicker thread work all the areas which are to be in the darkest tone, putting the stitches close together so that the gold is obliterated. The design lines can still be seen as the needle parts the gold threads. Next work the outlines to be carried out in the medium colour, and fill in the areas of the same colour, using a slightly finer thread and spacing the stitches a little further apart (28b). When this stage has been reached in the diagram, each colour is put in until the whole is completed, the very lightest being worked with a fine thread with stitches far apart.

The stitches should always remain at right angles to the gold and only when it is unavoidable should they be taken over only one thread of the gold, as this causes a bulge in the line.

These instructions refer to regular shapes which are covered entirely; when shaded gold is to fill an irregular shape introduced into an embroidery mainly composed of other stitchery, then the lines of gold can be horizontal or follow the contour.

The purls or bullion are twisted-wire threaded and are more properly used in regalia, heraldic and badge work, and less often in ecclesiastical embroidery; though the nature of these threads does make them very suitable as a means of interpreting the characteristics of design at the present day. There is no reason for not using them more widely for church work as they contain a proportion of gold and the range of possibilities is infinite. The technique will be discussed; it is for the creative worker to apply and develop the fundamental principles.

By referring to the photograph of the various threads (*XVI*), it will be seen that rough purl is dull and contrasts with the shine of the purl called smooth, and that bright check purl is rough and sparkling. Whole designs can be carried out using these and the bead purls exclusively; or alternatively smaller units worked in this way will give surfaces which offer a foil to other metal threads or to silk work or in relation to the background fabric.

The size of the purl should be in scale with the design. It has to be cut into short lengths as required; therefore the scissors should have firm sharp points, and a piece of card covered with felt to form a little cutting board will help, as

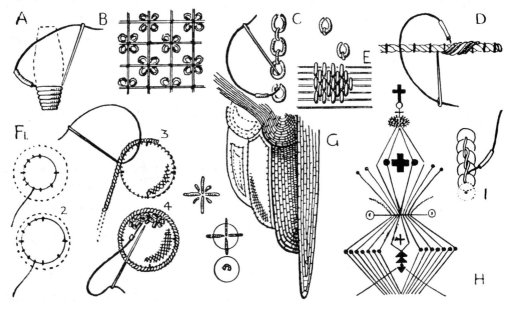

29   *Purl or Bullion work*

this prevents the tiny pieces from scattering, and they can more easily be picked up on the needle. The sewing thread, which can be horsetail (Maltese silk), cotton or sewing silk, should be passed through beeswax; this strengthens and prevents knotting. It is advisable to use a fairly fine needle.

When working satin stitch with purl, decide before starting in which direction to take the stitches; whether they should cover the shape diagonally or go into a vein or horizontally across (as shown in fig. *29a*). It takes practice to gauge and cut the lengths of purl to fit the shape. The needle, having been threaded with waxed horsetail, will be brought up through the fabric on the outline. It then picks up a piece of purl which has been cut to the required length, is threaded like a bead, and then the needle re-enters the material on the opposite side; this is repeated for each stitch. The stitches should be sufficiently far apart to lie flatly.

At fig. *29d* the satin stitch goes diagonally over a padding of string, giving a rope-like effect. Here two stitches of rough purl and one of check or smooth purl can be alternated. Another form of satin stitch sometimes referred to as "burden stitch" is illustrated at E. The long padding lines are worked in raising thread (which can be firmly couched down). The short lengths of purl, all cut to the same size, are sewn over the first and second lines of padding, leaving the width of the purl between each stitch; the stitches in the second row will be taken over the second and third lines of raising thread. This method is often used for working heraldic beasts. There is a use for the chain of smooth purl in heraldry too. This is shown at C. Longer pieces of purl have to be cut and threaded up in a loop, which is caught down with a smaller piece of purl.

An endless variety of little diaper patterns can be invented by working a foundation of laid stitches using Tambour and adding little loops of purl (*29b*) and spangles sewn with a small piece of purl or tiny bead.

A row of stem stitching worked with one of the purls forms a decorative means of attaching a row of spangles (*29i*). So-called sequins (actually the hole is near the edge of a sequin and in the centre of a spangle), sold for dress decoration, usually look too shiny unless attached by sewing with a coloured thread in the form of cross or star. There are several kinds of gold concave spangles sold for Church work; these are attached either with one or more self-coloured stitches or with a short length of purl.

String as a method of **padding** has been discussed in connection with basket stitch, but raising thread has only been mentioned because it is not in common use now, except for small and intricate details; for these a bunch of threads are cut to the exact size or shape and sewn down with a finer thread. For a circle the raising thread is wound round and round and laid in position. Where it is moulded into form, it is stitched over with a finer thread. When embroidering some emblems, including a small crown, a part of this modelled padding might be covered with velvet and pasted on the back. A further padding is then worked with raising thread sewn into place, which in its turn is covered with a satin stitch in one of the purls, the whole having been embroidered on to a backing of buckram, which is cut away to the edge of the emblem. It is then ready for applying to the object it is to decorate. Another method of padding with raising thread is to work laid stitches in the way described for white work.

Padding has become associated with a certain type of pretentious embroidery;

it has also been employed as a means for procuring additional realism; there are, in fact, examples where animal forms are almost three-dimensional, and some are in effect bas-reliefs built up with padding and covered with gold or silver embroidery. This misuse of the method obscures the advantages to be gained by introducing padding in moderation.

Where emphasis is needed in a design, the inclusion of padding is justified and added richness is achieved when the light catches the gold or silver.

Padding with felt, yellow for gold, white for silver, is the method most commonly used. When there are to be three thicknesses the first is cut smaller than the shape and sewn in place at the top and bottom, then both sides are hemmed round (as shown in the diagram 29, F1). The second layer of padding is cut a little larger, but still within the outline; it is stitched in the same way as at F2. Then the third and final thickness is cut exactly to the outline and stitched as shown at F3. When large areas are to be raised, there are frequently design-lines to be observed, either to be stitched in colour or defined with a cord ultimately. In this instance the original pricking is placed upon the felt, rubbed with pounce, and made permanent by painting, and the shape can then be cut out accurately. This is sewn in position as before, but it is necessary to stab-stitch at intervals along the design-lines to keep the thicknesses from shifting during the working. The same principle is applied when, for example, dealing with each of the feathers of which a bird's wing is composed. The diagram (G) shows stages in the working, and also the means of accentuating the form by the spacing (and change in the colour) of the stitches which couch down the metal thread.

Returning to F3, this shows **pearl or bead purl being sewn** to form an outline. Always stretch this type of purl before commencing to work, wax the sewing thread and take the first stitch through the little hook formed when cutting through the wire; the subsequent stitches are taken over and between every two or three twists in the pearl purl; a little click is felt as the thread is pulled into place. There are several advantages to be gained from using this form of outline; mainly the accuracy and cleanness of line; corners and points are bent into shape slightly in advance of the stitching and then the outlining of the circles, etc., can be joined invisibly.

Having completed the outline of the circle (29, F4) an attractive method for covering the area is shown. It consists of cutting many tiny pieces of check purl and sewing them at random like beads close together. It forms an excellent texture.

The type of decoration shown in the diagram at H could be carried out in the methods which have been discussed, using some of the threads and spangles

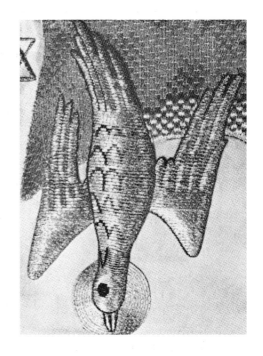

Banner of gold tissue worked entirely in gold couched with neutral colours. The Dove and surrounding wings (top right) are in relief to obtain the play of light upon the gold. The techniques employed are explained in Chapter 7. The enlarged detail of the Madonna's robe (right) shows several methods. The heads and hands are in long-and-short stitch (p. 112). Designed and executed by Beryl Dean

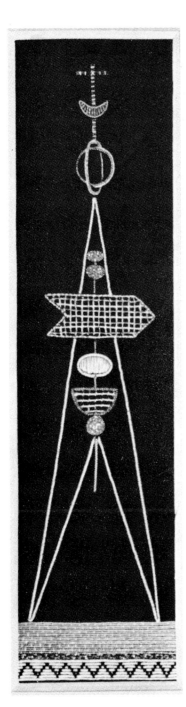 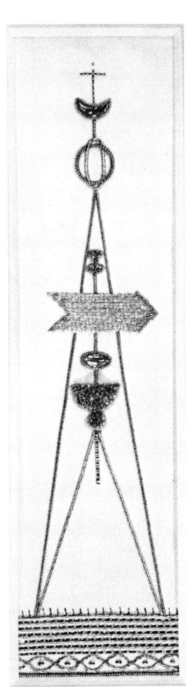 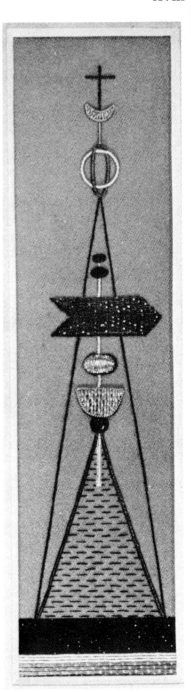

This decorative interpretation of a Church Steeple has been worked out to show: (a) Light on a dark woollen background, by means of Japanese silver, white "Lurex"-covered passing thread No. 13, silver bead-purl, and check purl. (b) Golds on white. Many of the threads and methods in Chapter 7 can be identified, including the use of plate. (c) The effect is dark on a medium-tone mass crêpe, obtained by using "Lurex"-covered passing thread No. 13 in gunmetal; also narrow strips of black "Lurex" couched down. Designed by Geraldine White

shown in the photograph (*XVI*). It is hoped that it should stimulate many more ideas in the idiom of the day.

The main points of the various techniques for dealing with metal threads having been considered, it is now for each individual worker to extract from these methods that which relates to his or her own problem or project. The aim should be to break through conventionalism when it stifles an enterprising approach to design and its interpretation. Of course the dangers inherent in experimentations are many, particularly in this somewhat specialised form of embroidery, but if the basic methods are mastered and the qualities peculiar to the metal threads appreciated, then there is no limit to the discoveries of new and dynamic means of expression in terms of gold work.

CHAPTER EIGHT

APPLIQUÉ

Undoubtedly much appliqué was produced in the Middle Ages but few early examples remain, due in part to the lack of durability and to the fact that it has never been esteemed as highly as stitchery. In English embroidery for the Church during the first half of the sixteenth century small units appear, applied in silk or satin. These are distinct from the solidly embroidered motifs worked separately and sewn on to the velvet backgrounds accompanied by the characteristic rays or scrolls. The subjects worked in appliqué often formed a decorative pun upon the name of the donor, in conformity with the prevailing practice fashionable at the time. The "Glover" chasuble is a most interesting example; found in a distillery in 1822 it is preserved at Downside Abbey. Gothic in shape, there are appliquéd formalised gloves at regular intervals in white satin on the red silk ground with its green orphreys; combined with this are repetitions of the letter "R" worked in gold. The blue linen lining forms an inch-wide border round the edge.

During the sixteenth and seventeenth centuries in Spain and France in particular (and in England for secular purposes, examples having been worked under the direction of Bess of Hardwick) abstract interlaced strapwork and arabesque designs were carried out in satin applied to velvet and outlined with fine cords, showing an Italian influence.

The series of large appliqué hangings at Hardwick Hall are unique, they represent classical and allegorical figures, typical of the spirit of the second half of the sixteenth century. Amongst the "cloth of golde, velvett and other like stuff" can be traced pieces of the thirty copes recorded as having been bought by Sir William Cavendish. The hoods and parts of the orphreys also remain.

Closely linked to appliqué is inlaid work, of which the many Italian pilaster hangings in satin are examples. The arabesque designs are outlined with cord, narrow ribbon or gold thongs. Of more interest are the Persian prayer mats; these are made from thick non-fraying woollen materials of clear brilliant colours combined with white and some black. Cords or rows of chain stitch form the outlines. To cut the inlay the two or more layers of material are laid one upon the other, with the design uppermost; this is cut round with a sharp knife, then the pattern of the first piece is fitted into the background, and overcast on the reverse side; this is neatened in various ways on the front. In the Italian examples the background and pasted satin pieces would have been mounted on a backing before being sewn together, using a frame.

An interesting fourteenth-century example in the Victoria and Albert Museum is of patchwork and appliqué in blue and red cloth, showing figures in splendid costumes, beneath arcading, it is of French or German origin.

Appliqué is the method most suited to the characteristic flatness and precision required when embroidering heraldry. An interesting early piece is that known as the Albemarle Fragment in the British Museum. This and other examples are discussed more fully in Chapter XII. To these may be added the large decorative emblems of the order of the Golden Fleece, worked in appliqué upon the velvet mantles, one of which is in the museum at Fribourg, and two portions are at Berne. These engage the attention, not only because there is a satisfactory inclusion of background material within the decoration, but also for the large-scale stitching executed with the metal thread; this breaks the surface of the cloth of gold and silver, adding a textural quality so often lacking.

Full of interest are the contemporary examples of ecclesiastical embroidery designed by architects who are artists too. They present a new and stimulating approach, requiring in the interpretation a sensitive and imaginative understanding on the part of the embroideress of today.

For the type of design frequently prepared by those architects who are not also artists, heraldry is usually included, appliqué is about the only suitable medium, as it is usually a matter of translating line and wash in terms of material and outlining cords.

It is regrettable that much of the perfectly executed applied work produced for sacred usage is uninfluenced by, and shows no infiltration of ideas from, the very real advances made in aesthetic expression through this technique for secular embroidery. During and onwards from the third decade of the twentieth-century appliqué stands out as being the typical mode of work, and full advantage has been taken to exploit the tremendous increase in the types of fabric available. Really significant works have been created in terms of applied materials, and in the use of the textures and the juxtaposition of the opaque, matt, shiny, transparent and the rough-surfaced fabrics a quality peculiar to the craft has been attained; something reaching far beyond the stereotyped traditional figure composed of pieces of arbitrarily chosen brocade placed upon a background of similar material of yet another pattern, encompassed with a hard outline.

For banners, frontals and hangings the large scale which appliqué makes possible commends it as an excellent method. If it is approached with imagination the result can be in perfect accord with the best contemporary architecture or with any period to which the interior surroundings belong. It is unnecessary to seek to imitate or reproduce a given style; it is perfectly possible to create a work which will harmonise with the prevailing character by producing a fitting design and selecting the right colours and fabrics.

Typical of the contemporary trend in appliqué is the impressive dossal hanging worked for the Chapel at the Pennsylvania State University, where Sybil D. Emerson, the designer, is Professor of Art Education. Measuring 28 feet by 12 feet wide, the impression is of light falling from the top and merging with the darker tones at the bottom. The abstract design is carried out in yarns of different weights threaded in various ways by hand through the zig-zag machine stitching, upon a ground of textured linen, applied to which are shapes in finer linens and silk organza in tones of grey and gold. The sensitive quality of the original design is retained by the interesting use made of the stitchery super-imposed upon the appliqué and carried over on to the background. The colours range from brown, through tan and gold to pale beige and white, with a little gold thread (the chapel is used for services of all faiths).

Miss Emerson's words, "It was felt that the design should be bold enough to be effective when seen at a distance, yet, on closer scrutiny should have a precious quality", have been fulfilled in this stimulating dossal, and they can bear for everyone a wider application.

When it has been decided that a **design** shall be worked out in appliqué certain modifications are advisable. First that it is conceived in terms of mass rather than indefinite linear effects (although this can be overcome by the use of transparent materials veiling parts, whilst the actual lines are accented by stitchery). Secondly that it is large enough in scale for the method. Thirdly, that the background and pattern are treated as parts of a whole. Then that the design is formalised, as this technique imposes a highly conventionalised rendering. Fifth, care must be taken that the scale of the materials used is right for the shapes into which they will be cut; it is unsatisfactory to select a loosely woven woollen fabric for an intricate detail.

As the inclusion of metal threads is an integral feature of embroidery for the Church, the **choice of materials** for appliqué may depend upon their texture in relation to these threads. A selection of materials collected together for their contrasting textural values can, when arranged, yield such unexpected and interesting results that an impetus is given to a further striving towards the creation of a design expressive of the best trends in the contemporary approach.

If this approach has never been attempted before, why not discover its possibilities and get the feel of really "using" materials by doing an exercise? Design a small unit and enlarge it to about 6 inches (Chapter II). Plan to work three variations. Then frame up a backing and put on to it the three different background pieces; one could be dull silk, another woven with a slight pattern and the other fine wool. Try out the effect of the variously textured pieces and select those which are most interesting on each of the three backgrounds, making use of transparency so that some edges are softened, and include surface stitchery. The method of working is given in the following pages. When complete have a coloured mount cut with three "windows" and stick the little exercises behind. When surveyed the result will stimulate you to develop the idea and to try out something larger, improving upon it as experience will have been gained.

THE TECHNIQUE

The reason for the conservative approach to the carrying out of sacred subjects in appliqué is understandable: by repeatedly using the same material its reactions can be anticipated. Whereas without previous experience of the other textiles it is impossible to foresee what will happen. But this will not deter the amateur (who has not got to work to a time schedule) if she is convinced that her embroidery will gain aesthetically by including some of the exciting fabrics now obtainable. But it must be realised that the total effect of a lovely combination of materials united with a perfect design can be ruined by puckering; extra care is needed in the preparation and some experimentation is first necessary to ascertain the best processes to employ. The following directions are the basic principles; to these each worker must add her own initiative and common sense, adapting the information to serve her own particular purpose:

1. Frame up the background material: or the backing if one is necessary (Chapter VI), stitching on the ground fabric.

2. Trace on the design (Chapter VI) (if required it can be traced on before framing). In the more unconventional work, where some edges simply merge away, or where the limits of an area of transparent material has to be indicated, paint guidance dots at intervals or tack in the particular lines. Tailor's chalk can be used to mark them temporarily.

3. When the fabrics to be applied are sufficiently firm, and do not fray too much, they can be used as they are.

Otherwise they must be pasted, but great discrimination must be exercised, as the nature of some materials is changed and they look hard. Avoid pasting unless it is deemed absolutely necessary, as for instance for very large shapes and "stretchy" materials.

For small pieces (also for gently rubbing over the back of the work on completion, covering with soft paper which has been crumpled up then smoothed out), some of the prepared pastes, such as Polywog or Gripfix will do. But for larger areas an embroidery paste should be mixed. The following is one recipe:

Take 3 oz. fine wheaten flour (not self-raising) and a small teaspoonful of powdered resin and ½ pint cold distilled or ordinary filtered water. Mix until absolutely smooth and strain if necessary. Then bring to the boil, stirring constantly to prevent lumps or burning. Lessen the amount of heat, so that the paste thickens equally and becomes slightly transparent. Turn it into an earthenware or heatproof glass bowl to cool. (A little boracic, formalin or a crystal of thymol added to the paste will prevent the growth of mould if the church is damp.)

Frame up a piece of fine muslin or bishop's lawn, keeping the frame tight. Apply the paste evenly with a large brush or palette knife. Place the piece or pieces of material on to this, and with an absolutely clean soft cloth stroke and smooth it out, working from the centre outwards; turn the frame over and remove any surplus paste with a bone folder or palette knife. Leave it to dry thoroughly.

Or, if practicable, the muslin can be pinned out on to a board, then after the paste has been applied and brushed out, the material is spread upon it, being pressed out with a cloth. It is then left to dry.

Alternatively, frame up the actual material (this is the best method for velvet), or pin it out, face down on a board. Well soak a piece of muslin in white rice starch, remove surplus moisture, spread it out and press it down smoothly on to the back of the material using a clean cloth. Allow to dry thoroughly before removing.

For small surfaces, pin out the material face down. Brush a white paste lightly over the back. The paste must not be too moist.

4. Place the tracing upon each piece so that when it is applied the grain of the fabric of each will correspond to that of the background. Pounce and paint (Chapter VI).

5. To cut, use a very sharp knife, razor blade or scissors. On all edges which are underneath and will be covered, leave about ¼-inch turnings.

Cut just a fraction outside the line for edges to be stitched then outlined.

When an edge is to be turned under, allow about ¼ inch (*30a*).

6. With the frame slightly slack, apply the pieces, commencing with the ones underneath; matching up the lines with those painted on the background material, pin (usually it is better to keep all the pins pointing in the same direction) (*30b*).

Tack, using slanting stitches in vertical lines over larger areas (*30b*).

7. Tighten up the frame. With tiny stitches on the right side and longer on

a

b

30   *Preparing the pieces to be applied*

the wrong, work outwards from the centre, hemming down the cut edges, and slip-stitch the turned-in ones, using self-coloured fine thread.

8. Decide which outlines are to be emphasised, working them in couching

(*34*) cords sewn down (*26h*) or any of the hand stitches which would be suitable, for example (*55c* and *d*, *56d* and *i*).

Sometimes a greater contrast is obtained by very freely working over the background, right up to and just over the edge of the appliqué (*33*).

A slanting satin stitch was often used, and where a line of varying colour or width is required it is still recommended.

31 *Appliqué, contrasting outlines*

Self-coloured couching serves to improve the drawing without attracting attention, but where detail and construction need to be indicated couching in a contrasting tone helps. As this reduces the apparent size of the area the edges should be cut a fraction beyond the traced line. In small-scale appliqué a stem stitch will also give a contrasting outline.

A cut edge can be left hemmed down, but this is not very strong. A turned-in edge, invisibly slip-stitched, is more satisfactory. (It is sometimes easier to do the

128

snipping for the concave and convex curves and the turning down and tacking first, before applying.) In some designs this type of edge is necessary when the addition of an outline would ruin the relative values of the contrast between line and mass (*31*).

For the rendering of a still softer edge, lines of self-coloured thread can be trammed down (*31a*), or modified with net or organza applied (*32*) or with detached chain or other similar stitches (*33*).

Faithfully to interpret and capture the sensitive lines used in the present idiom of design it is sometimes decided to work very strongly a line which is

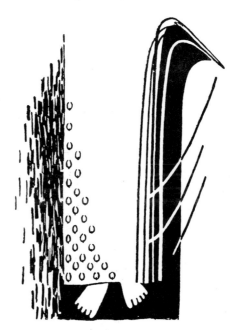

32   *Soft and hard edges*   33   *Treatment of edges*

neither a boundary of a shape or colour, yet is important to the "drawing" (*33*). Care must be taken to produce just the right weight, for example, the finest machine embroidery thread couched down will give the quality of the little scribble, or large free stitches worked with raffia or wool would best interpret the strength of the line conveyed with charcoal or paint (where to preserve such a characteristic is desirable). This treatment is far removed from the cold impersonality of the conventional approach, but by this or similar means something really worth while can be created.

With more imagination appliqué can translate exciting ideas in terms of colour, the shine of the fabric reflecting or dull woollens withdrawing, surrounded by stitchery to introduce tone or movement with the addition of textures, such as cords, weaving yarns, wools, velvety chenille or the subdued sparkle of black jet or Lurex; endless are the interesting effects, large or small, which can be carried out in this method of embroidery. If first-rate designers and the promising art students knew of the vast possibilities lying dormant and almost unrealised and became interested enough to give the subject their attention, there are usually responsive exponents, and with collaboration the resulting works would surely interest more of the artistically discriminating sponsors and patrons of religious embroidery.

CHAPTER NINE

LAIDWORK

Laidwork executed in wool, linen, silk or cotton threads has an early origin. This can be seen in extant examples. But it is with the later French hangings and the seventeenth-century ecclesiastical embroideries of Italy and Spain that it is most closely associated. Designs incorporating peonies, tulips, roses and spirally twisted acanthus-like leaves were worked in coloured floss silks upon backgrounds of cream satin or silk, or the whole was embroidered with basket stitch in silver thread. Seen in the environment for which they were intended these vestments and frontals would have presented a freshness and vitality which we do not, perhaps, appreciate, because of the endless reproductions which are still being worked.

But with unprejudiced consideration the immense possibilities of laidwork will be realised, both as an artistic expression and for interpreting the flat, semi-abstract pattern and treatment of design today. Whilst the scope made possible by the comparative speed of execution and breadth of scale attainable continue to make it suitable for the embroidery upon banners, frontals, hangings, copes and smaller pieces, which are unlikely to have excessive wear or rub. When laid-work is the method chosen as the most suitable, a design loses nothing aesthetically with its translation into stitchery, because the subtlety of the shapes and sensitivity of the lines can be retained. The play of light and shade introduced by changes of direction in the stitchery give a quality characteristic of the craft, and if the whole surface is to be embroidered this can be exploited to the fullest advantage.

Interest is added when stitchery of a different nature is introduced to act as a foil to the flatness of the laidwork. Some of the knotted or looped filling and line stitches enhance the effect, but as many of these are more conveniently worked in the hand—and laidwork is essentially a frame technique—this constitutes an unconventional suggestion. However, it is worth trying to overcome the difficulties if it will add to the aesthetic result, and with practice some of these stitches can be worked in the frame. Alternatively the hand stitchery can occasionally be done after the embroidery has been removed from the frame, always provided that the completed embroidery will not suffer damage by the pressing (on the wrong side and over several thicknesses of blanket) or stretching when applicable (see instructions, Chapter XIII) to remove the unavoidable creasing.

In the past it has been considered necessary to neaten all edges with a cord or couched outline stitched mechanically round the whole design. As the considera-

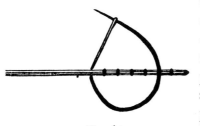

34 *Couching*

tion of technique does not dominate the exigencies of the design, **an outline is now only introduced where stress or accent is needed** in the conception of the whole composition. Sometimes this takes the form of a superimposed linear pattern coinciding for parts of the way with the outline, but crossing both the embroidery and the background if necessary. This line may have to vary in width;

accordingly some of the hand stitches are invaluable, for instance braid, pekinese, heavy chain, whipped run, satin, stem and rope, etc. For smooth continuous lines, cords (the composite cords used by upholsterers can be divided and used singly, and there are interesting cords covered with synthetic substances) and even buttonhole gimp, can be stitched down. Couching is also indispensable, especially because by its characteristics the line is left fluid; either a single thick or a group of finer threads are sewn over in the way shown in the diagram (*34*), the threads can be arranged to form a loop for the commencement and the ends are pulled through to the wrong side, and cut leaving about half an inch.

This leaves the treatment for the remaining edges unresolved; the query is whether they can be kept without outlines. If the design would suffer by drawing attention to the part of the pattern in dispute then it is preferable to choose the

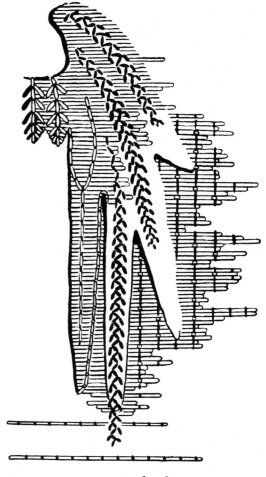

35 *Laidwork*

(a)   *A Banner carried out in appliqué, designed by the distinguished Swedish textilier, Sofia Widén*

(b)   *A Dossal Hanging, appliqué in brown, tan, gold through to white, with lines of zig-zag machine stitching interwoven with yarns. Designed by Sybil D. Emerson and carried out under her supervision by skilled seamstresses and art education students for the Chapel at the Pennsylvania State University*

(b) *Side panel of a Triptych worked in Or nué, mainly in jade greens, greys and orange on a dark-blue ground. Designed and worked by Beryl Dean*

(a) *St. Peter—an example of laid work in silk. Designed and worked by Beryl Dean for the Needlework Development Scheme*

incompleteness of the laid edge uncovered. There is a precedent to be found in Spanish and Portuguese secular laidwork. In any case a neater edge can be obtained by taking the laid stitches over a fine line of split stitching. Or if the laid stitching is so uneven that it is distracting, a fine self-coloured thread couched round will help.

In the idiom of contemporary design the freedom of an indefinite boundary to an area painted in water-colour can be interpreted (but not in the sense of copying in another medium that which is already complete as a work of art in its own right). This is achieved by terminating the laid stitches to form a deliberately broken edge. Long single stitches on the background are "trammed" down. This is useful for obtaining contrast (as in fig. 35). Another variation consists in working a decorative stitch extending beyond the confines of the area which it is tying down. This idea can be developed in many ways.

MATERIALS

Frame up the fabric (unless this is very firm and closely woven it should have a backing), then paint on. Laidwork is economical in time and thread, as the stitches are long and lie almost entirely upon the surface.

It is the nature of laidwork that large areas of flat colour in various textures (using an inconspicuous tying-down thread) can be obtained with the use of different experimental threads, and these are effective when contrasted with large or small shapes stitched with intricate laid fillings.

For the solid fillings untwisted threads are preferable. Stout floss silk is ideal, but the range is now very restricted and it is difficult to obtain.

There is a wider range of colour in filo floss. Two strands are used together, with one for tying down. This is a glossy silk slightly twisted.

In filoselle there is a wide range of colour, and the duller sheen and its adaptability make it easy to manipulate.

The enterprising worker will try out the effect of using cotton, linen, mercerised, wool and the threads with a matt finish; also raffia and man-made yarns manufactured for weaving.

Japanese gold and metal threads have been dealt with separately; their juxtaposition with the threads above mentioned will give most interesting surfaces.

THE TECHNIQUE

Solid Fillings. First consider the best direction to choose for the laid and tying down stitchery (the former can ultimately be the more dominant). Determine whether the preliminary stitches will need to be laid across or down the direction of the shape; or whether this shall be disregarded, and the stitches follow the grain of the fabric.

METHOD

If it has been decided to lay the foundation stitches horizontally, the thread is brought up on the left of the outline and is taken across the shape and put through the material on the right; the needle is then brought up exactly by the side as close as possible; it is returned across the surface to the left, the process being repeated. In this way only a tiny stitch on the two outlines will show on the reverse side of the fabric (36).

An alternative method is to leave a space the width of a thread between each stitch; these are filled on the return to the starting point. An advantage is gained by having a larger stitch through the material.

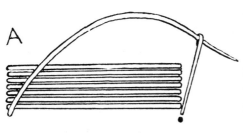

36   *The foundation*

These long threads (which must not be too tight) now have to be caught down; there are various methods, some inconspicuous, others decorative. A

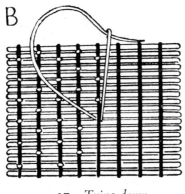

37   *Tying-down*

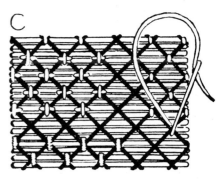

38   *Tying-down*

fine self-coloured or a rounder contrasting thread may be used. Fig. *37* shows the tying-down threads lying at right angles over the preliminary ground; these in their turn are caught down with tiny stitches at regular intervals, alternating with the previous row.

In fig. *38* the tying-down is taken diagonally and is then crossed to form a

136

lattice; this can either be tied down at the juncture with little stitches, crosses, or sewn with small pieces of check or rough purl, etc., as in the diagram.

When texture is required buttonhole stitching is worked over the surface; when going to the right the thread is taken under the needle from left to right as in fig. *39a* and on the return the loop goes from right to left. In fig. *39b* running stitches in alternating rows, taken through the fabric then over the laid foundation before returning through the material, give another texture which is pleasing.

Simple couched patterns are an effective means of tying down the laid-foundation. Fig. *40a* illustrates a repeating scroll; in this instance the thread forming the scroll is independent of that which ties it down and is taken through

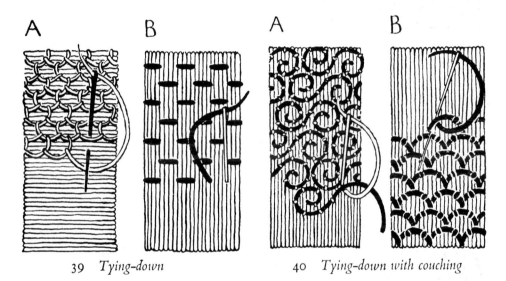

39 *Tying-down*   40 *Tying-down with couching*

the fabric as each scroll is finished, then brought up again for the next one. Whereas in fig. *40b* the same thread forms the scale and is used to couch it down. The decorative qualities of these and similar patterns hardly need to be pointed out; they are perfect for the treatment of robes and hangings when figures, etc., are introduced into design. Little isolated stars and other devices serve the same purpose, but they must be so spaced that the foundation threads left exposed are not too long.

Another virtue of laidwork lies in the fact that broken and irregular patches of colour can be introduced and subtle changes of tone, which, when sparingly employed, contrast with the areas of flat colour or gold. The principle on which this is achieved is set out in diagrammatic form in fig. *41*. Where the intermediate tones cannot be shown it must be understood that the fine lines tying down the foundation would be changed in colour as they cross this patch of colour, but usually one medium tone will suffice.

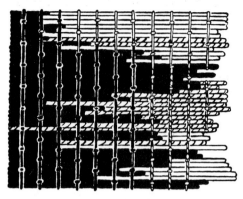

41 *Broken colour*

Where the movement of a curved shape needs to be further emphasised additional half-stitches have to be inserted on the convex side of the foundation, thus increasing the number on the outside of the curve, as in fig. *42*. Parallel lines of fine split stitching are generally used for the tying down; these stitches should be longer than usual and the needle is brought up about halfway through the previous stitch before being put into the material ahead. These lines follow the general direction and can converge or run off into the edge of the outline.

Couching is so closely allied to laidwork that three examples are included, even though these stitches are more conveniently worked in the hand. Bokhara couching is shown on the top right-hand side of fig. *43*, the thread being in position for the next stitch. Having been laid across the space from side to side, it is then couched down with slanting stitches at regular intervals across the laid stitch. An untwisted thread should be used.

Roumanian couching contributes another and contrasting texture; it is worked on the same principle as Bokhara couching. The needle brings the thread

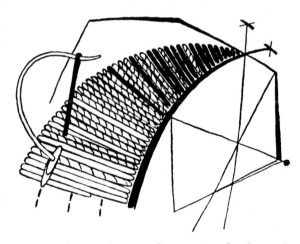

42 *Introducing direction by means of split stitch*

through the material on the left outline, is carried across, and put through on the right, being brought out again below and to the right of the laid thread which it crosses at a longer angle before going through the fabric in preparation for another stitch; this is repeated until the left-hand edge

138

is reached and another long laid stitch executed. A diagram is given in fig. *44a*.

Other surface textures are obtained by tying down with many of the open broad stitches; as shown in figs. *35* and *43* a group of laid threads are taken across from side to side and couched down with buttonhole stitches. It will be noted that the needle only enters the fabric at the beginning and end of the line, which is worked from left to right.

Open Laid Fillings. These are most effective for flat surfaces, as they are adaptable; the patterns can extend beyond the limits of an outline, thus giving a

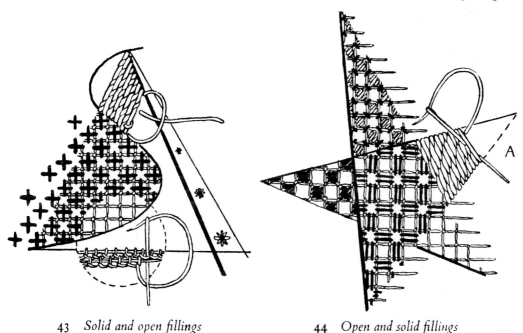

43 *Solid and open fillings*   44 *Open and solid fillings*

soft indefinite edge. The embroideress with imagination will find in these little pieces of decoration a way in which to work out patterns freely sketched on a design and not necessarily kept within the confines of an enclosed form. These open fillings possess the charm of the small-scale diaper patterns so prevalent in illuminated manuscripts, missals and paintings of the twelfth, thirteenth and fourteenth centuries. Their application to present-day Church embroidery is apparent. Usually these open fillings can be worked with any type of thread, and if metal threads or small spangles are introduced a rich jewel-like quality results. (This topic is developed in the chapter dealing with metal threads.) Many examples can be derived from Jacobean hangings and other historic embroideries.

METHOD

Straight threads are laid which are crossed at right angles; these are tied down with a small stitch as shown within the circle at the bottom of fig. 43. This forms the basis upon which the patterns are built up; in this example small crosses are worked across the lines.

In fig. 44 other fillings are worked upon the foundation in one or more operations; in the pattern on the left satin stitches form a check, whilst above a longer stitch is taken over the corners in a contrasting colour. In the centre is given one of a limitless number of arrangements which can include detached chain stitches, French knots, etc., and which are based upon the simple patterns given.

Though having a similar foundation of laid threads, caught down, fig. 45 gives a variation of chequer filling. This is worked in several operations. (1) Bring the needle out at the top right-hand side of the outline, put it through each succeeding tying-down stitch from right to left downwards, following diagonally through. (2) Complete by crossing with stitches made with the needle pointing from left to right; when the surface has once been covered these lines of stitches are crossed. The third and fourth lines are done in the same way but the diagonal is at right angles to the first two rows of stitching. Many different changes of spacing can give an entirely different appearance to this open filling.

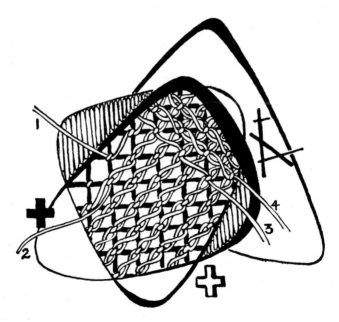

45   *A variation upon chequer filling*

CHAPTER TEN

FIGURE SUBJECTS

In religion representations of the human figure in terms of embroidery have an importance beyond the decorative. The subjects were selected as a visual means of religious teaching, the figures being easily identified by their respective symbols. The medieval convention of assigning given proportions to the relative size and placing of the features was a further aid to establishing designation and identity.

The characteristic impulses of each artistic phase can be discerned, motivating and inspiring the embroiderer through the human form.

The little saints on horseback depicted in the early Coptic tapestry weaving are allied to the figures so evidently developed from the Greco-Roman pre-Christian representatives of riders. One of the earliest pieces of actual embroidery is a fragment of a roundel of the sixth century from Egypt; the subject is Christian, and it is in the study room of the textile department at the Victoria and Albert Museum. The three figures are stitched very directly in silk; the background is also worked. There must have been an existing tradition of skill to lead to the production of such embroidery.

It is not always recognised that from the fourth to the twelfth centuries the artistic expression of the West developed as it did because of the influence derived from the established art of the Christian East. In order that the earlier medieval work of the West may be better understood, we shall progress chronologically, discussing first the treatment of the figure in Byzantine embroidery; because of its older origin, though the examples are later, the technique had remained almost unchanged.

The manipulation of the gold in the Byzantine religious embroideries imparts to the figures their own individuality, this preserves the richness associated with the paintings and mosaics and also with the Russian icons.

All the solid masses (including draperies) in the designs are worked flatly with fine gold threads surface couched double and stitched down in an endless variety of ways; the direction of the gold being changed to conform with the shape of the area being stitched, thus the clarity is retained with the addition of a strongly contrasted outline, and little touches of colour worked in silk. Where basket stitch and other raised effects have been used a foundation of rows of string would have been sewn down first and covered with the gold which is cool and slightly greenish in colour. When the background is also gold the direction of the working contrasts with that of the pattern, and narrower lines and shapes are worked by couching the gold in a zig-zag.

Another method is also found. It is simple in effect and very lovely. The outlines of the design are raised (this would have been done by first stitching down a string or linen thread), rows of gold were then laid straight across from side to side and with brick stitch couched down leaving the raised lines outlined with a stitch on either side to define them; the process would be repeated row by row until the whole had been solidly covered.

An outstanding example of Byzantine embroidery is the dalmatic of Charlemagne in the treasury of St. Peter's, Rome. It may date from the eighth century, but is more probably later. The technique and general arrangement of the design are typical; even with so many figures, the grouping is such that the effect is not crowded; actually the garment is so much larger than is the impression gained from reproductions. The touches of bright red on the clear blue silk ground act as a foil to the gold.

Characteristically the heads and limbs are worked in parallel lines of split stitch with silk (46a). For the heads these invariably run across the forehead, down the side of the face where the upper rows curve up to terminate under the nose, and the remainder continue round the chin. To fill the spaces additional rows of stitchery follow the existing directions. The features are defined with a dark line, heavier for the eyebrows and continuing in a finer line down the nose where it changes to a firmer line as it returns up the other side, widening for the second eyebrow, the wing of the nostril being worked afterwards. Usually black is used but in the head which forms the subject of the diagram (46) the outlines are of olive green. Characteristically the mouth is small and worked in a light pinkish colour, whereas the eyes are emphasised and are dark and expressive. The direction of the split stitch is indicated in the drawing with fine lines; similar lines show how the gold couching follows the lines of the drapery; the touches of blue split stitch and border of silver are also shown. The halo is couched in a chevron pattern. It is usual for the hair to be worked in alternating rows of dark and light colour: for the men, it is generally straight and the beards are arranged in various decorative ways; on the heads of angels and archangels curls are formally piled up, with a few longer curls falling on to the shoulders.

The late thirteenth- or early fourteenth-century frontal in the Historical Museum, Berne, is an inspiration of design, colour and workmanship. Unlike most Byzantine embroideries, much of the background is left without pattern; it is of purple silk, showing in parts the cyclamen pink weft. In the centre is a large-scale seated figure of the Virgin and Child, it is from plate XXI that fig. 46

is a detail. To the left is a tiny kneeling figure of the donor and two shields which establish the date and origin. On either side are delightful plant forms, growing from golden vases; the leaves are jade green, and almost luminous; each branch-

46 *Late thirteenth century—Byzantine*

ing terminates in a white roundel, giving a general effect of translucency. The archangels, one on either side, worked mainly in gold, with wings, the undersides of which are embroidered in narrow stripes of brown and white, and they swing censers. The broad orphreys at the ends of the frontal probably originated in Palermo and were added later, possibly in 1537 when it came to Berne from Lausanne Cathedral. For these designs of spiralling vines, growing from formal vases; the technique used for the gold is not unlike underside couching in effect and the background is of crimson silk.

Admittedly clumsy are some of the Byzantine embroideries, insufficient care having been taken to retain the clarity in the small-scale figure compositions. Yet there are examples which contain a wealth of interest. This can be judged from the Epitaphios Sindons in the Victoria and Albert Museum and at Canterbury Cathedral. The groups of figures will be seen to serve the same purpose as the iconography of the medieval Church in this country. Easily recognisable scenes enrich the stoles (*epitrachclion*), the diamond-shaped piece of stiffened silk worn suspended by a band (*epigonation*), bier palls (*Epitaphios sindon*), the dalmatic-like vestment (*salekos*), the mitre (*mitra*), and cuffs (*epimanika*), etc.

Similarities of grouping, proportion, posture and gesture are characteristic of all figures of the Gothic period, whether they be in sculpture, stained glass, wood, illuminated manuscripts, frescoes, mural paintings or embroideries. The S-bend, the high, broad forehead, the enlarged pupils of the eyes, and the arrangement of the folds in the draperies are general. To the embroideries of the Opus Anglicanum period (1250–1350) in particular there are certain characteristics. The flesh is worked in lines of fine split stitch which follows across the forehead, down the nose, then returns along the line of the brow. The cheeks are worked spirally (where the silk has worn away the painted linen shows that a deeper pink was introduced for younger people). The theory that these spirals were pressed with the heated point of an iron either inwards or outwards according to the age of the person depicted is no longer held. The general direction of the stitchery can be followed from the diagram (47). The hair and beards (the upper lip is shaven) are worked in alternating dark and light lines, either in green and yellow, brown and yellow, blue and white or black and white. In the treatment of the draperies lines of split stitch follow the direction, with the dark colour outside on the outline of each fold, and the lighter inside. The protruding pupils of the eyes were stitched spirally in black. The characteristic underside couching of the gold is discussed in Chapter VII. The head of the Archangel Gabriel (47) is taken from the cope of Pius II at Pienza and is of the first half of the fourteenth century; it is typical of the arcading type of spacing, which, in the intersections bears scenes from the Bible vividly depicted in stitchery which covers the ground entirely. There is a wealth of invention and interest in the design and the whole is a marvel in its richness of colour, incident and stitchery.

During the first part of the sixteenth century styles arose due in part to the introduction of new materials. In consequence other methods were adopted, leading to fresh conventions in the presentation of the human form, resulting in a certain charm which, as embroidery, is delightful; but spiritual values and

47   *Opus Anglicanum*

sincerity seem to be lacking and were being replaced by the Renaissance eye for "terrestrial beauty", which led to a poverty of inspiration in the subjects selected for embroidery design.

145

Worked separately on linen, the motif, when completed, was applied to the velvet ground, and in consequence the figure subjects lose rhythm and the delicacy of form. The head, hands and portions of drapery are worked in brick stitch (48a) with a fine, untwisted floss silk, and the features are outlined, with eyes and mouths, in split or satin stitch. The lavish draperies, contemporary dress, and heraldry are worked with surface-couched gold and silver gilt (this is gone into more fully in Chapter VII). There are examples showing figures standing on little swards done in laidwork, with tufts of flowers superimposed; typical examples are the St. Catherine of Alexandria, and the altar frontal depicting in the centre the Crucifixion, with Ralph, fourth Earl of Westmorland, and seven sons and also his wife with thirteen daughters. (This frontal is interesting for another reason, as it shows in the arrangement the same convention fashionable for monuments at the time.) These are to be found in the Northern Gothic section at the Victoria and Albert Museum.

In Europe the style contemporaneous with, and similar to, the Opus Anglicanum (but lacking the typical characteristics) continued and can be traced, for instance in Germany, from pieces in the galleries and study rooms in the Victoria and Albert Museum. The variety of methods used and the technical approach are interesting—it is noticeable that many of the embroideries have little or no gold thread and greater inventiveness of stitchery.

Other typical examples are two frontals of the fourteenth century, now in the Historical Museum, Berne; one shows a large-scale seated figure of the Virgin Mary and Child with St. John and John the Baptist against a background divided by arcading and including several beasts. The whole is almost entirely surface-couched in fine gold with details picked out in coral beads and this gives a lovely quality. The other frontal not so satisfactory as a design, nonetheless exhibits in the embroidery of the Crucifixion and figures of the saints, many interesting features. Fig. 48b is a detail which shows the direction of the split stitchery for the working of the head and hands. The treatment of the arcading is unusual; there is an almost round padding, over which gold plate has been passed back and forth to cover it; over this has been worked an open surface-buttonhole filling stitch with a fairly coarse round thread, and the capitals and surmounting pinnacles have been cut from flat, thin sheet metal, and sewn down on to the deep red velvet ground. The effect is uncommonly lovely. It is probable that both frontals were worked by Agnes, Queen of Hungary; the parchment backing had been cut from a letter written to her by Ludwig of Bavaria; it is known that she was a religious woman who did much embroidery.

Workers and designers were gradually absorbing the tendencies of increased

146

realism, until embroidery was completely under the influence of the Renaissance. The aim was to convey realism through the portrayal of third dimension, so the techniques employed were those with which gradation of colour could best be expressed, such as *or nué* (*28*), short stitch over lines of gold (*48c*), and long and short stitch (*49a, b, c*). The heads and hands being worked in long and short, or painted. This deplorable practice, incredible as it must seem, still persists!

A panel, worked by Edmund Harrison (in the Victoria and Albert Museum),

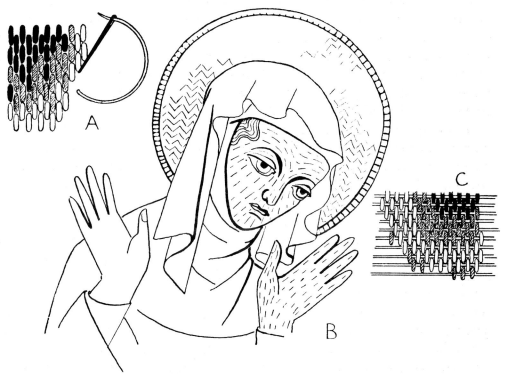

48 *To show the direction of the split stitching. Fourteenth century*

exhibits the impact of the influence of the later stages of the Renaissance in England. The subject is the Adoration and is a masterpiece of skill. Ever since it has been the aim of a minority of embroiderers to endeavour to paint with the needle to represent the modelling of the human figure and draperies in terms of light and shade, and to imitate perspective in stitchery. This is far removed from those early designers and workers who were intent upon conveying the story or incident simply and directly.

Another outstanding type of figure treatment is typical of the idealism inspired by the Pre-Raphaelites. It was adapted rather than created, but served to interpret faithfully the character of the designs, which are so well fitted for ecclesiastical embroidery. To describe but one example, a chalice veil, there are four formalised angels, very tall, heads towards the centre, their wings outspread to form a continuous and well-balanced design, the robes being white with gold, and the wings embroidered in a range of silks in wonderfully rich reds offset with a touch of orange. To counteract this brilliance there are slate greys, and the lighter bluish greys with which the central Agnus Dei is carried out. The significance of the design and its symbolism are typical of the best of the period; it is regrettable that the work of the imitators is, perhaps, more familiar.

The technique conventionally employed for the solid stitchery at this time consists mainly of **long and short** generally worked straight down with the grain of the material, or taking a direction. The diagram (*49a*) shows the stitches converging. To work, execute the edge in long and short stitches alternately, then bring the needle up through the stitches of the previous row, going well back into each stitch and not just into the end; the effect will be smoother; after the first row all the stitches are the same length (*49b*). To converge, gradually leave out stitches. Where one part of a design overlaps another it is important to work that which is behind first, then put a split stitch outline (*49c*) and work the first row of long and short stitches over it. Experienced workers all have their own systems, but this method is one way of obtaining a smooth finish and it is a good means of introducing additional tones gradually to procure gradation of colour when this is desirable. It is usual to use two threads together, and when large spaces have to be covered with long and short stitches following a curved direction, it is a great help to pencil in guiding lines, and to work these in split stitch, then to fill in and complete a section at a time.

To work a head in long and short stitch, it is essential to bear in mind the construction and structure of the head and to keep the form and symmetry (*49d, e, f*). (Those with little feeling for drawing will get a more satisfactory result with a less ambitious method.) All the stitches go straight down with the grain of the fabric; alternatively they can be taken straight through the face irrespective of the threads of the material.

Assuming that the head is turned slightly to the right and that the light is from the left-hand top corner, also that it has been decided to use four flesh tones: clearly determine in the mind where the darkest and the darker medium will come, then the lighter medium, and the lightest tone which will be used to pick out the highlights. Fig. *50b*, which is intentionally formalised, shows this distribution of the tones of colour in diagrammatic form.

148

THE WORKING

Bearing in mind the principle that the parts which come underneath are worked first, put long and short stitches under the chin and jaw: and, where there is sufficient space, below the brow also, otherwise put satin stitches, and then work down both sides of the nose. Sometimes split stitching is put along the line

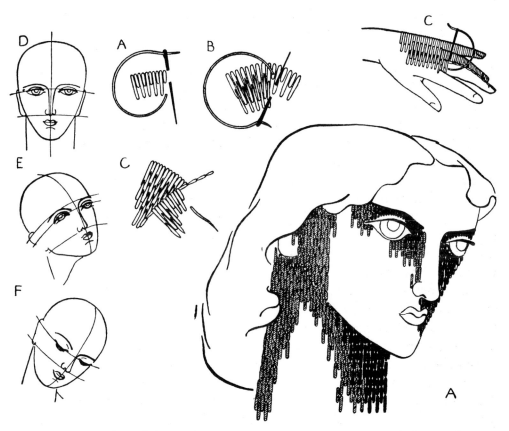

49 *Construction of the head*   *50a* and *c* *Long and short stitch*

of the jaw and the long and short stitches are taken over it; if this is not done then the stitches terminate to leave a narrow voided line (to be covered afterwards with an outline).

In fig. *50a* as much as possible of the two darker shades has been put in. The stage has been reached when the long and short edge at the hair line must next be worked, and it will be noticed in fig. *50b* that for this the lighter medium and lightest tints have been used, and that they are carried down to the eyebrows, where a narrow voided line is left. It is important to note that before commencing the nose a split-stitched line must be worked from the eyebrow down the outline of the nose and round the tip; also for the wing of the nostril. The subsequent long and short stitches are taken over it; this slightly raises the outline of the nose and "lifts it away" from the shadow side of the face. The filling in of the rest of spaces can be followed from the diagram. It is often preferred to introduce a pinker colour into the cheeks, though for an old person the lightest tone accenting the cheek bones is an advantage.

To keep the eyes symmetrical it is essential to work the same stage on both eyes as they progress. First work the whites of the eyes with satin stitches, using grey on the shadow side. The pupil and iris of the eye are worked in a spiral of split stitching, then the eyelid is outlined in a fine split stitch which is covered with satin stitches, using the darker medium and the lighter medium tones.

If the mouth is large enough, a fine split-stitch outline is used to "draw in" the shape and a very few satin stitches "sketch" in the colour, keeping the upper lip darker and the lower lighter, which can be worked with lines of split stitches following the contour across.

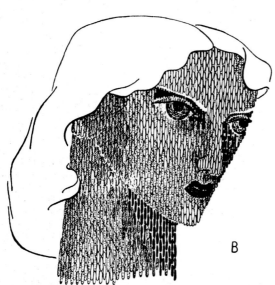

B

50b *Long and short stitch*

Starting from the ends work in the eyebrows; in a formalised head the line can continue down the shadow side of the nose. The wing of the nostril is outlined, so too are the eyes, keeping the upper lashes heavier. Just a few stitches in the right place along the centre of the mouth can alter the whole expression. So too can a white stitch to make the highlight in each eye.

Hair is usually worked in rows of split stitch starting from the ends each time.

Hands (50c) and feet can be worked in long and short, remembering to work that which is underneath first, then putting a split-stitch outline before working the next finger or toe.

150

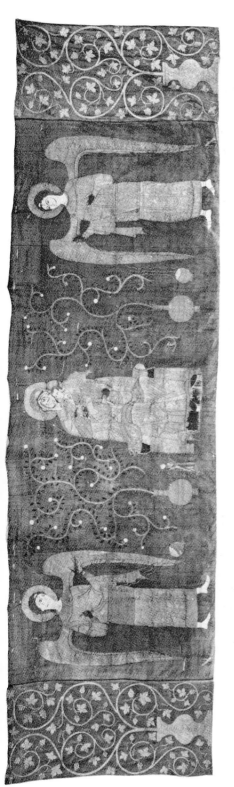

(a) Frontal (Byzantine, late thirteenth or early fourteenth century) (see p. 106). In the Historical Museum, Berne

(b) Frontal (fourteenth century). Probably worked by Agnes, Queen of Hungary. Historical Museum, Berne

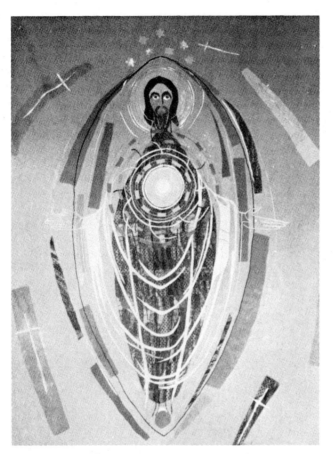

(a) *The Resurrection. Design in appliqué by David Holt. Commissioned by Sir Albert Richardson, P.P.R.A., and produced by Gerald Holtom Ltd*

(b) *A Panel, embroidered in very direct stitching, by Sister M. Regina, Kloster St. Ursula, Augsburg*

(a) *A formalisation, determined by the technique, of a Figure Subject. The pulled stitches, upon a loosely woven linen, require large unbroken shapes. Worked by Maria in der Afingstgeminde, and reproduced by permission of Schweizer Heimatwerk, Zürich*

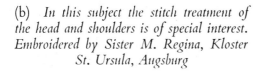

(b) *In this subject the stitch treatment of the head and shoulders is of special interest. Embroidered by Sister M. Regina, Kloster St. Ursula, Augsburg*

(a)   *The kneeling figure of Ralph, fourth Earl of Westmorland, with his seven sons, from a frontal of the mid-seventeenth century (see p. 110). The working of the couched gold, silver gilt and silver is of great interest*

(b)   *The fourteenth-century painting of St. Michael from the rood screen at Ranworth, Norfolk. This is but one example of medieval painting which is an inspiration to the designer of today*

The colours are a problem. There are no really satisfactory ranges, but there are separate colours in filoselle which are good. The conventional tram floss or flesh silk is so much too light and can only be procured where very old stock remains, and there are insufficient interesting and useful colours either in filo floss or any other silks. When the heads, conventionally carried out, are looked at really critically it is realised that the flesh colours are too insipid. However, unless the anaemic saints are to persist, some degree of improvisation is essential; skeins of silk and stocking dyes offer one solution.

Embroidering the whole figure in long and short has been misused as the means by which a painstaking effort has been made to imitate in one medium that which was conceived in another. But, if it is modified, and instead of aiming at imitation the impression of the slight degree of depth is introduced as an asset when used in conjunction with heavy gold work, then the effect is enhanced because the weight is equalised.

The preceding method is given as a guide to those who wish to work a head in this way and "simply do not know where to start". It is not intended as a formula, but just as a basis from which to work out a personal approach.

To have dealt with the subject of the head separately and the figure apart from the background may seem reactionary, because in the minds of the non-specialist there is no such distinction. Yet it would seem that an analysis of the techniques used in the past may extend the means of expression available. With imagination these methods can be adapted to interpret the concepts of the most forward-looking creative minds. But some finished results ineradicably associated with certain types of embroidery bring them into disrepute (not without cause when one sees some of the banners still used). With this prejudice it is difficult for the young student to appreciate or be receptive to the potentialities.

TO DESIGN

Saints with their symbols have been continuously employed as a subject for embroidery upon vestments, and furnishings for the altar. But many an able craftswoman needs some guidance in selecting and setting about the preparation of the design. So often the preconceived idea envisaged is really that of a complicated painting (usually Italian) and is quite unsuitable. Lacking an artistic training it is difficult to appreciate simplicity, yet it is the very essence of a satisfactory design embodying a figure to be embroidered. This very directness is to be found in primitive and early works, also the omission of inessentials and concentration upon the main idea: if this can be grasped and recognised in, for example, early Spanish religious carvings in wood, stained glass of the thirteenth and eighteenth centuries and illuminations of the eleventh and twelfth centuries, then inspiration can be found, adapted and applied to the particular problem.

If, when looking at a Gothic sculptured figure, the underlying rhythm is thought out, it will be seen that the direction of the body, head and limbs and the folds of the drapery all add up to a rhythmic whole, and that only those lines which contribute have been retained and then accentuated.

From the foregoing precept it can also be learnt that the **figure has to be treated as pattern,** the lines and shapes being selected and adapted to further the underlying and predetermined rhythm, and it must be planned as a whole in relation to the space it is to fill. If it is to form one unit in a group then there must be co-ordination between the component forms within the space. The medieval painted screen panels in the churches of Norfolk and Suffolk, for example, although not great works of art, do illustrate how the figures of the saints depicted have been planned to fill the space and how the symbols play an important part in the design. The painting of St. Michael at Ranworth, Norfolk, possesses the decorative qualities which could well be the inspiration for an embroidered figure. Another example in the Victoria and Albert is the altar piece—painted in tempera with scenes from the Apocalypse—German, late fourteenth century. And the treasures of Romanesque art, the churches and the decorations of Catalonia and Aragon in the north-east corner of Spain near the French frontier.

It is essential to choose a pose which makes a shape in itself, and to think of the figure as being composed of a series of related shapes. If this is established there is no possibility of reverting to the tendency to draw all round the outline. Therefore the main direction lines will be sketched in, and the figure constructed in terms of flat pattern, so that the movement will contribute to the rhythm. The drawing should be kept large, free and formalised so that it can be carried out within the conventions imposed by the limitations of the craft.

The practised designer may invent and create from the imagination, stimulated by the urge commonly shared, but expressed according to the tenets of the respective media. The less accomplished designer who wants to express an idea should be encouraged to have the confidence to strive to do so, even if, in the initial stages she finds her intention difficult to realise. This sincere attempt, and that of the experienced designer, or alternatively the design based upon an historical example, are all preferable to a copy, however accomplished. How can one make clear the distinction between imitation and inspiration to those whose appreciation is limited to, and only capable of recognising the technical achievement?

THE INTERPRETATION

Whether the design is original or the worker is carrying out one already prepared, the artist craftswoman will seek to divine the particular qualities with which the source of inspiration is endowed, and will aim at transmitting the spirit and movement, selecting that embroidery method which will best preserve the more elusive qualities during the process of interpretation, by means of stitchery.

51   *Characterisation*

To retain the characteristics either of the head alone, the figure or the group it is necessary to find the right embroidery method. First determine which is the most important quality. Take, for instance the head of Christ (*51*), the tragedy is conveyed by the vertical lines, therefore if the whole face was worked in horizontal stitchery, the superimposed downward lines, worked afterwards, would contrast much more effectively.

Next take the head of a saint from a twelfth-century Jugoslav fresco painting

52   *Characterisation*

157

(52). Suppose a design for a figure had been inspired by it, the exaggeration of underlying character and emotion would have to be conveyed in terms of embroidery. It would, of course, undergo further formalisation, and the movement could best be captured in rhythmical lines of split or stem stitch, using a few sharply defined tones of colour: a finer thread might have been used for working the long and short stitch of the flesh.

When the human form is presented as being somewhat static Laidwork (Chapter IX) or if larger and flat in treatment then appliqué (Chapter VIII) would be the most suitable method.

Only where the presentation is really formalised and the shapes are simple and material suitable can the interest be centred upon diaper patterns stitched in blackwork patterns, drawn or pulled stitches or laid fillings in gold threads or silk. There is a tradition of excellent linen work in Switzerland, where figure subjects are often incorporated with other decoration.

Sometimes a Botticelli-inspired decorative quality allied to delicacy is desired; for this a basis of appliqué with superimposed silk work and couching with metal threads would translate the convention.

In much modern design varying widths of outline stress and express the human form (and the surrounding design). Sometimes the background is done in paling (used in the sixteenth century) or areas of flat colour are applied, then these outlines can be couched threads or cords, or stitched lines superimposed.

The present tendency is for the drawing of the design of the figure to be carried out in a continuous line. Again line stitchery or couching a silk or metal thread, cord or wool is excellent. This is frequently accompanied by areas of flat colour (laidwork or appliqué) and texture (the knotted stitches, etc.). Ingenuity and skill are required to combine satisfactorily the various methods in order that the quality of the presentation of the design may be interpreted. The craft gains because the embroideress is forced to use her technique as a means to attaining something beyond the rut of the conventions.

53 *Characterisation*

The contemporary designer often combines very free pencil work to build up the background surrounding a figure which in its turn forms an independent pattern. If this quality is not to be lost then means must be found to interpret the

158

pencil or ink texture, generally stem, split or couching using interesting threads will put it in freely so that the background becomes something positive. The little figure of a saint (53) shows this tendency.

The nature of the way in which the head (54) has been drawn requires a very direct and free stitch treatment (possibly over an applied fabric for the face); a fairly coarse thread for the long stitches or lines of split stitches would give the almost brutal and stark force required.

For so long really interesting embroidery has been done in Germany and that is where we find some of the most vital examples of Church work being created. The figure subjects are treated with a wonderful sense of design and stitchery, and there is variety in the approach and outlook to a very great extent. The embroideries executed by and in the workrooms of Liesel Lechner are outstanding. The figure compositions and the methods of execution must surely be unsurpassed as examples of that type of contemporary ecclesiastical embroidery.

54 *Characterisation*

CHAPTER ELEVEN

WHITEWORK OR LINEN EMBROIDERY

From extant examples of early embroidery in monotone upon linen it is possible to estimate something of the wealth of "stitchcraft" and inventive pattern which grew out of the use of the clearly defined warp and weft threads characteristic of the weave. Comparatively little has been preserved, partly because it was less valued than embroideries upon silk with metal thread; also the constant use and subsequent laundering led to the more frequent renewal of altar linen. German examples from the thirteenth century onwards show a very interesting use of stitches worked in the hand, including interlacing stitch. A somewhat similar direct use of both line and counted thread filling stitches can be observed, particularly in sixteenth-century Swiss work. In much Italian and Sicilian, also some Spanish linen embroidery, the emphasis is upon the background, whether it be of drawn-thread or pulled work, cross or long-armed cross stitches, with an outline of fine chain or some other stitch to define the pattern which remains in the linen. Reticella and Richelieu work, also patterns carried out in back and other stitches to the counted thread, are methods typical of these countries to the present day. Early Scandinavian work was more closely allied to the weave, consisting of satin stitches and stem stitches formed round the warp threads, during the process of weaving, to make solid fillings. Many interesting vestments are today being embellished with mainly abstract ornament worked in ways developed from this beginning or in tapestry weaving. In England the whitework methods employed are those which were brought to such perfection in the late eighteenth and nineteenth centuries for secular use. The ground fabric was generally muslin and this gave scope for delightful shadow effects and pulled stitch fillings. The adaptation and application to Church linen is restricted not only by artistic but also liturgical principles. Some priests prefer the minimum of decoration, others admit some latitude, allowing for instance, the pall to be made of sheer linen or linen lawn, thereby making possible the introduction of the methods to which reference has been made. It should be perfectly clear that inspiration for whitework is derived only from certain of the types done in this country and copied in India, and it does not include the excesses of raised satin stitch, very wide drawn thread borders or the less practical fringes. This has, of necessity, been but a brief summary of linen embroidery from the past. There

160

are, however, many books which deal with the individual methods; and typical examples can be found in the Victoria and Albert Museum, in the primary collections and in the study rooms; most of the larger museums also possess specimens.

DESIGN

Limitations imposed by the ultimate purpose, the requirements of the liturgy, the nature of the material, and the method of work determine the type of design which is likely to be most suitable. The former two points will be covered when we consider each article of altar linen individually. Referring to the third limitation, that of the liturgical material, this is white linen, and (although not traditional and rarely used), "if this is particularly fine and closely woven, then it is lawn or cambric" (to quote Dom. E. A. Roulin, O.S.B.). Owing to the closeness of the weave of fair linen, the types of embroidery suitable are limited. The hempen fabric called canvas is equivalent to linen for these purposes. The methods employed for the embroidered decoration influence the suitability of design. If white stitchery upon white linen is appreciated as possessing a positive beauty of its own, then the worker has the right approach to this, which is one of the most interesting kinds of embroidery.

An understanding of the methods of work and the characteristics of the stitchery prior to designing will assist in producing patterns with additional individuality and suitability. The importance of choosing the right stitch for each unit in a design is obvious; for example, it will be seen that certain of the line stitches should be selected for expressing the freely drawn parts, some will interpret faithfully the movement of a sensitive linear quality, whilst many of the counted thread fillings are rigid and impart a geometrical formality unsuited to many designs. The diagrams illustrate various arrangements of stitches and their working; they are planned to indicate combinations of line and filling stitches. It will be observed that the shapes employed in the design should, preferably, be kept simple, as this shows the charm of the filling stitches to advantage.

Although it is permitted to work in a colour, usually red, green, yellow or blue, one is thinking in general terms of white on white, where the relative textural qualities of the surfaces are planned to give contrast and balance. Therefore it may help if we group the respective stitches according to weight.

THE CHARACTERISTICS OF STITCHES

The heavier, slightly raised surfaces or outlines are achieved with satin stitch, slanting or straight, if without a padding (*82*); first run small stitches round the shape. When a slight padding is needed, work double back stitch with a coarser thread (*60a*). Or make a few small laid stitches at right angles to the finished direction, B. Cross these with a second layer of stitches, C. Then these are crossed with stitches taken up to the outline, D. Unlike the laid the satin stitches are carried underneath, E.

It is generally advisable to execute the looped, knotted and chain and some pulled stitches in the hand: using a frame for satin stitch and drawn thread fillings because it is essential to avoid puckering. But as it is possible to work all the processes mentioned in hand, the diagrams show the needle in position for hand work.

In whitework it is usual to start by running the thread along the outline; or

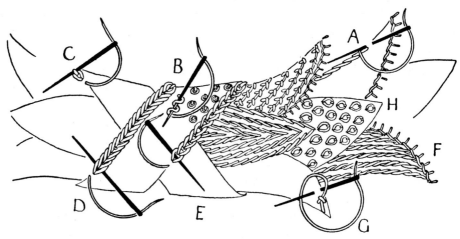

55   *Line and filling stitches*

when a knot is used, this remains on the right side until the thread has been secured by subsequent working; it is then cut off. Fasten off on the back or by working a few tiny stitches into a nearby outline where they will eventually be covered.

Rows of stem stitch, either close together, spaced or converging, make an interesting surface (*55a*). French knots, massed or singly, are effective. To commence, bring the thread through, hold it taut with the left hand and encircle the needle twice (*55b*). Whilst holding the thread, revolve the needle and put it down close to where it came up, and keeping the thumb over the twists, pass the needle through to the back. When not worked in a frame the material has to be held between the second and third finger of the left hand.

The slight shine of D.M.C. (red label) "coton floche" is ideal for working "burden stitch". First cover the ground with equally spaced laid threads, then make two satin stitches side by side over the first and second foundation rows (57a). Then work another two over the second and third rows, repeat over the first and second, and so on. Morris darning or brick stitch is similar but without the laid foundation; it is worked to the thread of the material, usually with one instead of two stitches.

Heavy chain stitch produces a wider continuous line. Start with a small running stitch, bring the needle out as if for a second, but instead put the needle underneath the running stitch, pull it through and take it down at the point when it last came through. Now bring the needle up a short distance ahead and pass it a second time through the running stitch (55c). Again put it down in the same hole and bring it out ahead; each time it passes behind two chain loops (55d). Broad chain is similar but instead of going back through the second chain loop, the needle is put through the previous stitch each time (55e).

Rosette chain is invaluable for giving a broken or decorative edge; a linen thread produces the best result. Having brought the thread up at the right-hand end of the line, pass it across to the left and hold it with the thumb. Put the needle into the fabric and bring it up through the loop formed by the thread and pull it through (56a). Then pass the needle under the thread to the right, as shown in (56b). Repeat at regular intervals.

Buttonhole is another heavier stitch. It can be used as an outline for cut or drawn thread work. First put small running stitches along the line; work the buttonhole stitches close together over this with the heading towards the cut edge, withdrawing the threads or cutting after completing the outline. As a ridged, solid filling, closely worked rows of buttonhole stitches are effective. And ordinary open buttonhole stitching done with sewing cotton gives a delightfully decorative edge (55f). There are many variations which can be used in different ways.

The line and filling stitches of medium weight form a large group; it is a characteristic that some fabric should show. Whether as an outline or repeated as a filling, coral stitch is useful; worked from right to left, the needle should be put into the material at right angles to the line and with the thread twisted round; the thumb must be kept over it as the needle is pulled through (55g). Detached chain stitches are invaluable for producing a regular or irregular powdering upon a surface (55h). Whilst chain stitch (56c) and zig-zag chain (56d) worked from right to left are also useful. So too is wheat-ear stitch (56e) and single feather stitch (56f) is effective when sewing cotton is used; it is executed by

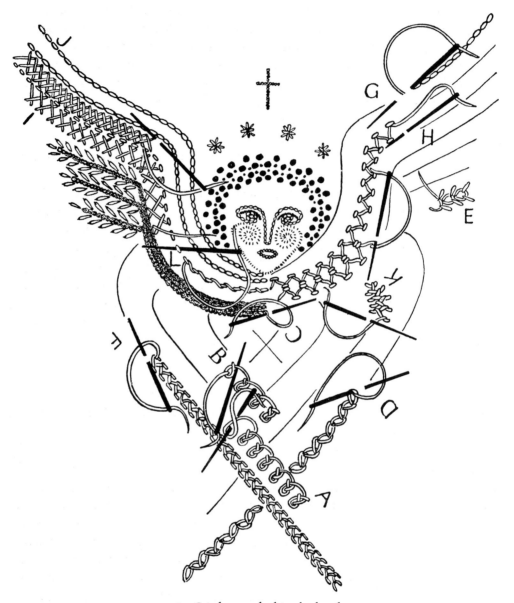

56 *Stitches worked in the hand*

placing the thread under the needle from left to right (the position shown in the diagram), then for the next stitch on the left of the line the thread will go under the needle from right to left; the left-hand thumb will be kept over the thread whilst the needle is pulled through. It should be stitched towards the worker.

164

Back stitch (56g) goes from right to left, but chevron (56h) either as a line or filling stitch is worked from left to right. Herringbone is also worked from left to right; here the spacing should be very regular (56i). Double back stitch (56j) is worked in the same way, but the new stitches come up through the holes made by the previous ones. Another decorative stitch which is well suited to whitework is Cretan stitch, as its width can be varied; in the diagram (56k) the needle is shown pointing downwards with the thread to the left; for the next stitch it will be inserted into the lower edge and point upwards; the thread will remain on the left of the needle as it is pulled through. Whipped run stitch can be varied according to the thread used (56l).

Also of medium weight are the immense variety of satin-stitch open fillings. These are worked to the counted thread (in 57 at B, C and D are shown three examples); either horizontal or vertical rows of evenly spaced slanting satin stitches act as an excellent foil to more elaborate patterning. And the little composite filling (57e) is slightly raised as a coarser, round thread (D.M.C. 70) is afterwards threaded through the groups of satin stitches. Plain bands of double back stitch, worked on the wrong side of the material and pulled rather tightly, present a ridged appearance on the right side, which shows to greater advantage when the material is semi-transparent (57f).

DRAWN AND PULLED WORK

The lightest effects are produced by withdrawing, or pulling, threads of the material together to form holes, hemstitching being the obvious example. When this is worked on one side only, two threads are taken out and two picked up each time, it is known as handkerchief hemstitching and is much used for Church linen (although one needs to avoid automatically finishing all hems in this way, as it draws attention from the main interest to the outer edges). With the hem held towards the worker and the wrong side uppermost, put a knot in the thread and start with a long stitch lying along the top of the hem, and bringing the needle up at the left-hand corner (58a), it will then pass diagonally across as the needle is put from right to left behind the first group of two threads. The needle is then brought out and inserted vertically as at B, ready to continue. Joining in a new thread is shown at C; when the hemstitches have secured the old and new threads they, like the commencing knot, are cut off on the right side. For spoke stitch four threads are usually withdrawn and the same groups of four are picked up and hemstitched on both sides (58d shows this from the right side of the work). For split group stitch, four threads are picked up on the first side, and on the second two threads from each group, so that a chevron is formed;

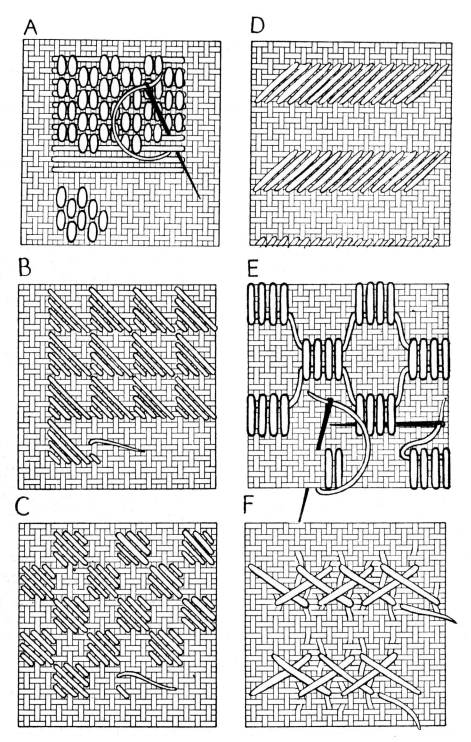

57 *Patterns worked to the counted thread*

its appearance on the right side is illustrated at E. Italian stitch or double hemstitch is similar. Draw out one thread, leave in three and draw out another one, working on the back make a back stitch over three threads at the bottom left-hand space (58f), and then take up the same three in the top space G, pass the needle

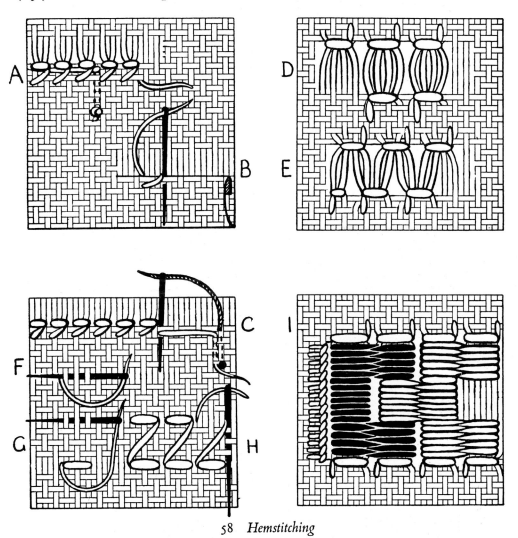

58 *Hemstitching*

vertically behind the three centre threads, H, and repeat. This can also make a decorative finish to a hem.

A woven hem is both ornamental and strong (but not light in effect). To work, first pull the top and bottom threads of the border, then strengthen the ends with

167

buttonhole stitching over small running stitches. Next, cut the horizontal threads close to the heading of the buttonhole stitching at both ends, and withdraw. (An alternative method is to make a cut vertically down the centre of the border and withdraw the horizontal threads to the left and right to the points marked for the two ends, then threading up each thread in turn, darn it back for a few stitches into the material and cut off on the back.) The groups of threads can be hemstitched or the weaving can be worked over groups of threads picked up by the needle. The diagram (58i) gives a simple woven border which when repeated would entirely cover the vertical threads. There is scope for the invention of many designs of greater complexity. This type of work looks very rich when other embroidered patterns are introduced as a part of the scheme.

Of the lovely pulled fabric stitches few lend themselves for the decoration of the linens in general use in this country. An exception is Double Faggot stitch, which is worked by completing first one then another stitch over two horizontal threads (59a), and passing the needle diagonally behind the intersection of the two warp and weft threads, making first one then another stitch over two vertical threads (59b), covering the ground with diagonally stitched rows. A fairly fine thread should be used, otherwise the perforations will not show. Another possibility is wave stitch filling, the working of which can be followed from the diagram (59c).

Many are the stitches which, pulled a little tighter (instead of withdrawing threads), can be executed upon ordinary linen. For example, fig. 59g and fig. 57f. Upon a loosely woven linen and linen lawn the immense variety of pulled fabric patterns can be executed.

DRAWN FABRIC FILLINGS

The outline of the area to be filled with a drawn fabric stitch should be completed first, but this presents a problem. The freedom of the design may be spoiled by the insistent and necessarily firm outline which this type of work really needs. Trailing (60f) is less likely to upset the balance than the inevitable buttonhole edge. But if one or two rows of very small running stitches are worked round the area first, to strengthen the edge, then there is greater latitude in the selection of outline.

If an embroidery frame is being used it should be slackened for the cutting and withdrawing of the threads (and for working pulled stitches).

The number of threads drawn out and the number left in depends upon the coarseness of the linen and the type of pattern. Most of these require an overcast foundation; this is worked on the wrong side, using a very fine thread. Fig. 59d shows a single stitch between each intersection of the fabric threads; the warp is usually whipped first, then the weft. Some patterns require a solidly overcast foundation, which resembles a square-meshed net when complete.

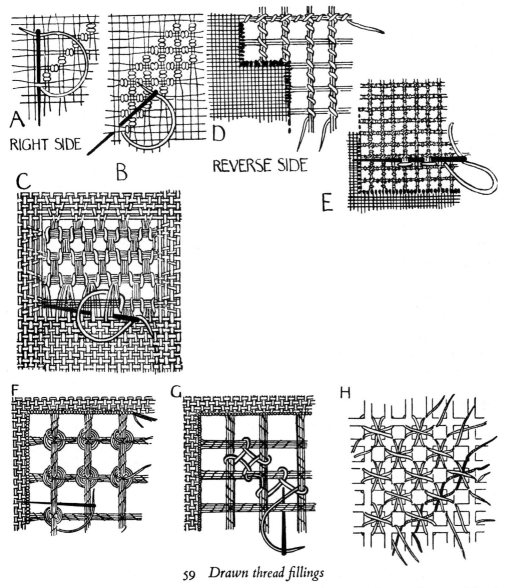

59   *Drawn thread fillings*

At fig. *59e* the beginning of a woven pattern is shown. This can be combined with other stitches; also the direction of the weaving can be varied. A lace thread is generally used for these drawn thread fillings.

169

In fig. *59f* the little spirals are worked on the wrong side to facilitate getting from one to another; it can be seen from the diagram that this is done by slipping the needle under the whipping stitches. For the same reason the looped stitch (it will be seen that it interlaces) is worked on the wrong side too. This can be varied by leaving in twice as many threads as are taken out and omitting the whipping. Each stitch goes over half the number each time, so dividing them and forming a diamond-shape hole.

At fig. *59h* another lace filling is shown (it may be more simple to follow the method where it is worked over a laid foundation, *45*). It is worked on the right side with a fine thread, diagonally across the mesh in four stages. The effect can be changed by altering the number of threads left in, and whether these are solidly overcast, lightly whipped or left plain as in the diagram.

The lightest and most delicate forms of embroidery are those which make use of transparency. As coarser linens are generally used it is seldom that the pall or "chalice veil" (second corporal, used sometimes in the Church of England) are made from linen lawn, grass lawn or cambric; when they are the characteristic methods can be employed; these will, to some extent, determine the nature and scale of the design. The cross is usually placed in the centre, and corner crosses or borders may be used.

As precision is necessary in the translating of the drawing to get the best results it is really essential to frame up for most of the processes. But when preparing shadow appliqué the frame should be slackened whilst the piece of opaque material is pinned, then tacked into place on the wrong side (this should be cut with the grain corresponding to that of the material to which it is applied, and large enough to cover all the parts to be treated in this method). The frame is then tightened up and the outline, usually trailing (*60f*), is worked. To do this thread up three threads and make a knot at the end, put the needle in a little beyond the line and bring it out actually on the line, then, using another and finer thread, with tiny satin stitches worked close together, cover the padding threads; at the finish of the line they are taken through to the back, where they and the commencing knot and end are cut off fairly close. The unwanted material can be cut away when the shadow appliqué is finished. In the diagram, one quarter is shown with the background treated in this way; and the other shaded part is the pattern.

The small leaves G would be carried out in needle shadowing; this is a double back stitch (*56j*) worked on the wrong side.

Seeding gives textural interest not only in whitework, but in all types of embroidery; it is invaluable to the embroideress of today as a means of producing

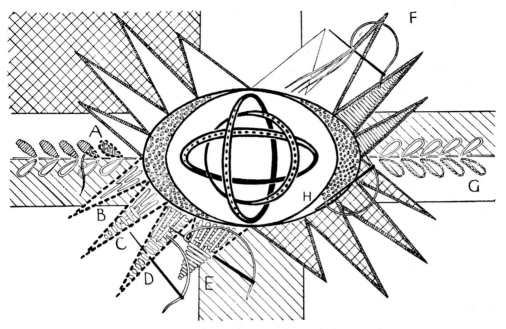

60   *Satin stitch, trailing, seeding, shadow work*

61   *Richelieu*

gradated massing and irregularity by the spacing and size of the stitches. To work, make a tiny back stitch, then another on top of the first (*60h*) to make a little raised spot. On transparent materials these must not be too far apart because the connecting thread would show through.

It has only been possible to give a few stitches, but they have been selected as the most likely to be used in the faithful interpretation of the spirit of a design.

Conversely, **certain techniques impose modifications** upon the design. In **Broderie Anglaise** it is the pattern, composed of eyelet holes, which is cut away; these should be large enough to show up, yet not too big for laundering. The material used should be closely woven, and the method of working can be followed from the diagram (*62a*). Outline the shape with small running stitches, B, pierce with a stiletto for a small eyelet, or C cut down and across from the centre for a larger one. Turn back a section at a time, and, using the same working thread, closely oversew through the double material. Fasten off at the back or carry the thread to the next hole. Cut away turnings on the wrong side.

62   *Broderie Anglaise*

The characteristic of **Richelieu** lies in the cutting away of the background, therefore these shapes should be good in themselves, and not too large: where needed, decorative bars, with or without picots are worked across for extra strength (*61*).

A shows one method. Put a running stitch round the outline, work small buttonhole stitches from left to right, with the heading towards the edge to be cut. When reaching the position for a bar take a stitch across into the other side and return on the surface, A. Repeat, but either whip or buttonhole stitch back, B over the three threads, finishing in a position to continue the buttonhole stitching of the edge. When complete cut away the areas of background C.

When it has been decided that the **emphasis shall be upon the**

172

background the shapes of the pattern and background must be designed to be simple (*63*). Suitable stitches for such a ground are: Double Faggot (*59a* and *b*). Also the drawn ground filling where two threads are withdrawn and two left in alternately, then whipping over twice over between the intersection of the warp and weft threads. In fact most small-scale drawn thread patterns and the simple pulled fillings could be used, including fig. *59d, e, g*. A further and

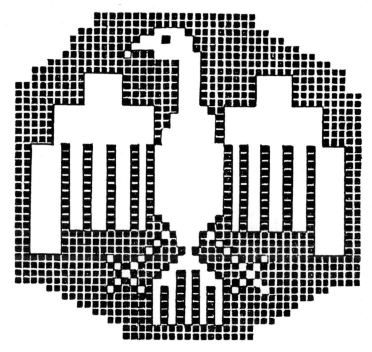

63   *Emphasis upon the background*

alternative means of emphasising the background is to work it solidly in long-armed cross or cross stitches, to the thread of the linen; these are given as canvas stitches (*91, 93*) and other stitches are equally suitable. It must be remembered that the outline should first be worked so that the shape shall be preserved.

Material—usually a fairly coarse white linen.

Threads

   A linen thread is more difficult to use and requires practice, but it is worth mastering. For some of the flat, looped, chained, knotted, etc., stitches which are preferably worked in the hand, the texture and roundness of a linen thread is an advantage. D.M.C. No. 20 is fairly coarse, Nos. 25 and 35 medium, and No. 40

fairly fine. For working some of the drawn fabric stitches a D.M.C. No. 60 can be used, but for finer pulled and drawn fillings a D.M.C. cotton lace thread No. 200 and for really fine work a reel of machine embroidery thread No. 30 or 50 is sometimes useful for whipping the foundation.

Satin stitch, trailing, seeding, and for surfaces which need to be smooth with a slight shine, D.M.C. coton floche à broder (Red Label) is excellent. No. 25 is fairly coarse, 35 medium and 40 fairly fine. There are, of course, many other sizes of all these threads. The numbers have been selected as a guide. A single thread of C.B. (Cartier-Bresson) mending is good for fine white embroidery, and Clark's Anchor stranded for coloured stitchery upon white.

Transferring

Frame up or pin out the linen, put the centre of the pricked tracing to the centre tack in the material, pounce and paint with blue water-colour. Where the material is sufficiently transparent, outline the design in ink, put it underneath and in contact with the back of the material; a finer outline can be achieved if a very hard pencil with a sharp point is used instead of a painted line. Where possible straight lines to the thread are better tacked instead of traced.

ALTAR-LINEN

THE FAIR LINEN OR ALTAR CLOTH

Finished the Fair Linen should measure the exact width of the altar, and hang almost to the ground or to within a few inches of it. For an average-size altar (6 ft. × 2 ft.) with 27 inches overhanging, the dimensions would be 25 inches wide by 27 inches+72 inches+27 inches. There should be five small crosses, placed so that one is in the centre and one at each corner when the cloth is in position on the altar.

It is fitting that there should be suitable embroidery to enhance the ends of the fair linen and a wider hem than the one down the sides, but the embroideress must decide whether a fringe is in keeping with the design.

In the Roman Church the crosses are not usually worked on the altar cloth, but it is fairly usual to have a narrow flat border embroidered on the inner side of the hem along the sides, in addition to the decoration at the ends.

THE CORPORAL

The corporal, on which rests the Body of Christ, is the most important item of Church linen. Originally quite large, it is often made rather too small. The size varies from 19 inches square to 24 inches square.

In the Roman Church it is about 21 inches square with a small cross placed in the centre of one side.

One fairly small cross worked in the centre of one side is normal. As the corporal is folded into three each way (it is kept in the burse) this cross should not exceed one-ninth of the total size. If there is to be such decoration the designer should be mindful of the sacred purpose, and the worker should avoid raised

64   *A typical altar of the sixth century, from the mosaics of St. Vitale;*
it shows the linen cloth ornamented with gammas and a star

embroidery and the type of drawn-thread work into which particles of the Host might adhere.

In the English Church, when there are two corporals, one takes the place of the silk chalice veil. The second may be used folded and is made of the same linen as the first, with which it forms a pair. Usually the cross is in the centre, with or without corner crosses or borders. Again the emblem of the cross should not take more than a third of the width and a third of the length. But when the

175

"chalice veil" is made of fine cambric or linen lawn it is from 20 to 24 inches square. Though it can be embroidered all over very delicately it must remain supple; the same limitations apply as to the silk veil. It can, of course, be of linen embroidered in one or more colours; conventionally the pattern is arranged as a border with a central ornament.

THE PALL

In the Roman Church the pall is a stiffened square, placed over the chalice. The size can vary from 4 to 6½ inches square, but 6 inches square is usual; it is determined by the size of the paten.

Although some clergy use it, the pall is not covered by the Ornaments Rubric in the Church of England. It is made of linen and generally a suitable design is derived from a cross, monogram or Passion symbol, usually embroidered in white. When the pall is entirely of linen it need not have cardboard, but may be stiffly starched.

There are several ways of making up a pall.

1. The upper embroidered square can be made separately, the edges being neatened in some suitable way, then a little bar is worked across each corner at the back. The square of cardboard is covered on both sides with linen and oversewn all round; when completed it is slipped into position under the bars.

2. A rectangle of linen cut twice the length plus hems, and the width of the square plus turnings. It is folded double and the sides overcast together, then the hems at the open end are completed. The cardboard is then slipped in. Alternately, about two inches extra of material can be left on the embroidered side, this forms a flap like an envelope, and is tucked in after the stiffening is in position; it is usually hemmed round after the sides of the pall have been overcast together, to enable the turnings to lie flatly: the little lay of the hem should be snipped.

Instead of a square of thin cardboard or celluloid, whether covered or not, a double fold of the stiffened material used for the interlining of linen collars can be used.

3. Take two squares of linen (one embroidered), turn in the half-inch turning all round each, place the cardboard between and oversew all round.

PURIFICATORS

These should be made of soft linen, the edges hemmed or fringed out: a small cross can be embroidered in the centre or at one corner. The size is usually 12 by 12 inches or 9 by 12 inches. In the Roman Church the size is about 13 by 20 inches, and can have a small cross in the centre and the hems at the ends are narrower than those at the sides.

Credence Cloth

The width of the cloth is determined by the width of the table the ends should hang down generously; they can be embroidered or finished with a hand-knotted fringe; whatever the treatment it should be in keeping with the altar cloth.

The Houseling Cloth

Where this is still used, the length is determined by the length of the altar rails and, again, the decoration, though more simple, matches the altar cloth.

The Communion Cloth

This is used in the Roman Church; if embroidered this needs to be very restrained, as it is intended to catch falling fragments of the Sacred Host.

Lavabo Towel

In the Church of England it should measure 2 feet by 10–15 inches wide.

This can have a little decoration above the hems, with or without a small cross at the ends. In the Roman Church it is made from linen diaper, 15 or 16 inches by 20 inches.

Hems

When making up altar linen the finishing of the hems calls for special attention. The most straightforward method is, of course, the ordinary hem, but as a ridge shows after laundering it is not entirely satisfactory.

Hemstitching (57a) is the conventional finish, and, as it is still widely used, the following directions for its preparation may be of assistance.

1. For a 1-inch hem finished, allow $1\frac{1}{4}$ inches all round the article.

2. Spread the material out, measure $2\frac{1}{4}$ inches inwards from each edge and mark with a pin.

3. Slightly lift and pull one thread in each direction so that they meet at the corner (65a).

4. Repeat at the diagonally opposite corner. The point at which these threads meet those of the first corner forms the position of the third and fourth corners.

5. Snip at each intersection and withdraw these threads, and draw out as many more as are required.

6. Fold the ¼-inch underlay and turn up the hem to the edge of the withdrawn threads. For a rectangle, arrange the opposite long sides first, then the shorter.

7. Slightly flatten the hems arranged as at B.

8. Then refold the corner as at C, making a crease.

9. Measure out ¼ inch from this crease and cut off the shaded portion D. Turn in this ¼ inch at the dotted line.

10. Refold the corner into a mitre, and slip-stitch on the wrong side, E.

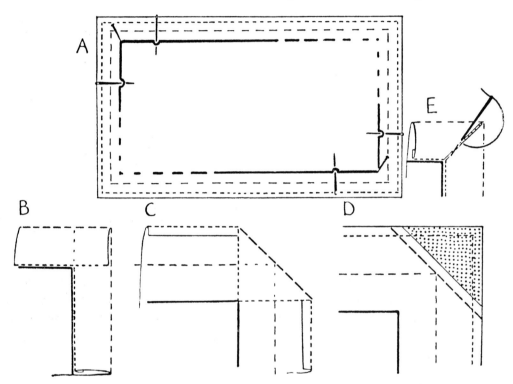

65   *The preparation of hemstitched hems and corners*

Many designs are planned to have a perfectly plain treatment for the edges. Where a certain emphasis would be an advantage a feature may be made of a length of hemstitching just where it is needed; this may, for instance, be terminated with a small raised circle or an eyelet hole. This raises its own problem because, if the remainder of the hem is simply hemmed down, the resultant ridge would spoil the effect. One way to overcome this is by omitting the underlay. Fold the hem into position, cut and stitch the mitred corner. Then pin and tack into place on the edge of the hem a narrow linen tape (folded diagonally at the corners). Attach it with hemming and lightly catch or slip hem the edge of the tape to the linen (*66a*), using fine sewing cotton as it is stronger.

Sometimes it is preferable to face up the edges on the reverse side with a fine, thin material cut to shape (*66b*).

For a narrow fringed hem, withdraw a couple of threads at the required measurement from the edge all round. Hemstitch on the inner side only, then withdraw the remaining threads to form a fringe. A few strands can either be woven or knotted in at the corners.

Lace edgings seem absolutely superfluous judged from any angle. Practically,

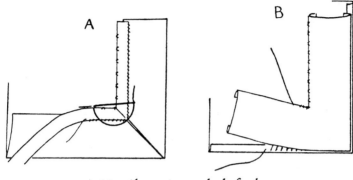

66   *Alternative methods for hems*

they quickly look "tatty" and crumpled before the linen requires laundering. Aesthetically, the texture (even of lovely handmade lace) does not accord well with either wood or stone or the materials against which it is seen. Beautiful as much real lace is in itself, as an addition to altar linen, or when it forms a superfrontal, it usually detracts from the general scheme.

THE ALB

One of the most important liturgical vestments is the alb. Originally worn in everyday life as the tunic by Greeks and Romans of the period, it is a long, flowing garment of white linen, with sleeves, and is held in at the waist with a girdle.

The pattern for an alb A (*67*) is to scale, and intended for 54-inch linen. Turnings must be added when cutting. Dotted lines should be placed to the fold, and both front and back yokes cut double. Extend the length to the measurement required, allowing for a hem of about 2 inches.

To make up, join front and back shoulder seams of both yokes; put the right sides together (inserting tapes across the shoulders, to come on the inside, for hangers). Then stitch round the neck, turn out and stitch on the right side for additional strength. Next turn up and tack the bottom edges of the yokes. Then gather up the whole width of material for the back and front, insert each between

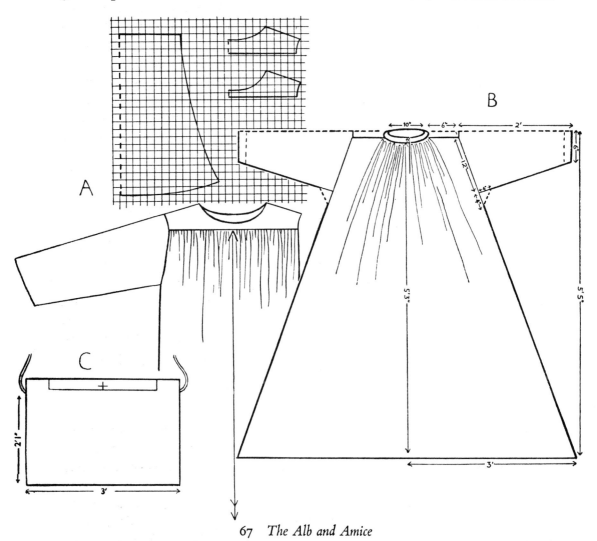

67   *The Alb and Amice*

the double yoke of front and back. Complete the sleeves as required using French seams, fit in place and join together the remainder of the side seams. Turn up and stitch hem.

When cut from 36-inch-wide material alb B takes from 7 to 9 yards. With a neckband into which the gathers are set, the seams are not shaped, except those of the sleeves (*67b*).

In making up, the selvedges are put together and oversewn with small stitches. For the sleeves a run and fell seam is neat and strong. It is preferable to sew the neck and shoulder bands by hand, using small back-stitching on the right side. The bottom hem can be between 1 and 3 inches deep. The sleeve, for convenience, is usually made from 12 to 14 inches round the wrist, but if it is to be tight-fitting, then an opening should be made in the seam, with fastenings.

The length measurement has to be adjusted to the height of the wearer.

The alb is a garment of greater dignity when it depends upon its own folds instead of having pieces of adornment sewn on. An exception being the type of embroidery worked directly on to the fabric. Because it becomes a part of it the whole is enriched, suitable techniques have been discussed in this chapter, whilst a washable thread must be used, it need not be limited to white, but if coloured it should harmonise with that of the appropriate season. A continuous apparel 1 to 3 inches deep and slightly above the hem is often preferred; sometimes a wider one is used for the priest and narrower ones for the deacon and sub-deacon; these can be embroidered directly upon the material, with perhaps smaller units of design above and at the wrist. If these consist of detachable bands of material or embroidery they are lightly attached and removed for washing. The rectangular apparels (the size is about 20 inches by 6 inches) are lined and attached on the back and front and a little above the hem of the alb. This practice has a Gothic origin, and is still in fairly common use in most cathedrals and many parish churches. In the Roman Church the alb is not ornamented with apparels but frequently there is embroidery in white or coloured threads.

THE AMICE

Worn as a neck-cloth the amice is a rectangle of white linen. The rubrics mention the addition of a cross only. The embroidered apparel dates from the Gothic period. Up to the middle of the twelfth century the amice remained simple and entirely white.

The size is usually 25 by 36 inches. It has a narrow hem all round, and two strings about 60 inches long are attached to the upper corners (*67c*). In the Roman Church the size is generally 32 inches long by 21 inches wide, with strings about 54 inches long.

In the most simple form the small cross is worked in the centre and slightly inwards from the top edge. When there is an embroidered border it is incorporated in the design. Sometimes the cross itself is enlarged as in the amice which belonged to St. Thomas of Canterbury. When the embroidery is in the form of a detachable apparel it is about 22 by 3 or 4 inches and is lightly sewn to the top edge of the amice. It can be worked in the colour of the season or something which will harmonise or in gold.

THE SURPLICE

This is similar to the alb, but it has large flowing sleeves and is also made from white linen. In fig. *68* the surplice, pattern A, is cut from 5½ yards of

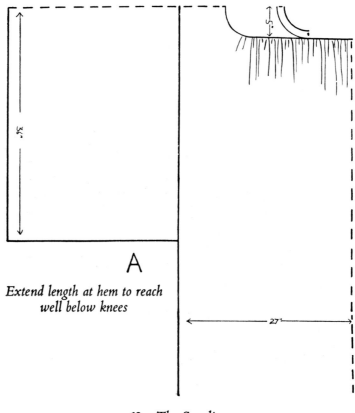

A

Extend length at hem to reach
well below knees

68   *The Surplice*

54-inch linen and allows for sleeves 27 inches long (from shoulder to wrist). The total length is not given as it should reach well below the knee and must depend upon the measurements of the wearer. The circular yoke is cut in four pieces, from the space remaining after shaping for the fullness at the neck. The construction is similar to that for alb A. The body part being gathered and fitted between the

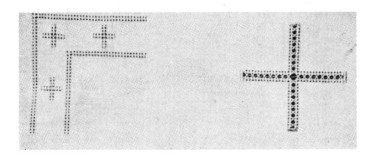

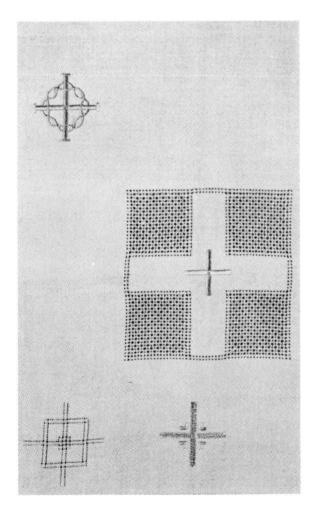

An immense variety of Borders and Crosses suitable for the decoration of Altar Linen can be evolved from combinations of simple stitches and drawn-thread work upon linen. Typical are these examples, worked by Joan Hansford on a sampler in the Embroiderers' Guild Collection

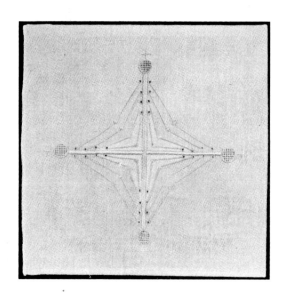
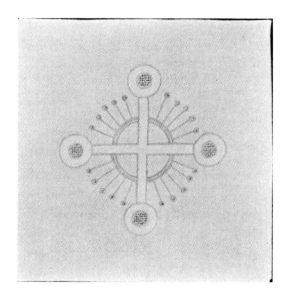

Palls, embroidered in satin-stitch, trailing, seeding, shadow-work, eyelets and drawn ground fillings: (a) Sister Kathleen Snelus, (b) Beryl Dean, (c) Katharine Bullock, (d) Walter W. Mitchell and (e) Guter Hirte, of Gertrudis Huber, Freiburg

double neckband. The selvedges of sleeves and sides are seamed together before the sleeves are joined and the side seams completed. In the diagram (*69b*) the dotted lines represent folds in the material. It should be cut longer, indeed the length varies according to the height of the wearer; this garment should reach well below the knees. If another width of material is inserted there would be a seam at the centre front and back in a 36-inch material. The circle for the neck is cut double, and where there is the extra fullness it would have to be wider. This should be halved and quartered, and marked with balance marks. The straight grain should run down the centre of the circles. Similar balance marks on the fullness are matched up with those on the circle. Before fixing this the

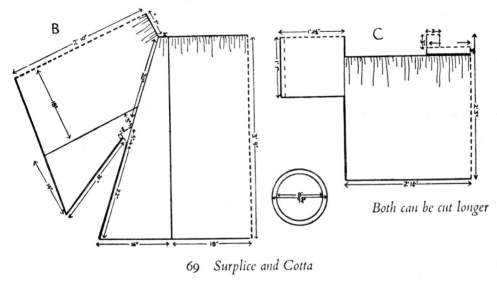

Both can be cut longer

69   *Surplice and Cotta*

neck circles are stitched together at the neckline and the turnings snipped before it is turned out. The making up of the surplice is like that described for the alb. The reducing of the fullness can be done with smocking.

THE COTTA

As there is seldom embroidery on the cotta (but it may have a border as on the bottom of the alb), the method of construction will be given only briefly. The cotta can have additional fullness; this is sometimes pressed into "accordion" pleats when lace is not used. The circumference is usually about 100 inches. The gathers are set into a front and a back band cut from 14 to 17 inches long and 3 to 4 inches wide, plus turnings; it is folded over on the upper edge, so that finished it is half the width. Two bands cut about 6 inches by 6 inches wide plus turnings form the shoulders and are attached to the top edge of the neckbands; into this the sleeves are set. When the neckband is cut to the shorter measurement the shoulder pieces are attached to the ends. The sleeves can be wider than indicated in the diagram. This garment, which is of such poor proportions, is usually made of nainsook (*69c*).

THE FINISHING AND CLEANING OF LINEN EMBROIDERY

Before taking the work out of the frame, cover the back with a damp cloth and press with a hot iron.

Using several layers of thick blanket covered with a clean cloth, embroidery which has not puckered can be placed face down and pressed on the back using a damp cloth, before making up.

Work which is clean but puckered can be pinned out, with the grain of the material straight down and across. First cover a drawing-board (or something suitable) with two or three layers of blanket and a clean white cloth. Place the work face downwards and stretch it out; pinning the edges with drawing-pins, thoroughly dampen the whole, and leave to dry for twenty-four hours.

When the embroidery has become grubby during the working, before making it up, prepare a basin of hot suds, and dip it up and down, but do not rub or squeeze. Rinse quickly and put the work face down on a well-padded surface which has over it two layers of clean dry cloth. Cover the reverse side of the work with another cloth and dry it off with a hot iron.

CHAPTER TWELVE

LETTERING, HERALDRY AND CEREMONIAL EMBROIDERY

As a means of communication embroidered lettering has been and still is important, whether it be to convey a symbol or message from the Scriptures, identify
a saint, record the date or name the place of origin.

To take the first of but a few examples from the past, the early tenth-century
stole and maniple from the tomb of St. Cuthbert at Durham: here the letters of
the inscription and the names against the figures of the prophets are fairly large;
by their placing upon the background they form an integral part of the whole
design. One of the typical features of the Opus Anglicanum period is the written
and embroidered identification of the saints in addition to the inclusion of their
respective symbols. The Byzantine and Greek embroideries both frequently
show lettering included as a part of the content of the design, sometimes arranged
to form a border (as in the Epitaphios Sindon dated 1407 in the possession of the
Victoria and Albert Museum and the piece showing similar characteristics in
the Lady Chapel, Canterbury Cathedral) or grouped upon the background. The
nature of Arabic characters can be a complete decoration in itself; this may be
heightened by the stitch treatment, as it is usual to find the metal thread passed
backwards and forwards across the wider heavier types, whether or not there is a
padding; for the lighter forms a single thread may suffice.

To return to European, and in particular English ecclesiastical embroidery of
the fifteenth and first half of the sixteenth century, when figures were included
it is characteristic to find an inscribed scroll either held by or planned in conjunction with the figures depicted. In the latter part of the nineteenth century
the style of lettering deteriorated. Repeated as authentic, we are all too familiar
with variants of bastard-Lombardic scripts "invented" by the Victorians and the
type of pseudo-Gothic letters of which the sacred monogram (*81*) is composed,
reference should be made to examples of the Lombardic painted initials and
versals of the eighth to eleventh centuries and Gothic of the eleventh and twelfth.
There is a renewal of interest in good lettering; in some examples it is the main
feature of the design.

To assist those who are unfamiliar with the subject the following brief
information is offered as an introduction and guide. There are many methods of
working letters in embroidery and each will have its influence on the design.

Writing has changed slowly through its many stages in history. There are several forms of writing. The letters which we use in our time come directly from Roman letters; the designer therefore cannot do better than to look for inspiration to inscription letters of the Roman period.

Drawing the skeleton shapes as in fig. *70a* will give practice in good **spacing** and in giving to each letter its correct breadth. The relative widths are shown in fig. *70b*. The narrow letters are about twice their width in height; the wide letters approximately a square or circle, except the M and W which are a little wider (*71a*).

The form of our letters has evolved by means of the tools used in making them. The wide pen quite naturally gives thick down strokes and thin up strokes.

a ABCDEFGHIJKLMN
OPQRSTUVWXYZ

b ABCDEFGHIJKLMN
OPQRSTUVWXYZ

70 *Spacing*

To understand this, practise the letters according to the skeleton guide, with two pencils tied together.

The words "Mothers' Union" written twice show different **proportions** (*71b*). In the first line the O is a circle and the other letters are in relation to it. In the second line, the O has become oval and all the other letters narrower and taller, but the whole taking up the same line space. Proportions may vary greatly and will be suggested by the purpose and method of work.

Good spacing is of the utmost importance. Each letter should be spaced in relation to the one before and in relation to the whole, leaving a narrow letter interval between words. The strokes should be evenly spaced, having neither voids nor dense masses caused by being wide apart or close together in the same piece of lettering. The letter I is often given too little room.

The embroideress who would design letters should practise drawing them freely, developing judgement of eye and a flowing rhythmic use of the hand, remembering that distortion may mean illegibility and consequent loss of meaning and purpose.

So will she be able to take advantage in full of the freedom given to her by her craft. These principles should apply in the utmost degree when planning banners, but all too frequently the results are unsatisfactory because the interest is equally divided between the figure or ornament and the wording; each has to strive for dominance and this leads to a restless composition. To look right and thereby

a

CDGOQU *Round letters* TXZ *may also be narrow*

AHKMNTVWXZ *Wide letters*

BEFIJLPRSY *Narrow letters* JLPY *may be widened*

b

MOTHERS UNION

MOTHERS UNION

71 *Proportions*

pleasing, the **scale of lettering,** and its position and proportion, must be judged in relation to the rest of the decoration. There are advantages in having some or all of the lettering on the back of the banner; this adds interest and character to the reverse side and the increased space leads to a better arrangement and offers a solution to the problem of overcrowding on the front.

The layout of an embroidery must be planned as a whole, and the wording treated as a part of the pattern: its size is to some extent determined by the distance from which it is generally to be viewed. To preserve an underlying unity the method of working the lettering should be in keeping with the rest of the embroidery, therefore the design of the letters is adapted to the stitch treatment.

METHOD OF WORKING

Slanting **satin stitches** are most commonly used for working types of lettering such as the INRI shown in fig. *72*; the slant is increased in order to get round the curves, the stitches being closer together on the inner edge and

INRI

72   *Method of working—satin stitch*

further apart on the outer; this is given in diagrammatic form in the letter R (*74*). If the satin stitch is worked over a split-stitched outline the shape is kept and it is raised from the background. A padding composed of a group of coton-à-broder threads sewn down, then covered with a layer of felt, is sometimes essential, particularly upon a material with a pile. If a final outline is to be added it is

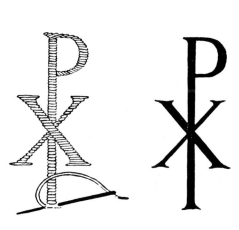

73   *Satin stitch (straight)*

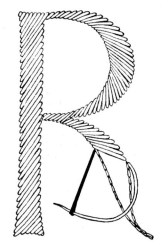

74   *Satin stitch with no outline*

unnecessary to have the split stitch. There are occasions when the direction of the satin stitch is kept straight, but for contriving curves and the serifs a slight slant assists (*73*).

Appliqué is the most suitable method of interpreting large-scale lettering.

The A given as an example (*75*) is simple and well suited to be treated in this way. Generally the material should first be pasted to muslin; it is more satisfactory. When the letters have been cut out and stitched in place the question of outlining arises; all too often one, two and even three cords are couched all round and refinements of drawing and proportion are thus lost. It is often more effective

to make a feature of the shadow side, either with satin stitch or cords, and neatening without stressing the other side of the letters. Legibility from a distance is a problem common to most lettering if there is insufficient contrast of tone; gold on white or ivory usually requires some extra emphasis to lift it away from the background. In fig. *76* the symbolic AM lends itself for a solid **gold couching** around the outlines, the remaining spaces being filled in with short lengths of gold. This can be complete in itself, but when a neatening outlining

75   *Appliqué*

will be used, the gold runs through the centre of each part, the remainder being filled up with parallel rows on either side; the gleam is then unbroken.

The Alpha and Omega symbol (*77*) shows a decorative treatment evolved with couched metal threads from the nature of the letters. This is complete in itself, though a touch of emphasis here and there may be added.

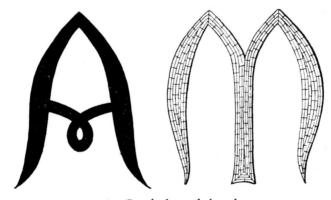

76   *Couched metal threads*

When rough or smooth **purl or bullion** are used for the working, the short lengths are cut and threaded up and sewn in the usual way. The type of lettering determines the direction of the stitches. Fig. *78* requires a uniform width and straight stitch except for the curves, where they are close together on the inside and are spaced on the outer edges. In this example a single layer of parchment or felt has first been stitched in place.

The slanting satin stitch in a purl worked over a padding consisting of a bunch of coton-à-broder or a single raising thread covered with a layer of felt is the method which is suitable for a background of velvet or some such material.

77   *A decorative treatment*

The cypher (79) lends itself to this treatment as the slanting satin stitch can narrow into stem stitch.

In **whitework** approach to the lettering is altogether different, being stitched in self colour; contrast must be obtained by the techniques employed. One suggestion is to emphasise the background by working in pulled or drawn

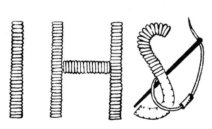

78   *Satin stitch with rough purl*

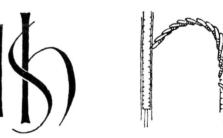

79   *Manipulating a curve*

filling stitches, throwing the letters into relief. This calls for a design which produces good shapes in the background; the monogram giving the IHS interlaced is entirely suitable (*80*). These contemporary examples are legible, decorative, restrained and suited to the methods for which they are designed. These points are illustrated more clearly by comparison with the neo-Gothic

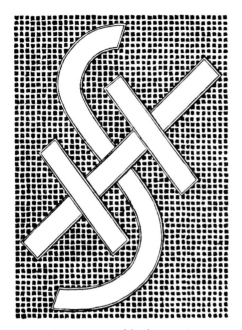

80 *Accented background*

81 *Neo-Gothic*

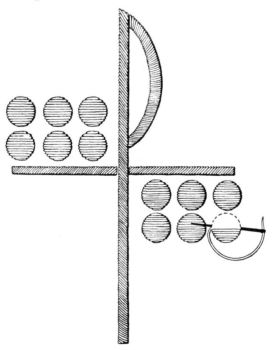

82 *Satin stitch*

193

specimen (*81*), variations of which linger on to be embroidered anew even to this day.

The perfect simplicity of the variation upon the Chi Rho of Constantine and grapes, an example from France, was worked in slanting satin stitch over a running stitched outline but with no padding; being whitework, this treatment accorded with the character of the letters (*82*).

HERALDRY

Heraldry has constantly been combined with other forms of decoration for the Church and this applies equally to embroidery. On furnishings and vestments alike the arms of donors or associated families appear. Further evidence of this widespread usage can be gained by referring to inventories of the time; extant examples abound all over Europe, none being more obvious than the English early fourteenth-century orphrey on the Syon cope and the stole placed alongside it in the Victoria and Albert Museum, which is of the same date. On the City Guild and Company palls the arms are generally prominent. The civic aspect of heraldry is very much alive today, a reason which justifies this digression from strictly ecclesiastical embroidery. The following brief introduction may stimulate an interest in the subject.

The gay art of heraldry, anciently called armoury, appeared upon the scene of history during the twelfth century A.D. and that it has survived until our own time is a tribute to its vitality.

Signs and symbols used as personal marks are older than writing but the precise origin of heraldry as we know it, with a system and order, is unknown. It became established when it came to be hereditary, and it developed into its particular form because the time and circumstances were suited to it. In tournaments and in knightly exercises and in battle, the man inside armour needed a means to show his identity and so he claimed his particular mark which became his coat-of-arms, and it was painted on his shield, embroidered on his surcoat and on to the trappings of his horse. He also adopted a crest to wear upon his helm.

It is to these early times, from about the middle of the twelfth century to the fourteenth and fifteenth centuries, that the heraldic artist should look to see the beauty and simplicity of heraldry, for later its purpose diminished, only the hereditary aspect remained, and it became complicated by family relationships and varying fashions.

To draw heraldry it is necessary to study the basic rules which govern the arrangement of a coat-of-arms. The **colours** used are few: red, blue, black, green and purple, called gules, azure, sable, vert and purpure. There are two metals, silver and gold, called argent and or. There are two furs, ermine and vair, of which there are many variations having different names.

Fig. *83* shows first the **divisions** then the **ordinaries** which developed from them, and then some **parti-coloured fields**. To make greater variety, as every man must have a different coat, there were patterned dividing lines of which a few are given.

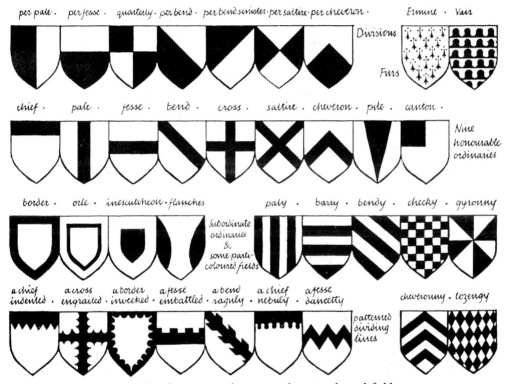

83 *The divisions, ordinaries and parti-coloured fields*

Then there were innumerable **charges**: animals, birds, fishes, flowers, celestial bodies, and fabulous beasts; also many small inanimate charges such as bosses and roundels, keys and many beautiful crosses. All these things may be adapted for embroidery and a few are shown in fig. *84*.

To learn more of heraldic rules there are many books to study from. To learn to draw it study from heraldry as it has been drawn through the years; the old heraldic rolls or records, heraldic seals and badges; also heraldry as it has been

195

used in many crafts, stained glass, wood and stone carving, illuminated MSS. and, of course, embroidery.

In the Bayeux Tapestry (so-called; actually it is embroidered) many of the shields show a personal device which would have been painted on, and the lances often bear a small pennon; one such bears a device which comes near to true heraldry and this would have been embroidered. A very interesting example of appliqué in silk upon two layers of linen backing is the fragment from the trappings bearing the arms of William de Fortibus, third Earl of Albemarle, of the latter half of the thirteenth century and is in the British Museum. The original (and the replica over his tomb in Canterbury Cathedral) fourteenth-century jupon which belonged to the Black Prince shows another method of working heraldry, on a foundation of linen; the blue and red velvet is arranged quarterly; over an interlining of wool, the whole is quilted. The three lions or leopards and the fleurs-de-lis are worked separately and applied. Another interesting example to which reference has already been made from the fourteenth century is the horse trapper, as it was originally, belonging to the second son of Edward II, and in the Cluny Museum. It is a wonderful piece of embroidery; the three lions guardant were worked with gold directly upon the fine velvet background. The embroidery of the arms upon the eighteenth-century tabards in the Victoria and Albert Museum is of interest also; here the quarterings are applied and the charges worked over padding.

THE TECHNIQUES

The method generally suitable for working heraldry is **appliqué,** as the large flat surfaces can be represented; also interest can be introduced with materials of contrasting textures; care should be taken that the colours conform to the rules of heraldry. When applicable white or pale grey can represent silver and yellow for gold. It is advisable to paste the fabrics; the method of working is described in Chapter VIII. As precise edges are required, satin stitch, couching, cords or bead purl or bullion are good for outlining. If on a large enough scale the whole coat-of-arms can be carried out in appliqué.

On a smaller scale the divisions of the field can be applied and the devices worked in satin stitch (*85d*) and/or outlined in bead purl (*85c*). Though sometimes they are worked with tambour or passing thread, or alternatively this may be bent backwards and forwards across a foundation of card or felt, being stitched twice at each turn as in fig. *85e*. This requires an outline to neaten it. Details of drawing are put in freely with fairly long stitches in a dark thread. An examination of a blazer badge will make this clear.

(a)   *One end of a fair Linen cloth by Katharine Bullock*

(b)   *Pall and Corporal, in shadow work, trailing and seeding by Vivienne Tuddenham. Also, cloth for a baptismal candle embroidered in white, by Lydia Jungmann, Cologne*

(a) *The Frontal Monogram from the War Memorial Chapel, Selby Abbey, Yorkshire. Designed by George G. Pace*

(b) *Another example of Lettering. Embroidered upon a white frontal in red, gold and green, by Marta Afzelius for Sofia Widén, Stockholm*

(c) *An Altar Frontal, worked by Anna-Lisa Odelquist-Ekström, of Libraria, Stockholm*

When the above methods are judged to be inapplicable, **laidwork** is generally suitable for working devices such as F, I, N and O; also the mantling and helm in G, all in fig. *84*. Various forms of tying down could be incorporated in an imaginative way (see Chapter IX). Ermine lends itself to this treatment, whilst laidwork, combined with graduated colour introduced by means of long and short for mantling, is very interesting.

Either the whole or a part of a coat-of-arms can be carried out in long and

84 *Some charges*

short stitch using silk or wool. Badges and emblems worked for **Regimental colours** must be the same on both sides; this is a very specialised type of embroidery, requiring skill and concentration. Where there is lettering, that for the reverse side is carried out on a separate piece of material, which is then invisibly stitched over the back of the lettering of the front. As Masonic banners are lined this procedure is unnecessary.

The formality of canvas work renders it very suitable for the interpretation of heraldry.

When the charges are to be **worked in gold,** whether directly upon the fabric or embroidered separately and applied, the methods are adapted from those set out in Chapter VII, except that passing thread or tambour usually replaces Japanese gold. A device such as the fleur-de-lis (*84j*) may, if not too heavy, be carried out in basket stitch. The fret (*84b*) might be in metal and colour interlaced. There is a ruling that one metal must be separated from another by a colour.

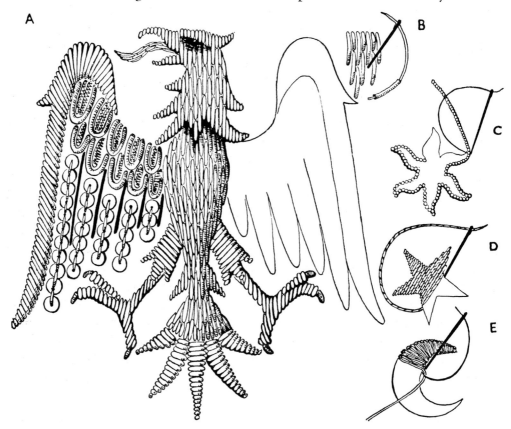

85   *Purl or bullion work*

Beasts and birds, when they have to be worked in metal threads, are difficult, but if the embroideress will think of them as pattern and treat them flatly, bringing out and emphasising the decorative features, the result will be in keeping with the whole feeling of heraldry. It must first be decided whether the direction to be taken by the metal thread shall be straight with the thread of the fabric throughout; or whether it shall go through the centre of the main form, the rest being filled in with parallel rows; an outline to neaten and bring out the drawing is essential. The dotted lines at fig. *84l* give some indication of this approach.

For clarity it is usual to denote the features and accent the drawing with stitchery in silk. Another way to work a beast with metal threads is to couch them down in rows following the contours, forming spirals where possible; this adds to the decorative value, but the shapes which remain are awkward to fill; with forethought these can be turned to advantage. As an example a more formalised animal would lend itself to this treatment (worked in silk, there is a delightful horse on the Steeple Aston frontal); however, the dotted lines on the unicorn, fig. *84l*, denote the direction which the threads might follow. A straightforward simplified form of stitchery is more suited to heraldic interpretation than the realistically moulded beasts which are feats of technical skill.

In fig. *85* the eagle, displayed, incorporates the main points to be considered when working beasts or birds using **the wire threads**. This applies when they are to be embroidered upon regalia also. The body in this example is raised, the head and body are worked with a fairly fine rough purl stitched as described in Chapter VII, also at B in fig. *85*. This combination of long and short satin and brick stitches are contrived so that they cover the shape. It will be noticed that at the top of the tail an interesting irregularity is introduced by having the purl longer than the stitch, so that it is slightly looped (this can be developed with advantage for a lion's mane, etc.). The slant of the satin stitch has to be regulated whilst negotiating the curve of the wings and the feathers are represented by threading up a longer piece of purl; the needle then goes down through the hole from which it emerged and this leaves a loop which is caught down with a small stitch made with the working thread. One or two shorter lengths of bright check purl fill in the centre. The spangles are attached by means of back stitches with a fine rough purl. Long stitches in black silk give accent and it is used again for the eye.

EMBROIDERY FOR REGALIA

Although the type of embroidery for regalia and ceremonial usage is really outside the scope of this book the following brief introduction may serve to increase through understanding the appreciation of this highly skilled and specialised work, which can be seen at its best on the Coronation robes in the London Museum. Each Privy purse was (and still is) embroidered with the arms in high relief. There are interesting ceremonial robes in the Cluny Museum too, and Italian, Spanish and Portuguese examples are richly ornate. This embroidery is to be found on Masonic regalia, the insignia of various orders and on naval and military uniforms, etc. Many earlier examples were destroyed when, in the eighteenth century, there was the craze for "drizzling": the fashionable ladies unpicked the gold for its value when melted down. Some embroidered gloves escaped their attention, as the bestowing of these had an important significance, which survives to this day in the Coronation ceremony.

Bullion work, comprising the use of wire threads, the purls and bullion, tambour and passing, the Grecian and other cords, the check twists, spangles and jewels, have been discussed in Chapter VII, where the technique is also explained.

Having in fig. *85* considered in detail the more conventional application of the methods employed, it will readily be understood that the embroideress thinks out the most direct way

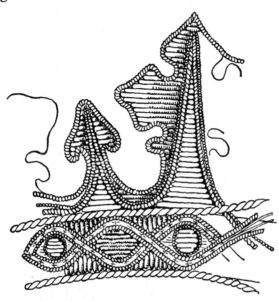

86 *Satin stitch with outlines of various purls*

to fill each space, obtaining contrast by changes of thread and direction. In fig. *86* the coronet (which is not a coronet of rank) is outlined with bead purl of three sizes; the greater area is filled with satin stitches of rough purl. A double passing thread is couched down, and a cord is sewn on either side to complete the whole; these and the other processes are given in diagrams and explanation in Chapter VII. When repetitions of the same unit are undertaken commercially instead of tracing the outline on to the fabric, the design is stamped on to paper cut to shape and attached to the material, then the stitches are taken right over it.

87 *A coronet*

These methods are repeated in working the orb (*88a*) with the addition of satin stitch in silk outlined in the finest bead purl for the jewels. In the sword, the stitching and bending of the plate will be recognised, the "chips" of bright check purl, and satin stitch using two stitches in bright check purl alternatively with one of smooth. Working diagrams in Chapter VII explain all these and the following processes. In the thistle (*88d*) the change from

202

smooth to rough purl is effective, and the long stitches made with tambour thread alternating with others in filoselle add variety. The finer lines of the rose (F) are worked with passing thread. In the acorn a wider plate has been taken over a slight padding, and the contrast of texture has been accentuated by the little loops of rough purl of which the cup is composed; this is achieved by threading up a longer piece of purl and returning the needle next to the spot from which

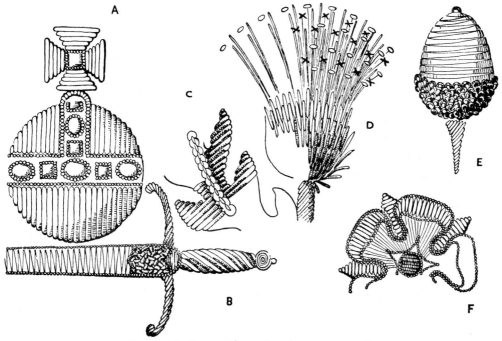

88   *Methods used for embroidery upon regalia*

it came up. The stem is in satin stitch using rough purl. It will be realised that, with the exception of the rose, these examples would be worked directly on to the fabric.

Something of the basis of the technique has been covered; only practice and skill can achieve the regularity required and a wider knowledge of the intricacies of padding, raising, pasting and in some instances working units on velvet over a foundation of buckram, or upon kid and other leathers.

CHAPTER THIRTEEN

CANVAS WORK

The group of stitches which constitute what we now term canvas work was frequently incorporated into other forms of embroidery for the enrichment of medieval vestments; this was made possible by the nature of the handwoven linens which formed the background: the whole surface was covered with stitches worked to the counted thread with silk. It remained supple and light enough to hang in folds; this is exemplified in the mid-fourteenth-century Hildesheim cope, the subject of the design being the Martyrdom of the Saints, and it is characteristic of much German needlework upon linen.

Heraldry was important as it formed the means by which particular persons or families were associated with embroideries. Both these points are illustrated in the magnificent early fourteenth-century Syon cope. The orphrey and border are composed of coats-of-arms mostly blazoned on lozenge-shaped shields worked in tent stitch with silk, the gold and silver being in underside couching: these are probably somewhat later in date than the cope as a whole; the ground is divided into barbed quatrefoils, each containing the figure of one or more saints, displaying the characteristics typical of the Opus Anglicanum work; the background is entirely covered with a stitch resembling Florentine and forming chevrons but worked with an upper and lower thread; these are in red silk with the alternating spaces having backgrounds worked in green silk. Another piece of work of the same type is a fourteenth-century English Burse or Corporal case; it is worked completely in reversed tent stitch, resembling a plait (see the chapter on Symbolism). On one side is shown the handkerchief of St. Veronica with the impression of the head of Christ, and on the other the Agnus Dei; many symbols are incorporated in a way both interesting and fitting: they are most beautifully formalised and adapted to the medium. These and other specimens of canvas work are to be found in the Victoria and Albert Museum.

Later, large wall-hangings were embroidered in tent stitch the style of, and as a substitute for, the more costly and highly treasured tapestries. Which is an entirely different process entailing a warp of string threaded upon a loom, the pattern being woven in wool or silk to cover the warp. When the difference between the two techniques is pointed out the inaccuracy of the prevalent misnomer (i.e. canvas embroidery called tapestry work) is obvious.

For Church and secular usage a great variety of stitches were tried out on samplers. Cross, long-armed cross, plait, tent and many other stitches were

89   *Diaper patterns*

incorporated into the working of large and small wool or silk embroideries of the sixteenth and seventeenth centuries. Burses, cushion covers, bags and table and floor carpets were stitched in this method.

The popularity of Berlin wool work, coupled with the production of colours reflecting the crudity of aniline dyes in their early form, also the introduction of stiffened canvas in the mid-nineteenth century, may not have made any outstanding contribution to embroidery for the Church, but the great variety of little diaper patterns do serve today as a source of inspiration to those not wishing to embark upon more ambitious designs. A few of these **groundings** are given

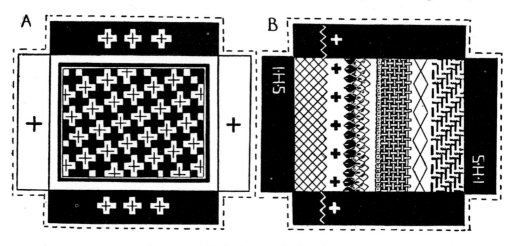

90   *Simple designs for kneelers*

in fig. *89*: the working can be followed from the diagram. The adaptation of some of the patterns implemented with stripes, borders or symbols in plain colour can be charming. Fig. *90a* and *b* gives some suggestions. When the proportions are good, these arrangements are infinitely preferable to over-elaborate representational subjects.

Canvas work when used in the service of the Church is now confined chiefly to kneelers, communicants' rail kneelers, and for alms bags when finely worked and not too bulky for making-up. It is chosen as the most suitable method for these purposes because of the durability.

DESIGNING A KNEELER

Before setting out to prepare a **design** for canvas work the limitations imposed by the method must be considered; this is even more important with the coarser meshes. The character peculiar to this form of embroidery is inherent in the stitches which are based upon counted threads; this leads to a somewhat geometrical or formalised treatment. The stitches are in themselves decorative, therefore the greatest value is derived when the design is straightforward and composed of uncomplicated shapes. But frequently the nature of the design is such that the flatness and detail made possible by working mainly in tent stitch is deliberate and justified. For example, much of the "readability" might be obscured or muddled if several ornamental canvas stitches were used for working a coat-of-arms. Too often tent and cross stitches have to be resorted to for a design which is unsuitable by virtue of the complexity of line and excess of "movement" in the subject matter. When the emphasis is upon line rather than mass, much of the delight gained from using stitches with a textural quality is lost.

For a kneeler which is to be worked in one piece: draw out on paper the rectangle 9 by 12 inches for the top, extend each line by 2 inches to form the depth of the gusset, join each to complete the four side pieces. When starting to design the beginner will find it a good plan to cut out several simple shapes or templates in paper, keeping them based to some extent upon the vertical or horizontal and diagonal, rather than the oblique and small complicated curves. Abstract shapes can be combined to form design, or formalised symbols or some characteristic detail typical of the church or locality if suitable for such simplification, for example at Guildford Cathedral, that monumental pile set upon a hill. Having cut out these component parts they are moved around until a satisfactory composition has been achieved. (It is advisable to avoid more than occasional overlapping of the lines.) Draw round the paper shapes whilst they are still in position, and with black ink or paint thicken the outlines.

When attempting to draw a design there is a tendency to include too many ideas which become small and overcrowded for the scale of the work. This can be overcome by using the cut paper templates, as the emphasis is upon the form rather than the outline.

Some patterns are better drawn out on graph paper and worked out directly upon the canvas by counting, usually working outwards from the centre.

In general the tones of each colour should be defined. The little groundings derived from Berlin wool-work samplers depend upon the use of dark, medium and light tones of one or more hues. For most of the more decorative stitches it is well to keep to flat colour: tent and cross stitch give the most satisfactory graduated effect. It is advisable to make a coloured sketch before commencing, as it is not easy to unpick.

MATERIALS

The size of the linen or Italian hemp canvas is determined by the number of threads to the inch. Choose one which is in scale with the design; a single-thread canvas is generally preferable to the double or Penelope. And the natural or buff colour is stronger than the white.

It is only by working with the correct thickness of thread that the canvas is completely covered. For a coarse canvas tapestry wool or three threads of crewel wool should be used, threaded into a tapestry needle, which has a long eye and blunt point. For a medium canvas (18 threads to 1 inch) use two threads of crewel or three of Medici and French wools; this is usually satisfactory but can, of course, be varied and one of crewel or two of Medici for a very fine canvas. Filoselle and stranded cottons are effective for the whole work or when combined with wool. (See also the Appendix.)

METHOD

For the kneeler, cut a piece of canvas or other suitable material, leaving about 2 inches to spare beyond the actual size of the design; cut off or snip the selvedge. It is advisable to frame up the work as the correct shape is retained and also it can be executed much more speedily.

To **transfer** the design, place the frame over the outlined design, building it up from underneath until the paper is in contact with the canvas. Then paint over the outline on the canvas with a fine brush, watching to see that straight lines in either direction are parallel with the threads. To paint on without framing, pin out the canvas over the drawing so that it is taut, and paint in the outline.

STITCHES

Many of the canvas stitches are derived from samplers of the late seventeenth century onwards to the mid-eighteenth century and from chair seats; also the famous Hatton Garden hangings in the Victoria and Albert Museum. The embroideries typical of several countries were and still are based upon these stitches and designs which were worked upon linen.

In the accompanying composite diagrams (91, 92) numerous stitches are shown in juxtaposition in order that the relative characteristics can better be appreciated, although it must be noted that they are primarily working diagrams and there has been no attempt at conformity of scale; the object is to indicate the immense variety of textural surfaces. In the convention of the diagrammatic form the needle is shown (in most instances) entering the material, with a small cross

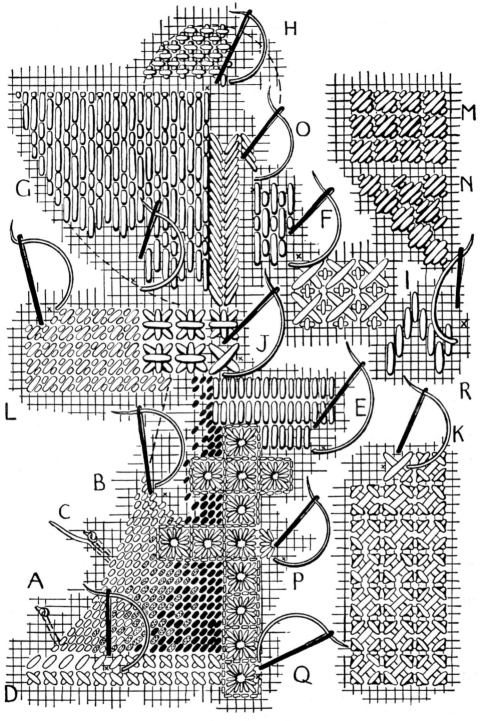

91 *Stitches and groundings*

to indicate where it will emerge. The method of working is usually evident and needs little explanation.

When working it is essential that all the stitches of one pattern should be formed in exactly the same order each time; if changed the alteration may not be observable at once, but will show up later when a large area has been covered. This can be checked up by looking at the reverse side which should be regular and alike.

A. To commence, knot the end of the wool, take the thread through to the wrong side at least half an inch from the point where the needle will be brought up for the first stitch. This length of thread lying on the back will be worked in as it is covered, and the knot can then be cut off.

B. Tent Stitch (formerly embroidery mounted on a frame was referred to as tent work) or Petit Point: the finest of the canvas stitches, in the English form, the direction is taken from the top right-hand to the bottom left. Worked in diagonal lines across the canvas it may be stronger than when worked in horizontal rows.

C. For joining, bring the old thread up, half an inch away (finish off in the same way). Start the new thread as for the commencement. They will be covered as the work progresses.

D. At the base of fig. *91* will be found at D Cross Stitch or Gros Point, which is the commonest of all the stitches: it can be worked upon single or double canvas. The final crossing stitch must always be in the same direction.

E. Upright or Straight Gobelin: though the stitches are usually taken over two threads of the canvas, they can be worked over three if the ground is completely covered.

F. Parisian Stitch: this is worked over two and four threads of the canvas alternately.

G. Hungarian Stitch: several groundings can be made by varying the length and order of the stitches but they are all more suited to larger areas.

H. Straight or Upright Cross: as the name implies, the stitches are taken vertically and crossed horizontally over two threads of the canvas. It is usually found more satisfactory to complete each stitch before proceeding to the next (as shown in the diagram)—though this gives one of the most delightful textures it does take longer to work.

I. This grounding is composed of large cross stitches and small straight crosses.

J. Smyrna or Double-cross Stitch: this is a diagonal cross with a straight cross worked over it. An attractive variation can be obtained by using a single strand of crewel wool worked over two instead of four threads, two colours alternating heighten the effect.

K. Rice, Crossed Corners or William and Mary: this is suitable for large spaces and it has the advantage of covering the ground quickly.

L. Mosaic Stitch: the smallness of the scale renders it useful for intricate shapes.

M. A variation of Mosaic, but with the stitches taken diagonally across first one then two, three, two and again one thread of the canvas.

N. Diagonal Stitch: this is worked across the material diagonally over two, then three and four, decreasing to three, then two threads of the canvas.

O. Diagonal Satin Stitches, worked in lines over two vertical and three horizontal threads of the canvas.

P. This Cross Lorraine is composed of eye stitches.

Q. The outlines are worked in back stitches. When these are combined to form a grounding, contrasting colours add interest.

R. Florentine: this is one of the most characteristic of the canvas stitches and must be worked over an even number of threads. Very elaborate patterns covering the whole surface and worked in untwisted silk were very popular in the eighteenth century and again in the middle nineteenth century when interest was revived with the graduations of colour possible with Berlin wools.

The following stitches in common with those already shown were frequently used in the early seventeenth century onwards and some are associated with the little purses, bags and pincushions which were given as christening presents; they were finely worked in silk with the addition of metal threads.

In the diagram (92) the arcading at the top is filled with Encroaching Gobelin at A. The stitches should slant across one vertical and four or five horizontal threads; the stitches of each succeeding row encroach between those of the previous one. The resultant smooth surface acts as a foil to the more ornamental textures.

B. Gobelin Stitch: to work, begin at the point marked with an arrow, then take the thread obliquely down and back over two horizontal and one vertical threads of the canvas. Next, pass the needle underneath and forward under two vertical and two horizontal threads, bringing it up next to the point of commencement, and repeat. The working is reversed for the second row. It will be observed that the stitch is longer on the reverse side.

C. Upright Gobelin: though this is a useful stitch it does not always completely cover the canvas. This disadvantage can be obviated by laying a self-coloured thread along the line and working over it; this is shown at D, where it has been used to work the capital of the central column in the diagram.

E. Another variation of Upright Gobelin: here, too, the ground fabric may be exposed; when this is likely to happen the shape may be painted with a little oil or water-colour before working.

F. Plaited Gobelin: the stitches all face in the same direction for one row and in the opposite way for the next.

G. Chequer Stitch: composed of alternating stitches of satin and tent stitches.

H and I are variations of chequer stitch.

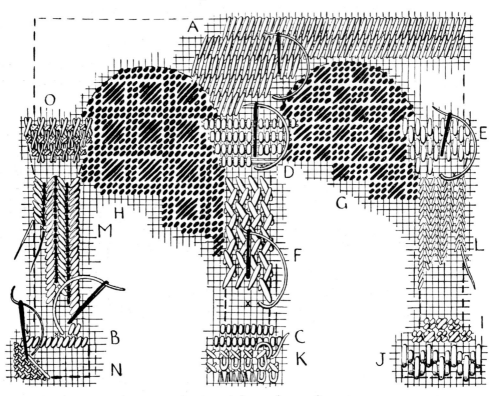

92   *Canvas stitches and groundings*

J. Hungarian Stitch: this is very adaptable, by changing the colours, decorative patterns can be formed.

K. Velvet or Astrakhan Stitch: produces a cut pile texture, and consists of loops each secured by a cross stitch; these loops are cut afterwards to form the pile. Commence with a cross stitch, bringing the needle out at the bottom left-hand corner, make a loop (these can be formed round a strip of whalebone) and insert the needle above and across two threads of the canvas in each direction, then bring it out again at the bottom left-hand corner. Take a stitch diagonally across, re-entering the material at the top right-hand corner and emerging at the bottom right-hand corner. Next, complete the cross stitch as shown in the diagram.

L. Reverse Tent Stitch: in each vertical line the direction of the stitch is changed, giving a striped effect.

M. Stem Stitch: this grounding is worked with vertical rows of slanting stitches taken over two or four threads of the canvas as shown in the diagram. Lines of back stitching are afterwards worked between the rows.

N. Web Stitch: diagonal threads are laid across the shape to be filled, and tent stitches are worked across, the stitches of each row alternating.

O. Double Stitch: make a row of cross stiches over one thread, leaving one thread of canvas between each. Return, filling the spaces with a long cross stitch

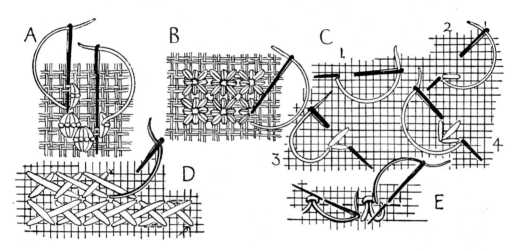

93   *Canvas stitches*

over three horizontal and one vertical thread of the canvas. In the next row work the small crosses directly at the base of the long ones, and return, fitting the long crosses in between those of the first row.

Rococo Stitch (*93a*): was universally popular for small articles and was usually worked on linen of open weave with silk. Stiff canvas is unsuitable. The material is completely covered, the pattern being formed by the change of colour. In the diagram the upper needle is shown in position for working the first stage, and the one on the right illustrates the formation of the small stitch which keeps the longer one in position. Groups of four stitches surround and make each hole; they should be worked in slanting rows.

B. Algerian Eye Stitch: can be worked to cover the entire ground, or each eye stitch can alternate with a square of material left plain; this is typical of the Algerian examples. Each of the eight stitches is worked over twice from the outer edge to make the centre hole; they should be slightly pulled in the working.

C. Two-sided Italian Cross: can be found utilised in several different ways. When worked upon canvas the texture produced has individuality. Each stage in the working of the back stitches of which it is composed can be followed from the diagram.

D. Long-armed Cross or Greek Stitch: commence by bringing the needle up at the point marked by the arrow, then take the thread over a square of four threads of the canvas, putting the needle through the material, bringing it out four threads back; this thread will then be taken obliquely forward over eight vertical and four horizontal canvas threads and brought out four threads back; this is then repeated and for the next row it is reversed as shown in the diagram. When worked by this method two parallel lines of back stitches are made on the reverse side.

E. Single Knotted Stitches: one or more of these stitches can be introduced into a piece of work to add interest. They are worked in the same way as a single Maltese stitch. It should be realised that, whereas in the diagram a single thread is illustrated, to be effective, a group of several strands would, in reality be used; when the loops are cut little tassels are formed. The needle is shown in position for the first stage of a second stitch, and the one on the right shows the completion.

STRETCHING

When a piece of canvas work is finished, it should be kept in the frame, but unrolled and straightened up if necessary. It should then be turned with the reverse side upwards, and thoroughly dampened with a sponge and water, and allowed to dry off, for about twenty-four hours.

If, however, it has been worked in the hand and is badly misshapen it is necessary to pin or nail the work out upon a wooden surface. Place the embroidery face upwards with one straight selvedge side to the edge of the board, stretch it and pin or nail out the second edge at right angles to the first. Do the same with the third and fourth sides; these will require more pulling to get the shape accurate. Fig. *94* shows this process. Thoroughly dampen with a sponge and water, being sure to dab rather than rub; the latter would cause the wool to fluff up. Allow to dry for about twenty-four hours.

The threads should be tested first, and if likely to run a cloth should be placed underneath; this absorbs the surplus dye and moisture.

Kneelers, worked in stitches mentioned in Chapter 13, by Sister Kathleen Snelus, Joan Nicholson (for the Needlework Development Scheme), Mary Lewis, and Harrie Nimmo

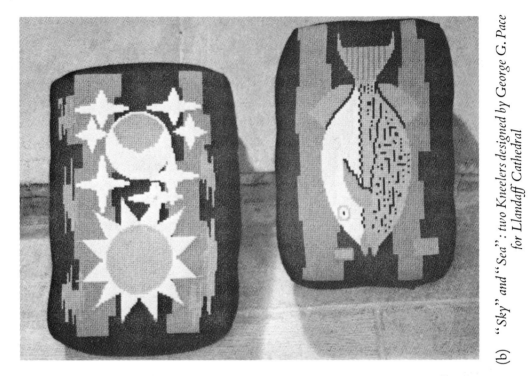

(b) *"Sky" and "Sea": two Kneelers designed by George G. Pace for Llandaff Cathedral*

(a) *Kneelers of differing designs and treatment, designed by Beryl Dean and carried out by John W. Brown, Mary Bates and Mildred Foord*

This process is used if stretching as a method is suitable, though for work on linen the embroidery is put face down. For light materials sometimes it is sufficient to pin out over damp clean blotting-paper or cloth.

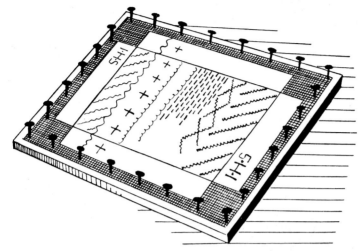

94   *Stretching the work*

MAKING-UP

To make-up a kneeler which has been worked in one piece, after stretching cut the canvas, leaving three-quarters of an inch turning all round. Stitch the corner seams, press flatly and turn out.

Having selected plastic foam sheeting, two inches thick for the filling, it can be cut to shape with large very sharp scissors or a knife. Alternative fillings would be layers of thick felt cut to shape, Latex foam rubber, rubberised hair or horse-hair. When the latter is used it is shaped about two inches longer than the actual measurement. When it is placed inside the covering it has to be pressed well down to fit right into the corners. (Supplement plastic or foam rubber with several thicknesses of felt.)

The next stage, after pressing it into the cover, is to keep it in place; this is done by bending the turnings of the gusset over, then (if the interior is firm) they can be laced from side to side with strong thread and long stitches, starting from the centre and working outwards. This is shown in fig. 95. After completing the long sides, the short ones are stitched in the same way. When plastic or foam rubber has been used the turnings should be catch-stitched or hemmed to the interior. With experience this part of the preparation may be omitted.

To neaten, cut a rectangle, the size of the kneeler, plus turnings, using the black upholsterer's linen. Press under the turnings, mark the centres, match up with the centres of the sides of the gusset, then pin in position and hem.

TO MAKE-UP A KNEELER WITH SEPARATE TOP AND SIDES

If the top and sides of the kneeler are separate, the gusset pieces should be joined and pressed, and the centre of each marked. The centres of the sides of the top should also be marked. Place the right side of the gusset to the right side of the top, match up the corresponding corners and centres, pin with the pins at right angles to the edge, tack and machine stitch or back stitch, press and turn out. Proceed as before. Many designs are enhanced by having two sides of one colour and the other two of another, and each side of the gusset can be of a different colour, when material is used; the method described would be applicable.

When a **piping** is to be inserted, cut the strips on the true cross of the material, measure for the length of the gusset, allowing turnings and stitch the join, putting the straight grain of both edges together before stitching; this makes a diagonal

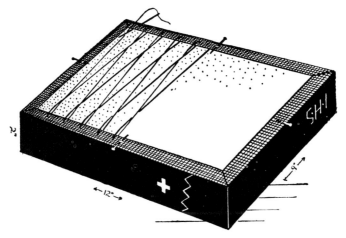

95 *Making-up a kneeler*

join. Press, and cut the piping cord to the same measurement. Cover the piping cord, tack and stitch. Pin the piping in position round the top, keeping it taut, snip the turning at the corners and tack. Experienced workers prefer not to do this preliminary fixing. Next, stitch, using a piping presser foot on the sewing machine. Then, putting the right side of the gusset to the right side of the top and matching up centres and corners, tack and stitch on the previous line of stitching. After pressing the cover is ready for the filling, lacing and lining. Should a button or little tassel be needed to keep the whole firm and in position, then it can be decorative if applicable. If the kneeler is in a plain colour the button and piping might introduce a contrasting note of colour. Usually the long stitch

218

which secures and makes the kneeler firm is only necessary when hair or felt has been used for the interior. If the kneeler is to hang on a hook, a curtain ring should be securely stitched on the back, making sure that it is attached through to the interior.

The same principles apply for making up the small flatter pad type of kneeler, without a gusset. When both sides are of material there is usually a piping which also makes a good finish when the top is embroidered and the under-side is of material. It is necessary to attach a ring for hanging this kind of kneeler.

CHAPTER FOURTEEN

MAKING-UP AND MOUNTING

With care and thought the finish can look really "professional" and yet show those touches of individuality which add interest. The function of each article usually determines the general form, and where slight variants are permissible the proportions and shapes should be considered in relation to the design as a whole and the finishings given special attention so that they become an integral part of the scheme. Thus avoiding the thoughtless and mechanical application of machine-made fringes, braids, galloons, gimps and cords.

There are usually several ways of approaching and doing most jobs; no two people set about making-up by exactly the same means and this is of no consequence if the ultimate result is flat, hangs well and is without puckers. The beginner may find the following suggestions helpful, until, with experience, she evolves her own method.

The directions for making up a banner will be given first and in detail because most of the basic processes are incorporated and the principles can be applied to the making-up of other goods.

A BANNER

The size is determined according to the purpose which it is to fulfil, and the shape of the banner should be carefully deliberated; the most straightforward form is a rectangle, with a basic proportion of two in width and not less than three and a half in length—or it can be longer, to allow for the foreshortening. The bottom edge can be finished as a curve or a point or given some other treatment such as a series of small points; if designed as a part of the whole this contributes visually, for instance a handsome handmade fringe or one knotted from the warp threads of hand-woven (or any loosely woven) material. Too often at the bottom of banners there is a collection of unrelated points, curves, angles, indentations and corners, further emphasised with fringes and tassels, mostly quite unnecessary, in poor taste and detracting from the main interest which should be centred in the design.

The Method

1. Press over the back of the embroidery with a warm (not hot) iron. Paste the ends on the reverse side of the work, taking care that no dampness penetrates to the front. (Press while in the frame.)

2. If preferred any orphreys can be attached whilst the work is still in the frame.

3. Tack round for the outside shape, and put a light tack (using sewing silk) down the centre and another across. (When, if absolutely necessary, due to puckering, the backing has to be cut it is taken away as near to the work as possible. This would be done before putting in the tacks.)

4. Select the material for interlining, dowlais (when procurable), deck-chair canvas, cotton duck, tailor's canvas, heavy holland or unbleached calico, and for weighty works, sail cloth. A good material should not need shrinking, but if it is decided to do so it is framed up for the operation.

5. Cut the interlining very slightly smaller (about $\frac{1}{12}$ inch) than the actual size of the banner. Mark centres, as for the front.

6. Remove the embroidery from the frame, cut leaving about 1-inch turnings all round. Spread out on a clean surface, face down. Put the interlining on the back, matching up the centres, pinning (using needles as they mark less) or keeping in place with lead weights. It can be tacked down the centre but with a thick interlining it is impracticable (96).

7. Turn over the edges on to the interlining, cutting diagonally across or snipping into corners (96a and b) (the treatment for convex and concave curves is also shown).

8. Arrange the corners, pin the edges, turn the work over, hold it up, look to see that the front is neither too tight nor too loose, remedy any defects. (With a large banner it is advisable to do the top first, then the sides and lastly the bottom.) Tack the turnings and catch-stitch or herringbone to the back of the interlining, in the order previously mentioned (96c). Lightly press the edges on the wrong side (but not for velvet).

9. Prepare the strips (called sleeves) which will form the loops. There should be an equal number, arranged at regular intervals leaving a space in the centre wide enough for the suspender fitment. An average width for the interlining might be 3 inches wide and 4 inches to 5 inches long plus 1 inch turnings at either end; these would be covered according to the method given, and lined with self or a contrasting colour. The loops are then firmly attached to the top edge (96d).

Some more ingenious method for fixing the banner to the crossbar of the pole may be thought out, bearing in mind the weight and the fact that it must hang slightly outwards.

If there is a fringe, it may be sewn on to the interlining or on the front, with the heading showing.

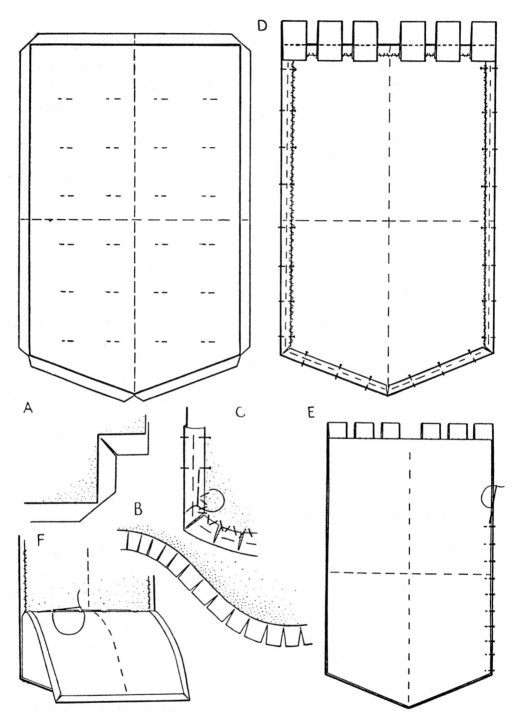

96   *Making-up a banner*

10. Cut the lining with ½-inch turnings. In theory these edges are turned in and tacked; a centre is marked down and across; it is pinned, then tacked in place, after matching up the centres, and the edges slip stitched. But in practice the actual size is marked, the centre is put to the centre of the interlining, and it is smoothed outwards from the centre. Then, starting at the top edge, it is turned in and pinned, the bottom being done last. It can be tacked a few inches in from the edge but it is not really advisable. Slip-stitch the edge (*96e*). (Top edge first, then downwards, pulling a little outwards from the centre. The edge of the lining may be a fraction inside the edge of the banner, especially if it is of a contrasting colour.) A loop should be sewn on the back and about two-thirds of the way down. This goes round the pole and prevents it hanging too far from it.

Suppose a lining, unsuitable because it is "floppy", has to be used for this or any other large article. Put the centre to the centre of the interlining, fold back the lining and loosely catch it with a matching thread, using a tiny stitch when penetrating the material or lining and a long one across the interlining (*96f*), commencing and finishing within about 3 inches of the edge; this is repeated at intervals of about 9 inches over the whole surface. The outside edges are then turned in and slip-stitched.

Much depends upon the choice of lining material: for a banner a stiff poult or even rayon taffeta can be used. Polonaise and glazed cotton are the conventional materials. But where it is to hang in folds it must be firm yet not stiff and never too thick. For softly draping chasubles or veils shantung or some fabric with "body" yet pliability is required.

THE CHASUBLE

When a medallion or other pieces of embroidery have been worked separately, and cut out and pasted on the back round the edges and in the centre, they should then be applied. But when there is in addition embroidery involved in the process, first attach the back of the chasuble to a backing (large enough to take the area) which has already been framed up. Usually the orphreys would have been stitched on or they may be put on in the frame. The medallion is fixed in place with pins stuck in vertically, then it is sewn with tiny stitches on the right side and larger on the back at intervals all over, working out from the centre; finally the edges are stitched, and the surrounding embroidery completed, before cutting away the surplus backing.

THE GOTHIC SHAPE

The diagram (*97*) is to scale, but these measurements and those of the following patterns must, to some extent, depend upon the height and preferences of the wearer. The dotted line down the centre represents the fold, and the back is slightly longer than the front, and the neck is shown with another dotted line. The bottom can be taken to a point or finished in a rounded curve.

First, cut out the shape of back and front, leaving about ¾-inch turnings.

(If there is to be an interlining it should be light and soft; it is cut without turnings and can be very lightly attached just to the back of the silk itself, invisibly.)

Nick and turn up the edges, catch-stitch, taking care not to stretch the parts on the cross (96b and c), then press on the wrong side.

The lining, which can be of a contrasting colour, should be soft, such as shantung silk; it is cut, leaving the usual turnings, the centre line is tacked in and the edges can be turned in and tacked at this stage, or later.

Then, with the front and the back of the chasuble lying face down, put the linings in position, matching up the centres, pinning and tacking, smooth out from the centre and pin at intervals, keeping the pins (or needles) all in the same direction; then put in a tack about 4 inches from the edge, and, if the lining turnings are prepared, the edge is put to the edge and slip-stitched. Some workers prefer to turn in the edge, section by section, so that it is just inside the edge of the chasuble, pinning with the pins pointing inwards, then slip-stitching. However this is done, if all the lines of stitches start and finish a few inches short of the shoulder seam a much neater edge will result.

Place the right sides of the front and back together, first folding back the linings, matching up the shoulder seam fitting lines, pin, tack and stitch the seams on the line, and press open. Then turn up and complete the hem, catch-stitching the remaining portions, and press.

Bring the back lining to lie over the seam and stitch it in self colour along the seam line. Fold in the remaining few inches of the outside edge and the shoulder turnings of the front lining; put the fold to the seam line, tack and hem, taking the stitches through the turnings but not allowing them to penetrate to the front of the chasuble.

When the material is suitable the chasuble can be unlined, then the edges can be neatened with a narrow hem, care being taken not to stretch the parts on the bias. Or the outside edges can be finished with a narrow shaped facing or faced with a cross-cut strip, or with a decorative braid (provided that it is sufficiently pliant).

Whether lined or unlined the measurement of a round neck must be large enough (about 22 to 25 inches proves satisfactory). It can be finished with a piping. To prepare this cut a strip of material on the true cross, 1 inch wide, fold

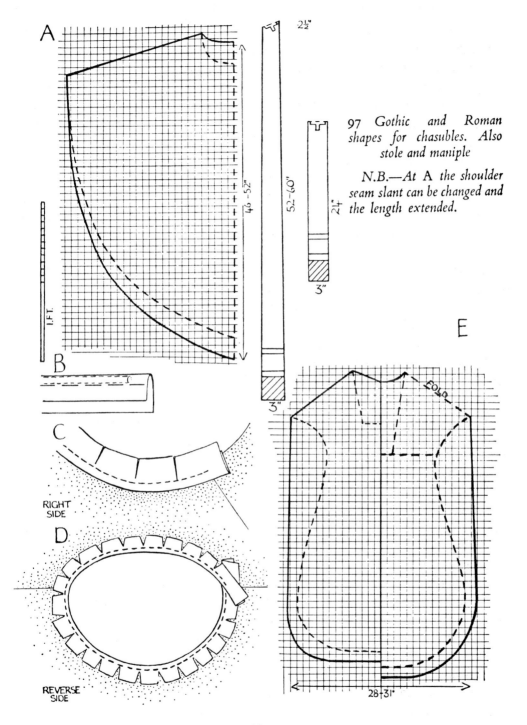

A

2½"

3"

97 *Gothic and Roman shapes for chasubles. Also stole and maniple*

N.B.—At A *the shoulder seam slant can be changed and the length extended.*

24"

3"

1. FT.

46"–52"

52"–60"

B

C

RIGHT SIDE

D

REVERSE SIDE

E

FOLD

28"–31"

this over the cord so that the edges do not come exactly together; do not let the cord go right to the end either at the beginning or finish, as this will make a neater join when overlapped—tack along (97b). Starting at one shoulder sew the piping on to the right side of the garment (97c), overlapping for the join. When complete, turn it over and press the turnings down on to the wrong side of the chasuble; the turnings of the neck should first be snipped (97d). Next snip round the neck turnings of the lining, fold them in and hem to the stitching of the piping.

Where the shape of the neck or the nature of the material calls for a facing this is cut to fit in self material and placed right sides together at the neck opening; it is then stitched on to the fitting line, the turnings are snipped, it is turned out and pressed. The outer edges are then invisibly caught down to the vestment and the lining hemmed into position.

When the seams of the chasuble are down the centre of the back and centre front the process of making-up is different, as the lining joins must be completed and it is necessary to catch the lining to the back of the fabric, as in fig 96f.

When completed the whole vestment can be lightly pressed on the wrong side with a warm (not hot) iron.

To make up a Roman-shape chasuble (now less often used), two alternatives are given in fig. 97e (no turnings allowed; the process is similar, but an inter-lining is used. Whether the seam is on the shoulder or at the base of the front neck opening, the lining would follow the same construction. The Spanish chasuble (99a) is made up in the same way. Turnings have not been included in the patterns.

The Stole

The stole should not be less than 100 inches; 9 feet is the usual length, as the ends should show below the chasuble. They can be from 3 up to 4½ inches wide at the bottom narrowing from 2 to 2½ inches at the neck, but the simple straight or only slightly widening ends are generally preferred to unnecessarily complicated and sometimes vulgar variants. All good traditional and modern Continental stoles are nearly the same width all the way down, 3 inches to 3½ inches from neck to end. The "spade-ended" stole is a piece of real Baroque decadence.

The general rules for making-up apply to the stole; a difference is introduced for the slight shaping at the neck. Although some stoles are made without this shaping.

After cutting away the backing from the embroidery, put the two embroidered sides together and make a seam at a slight slant, press open and embroider the cross over the centre seam.

Cut the interlining, allowing an extra 2 inches beyond the narrow ends. Spread the stole out, face down, put the interlining pieces in place working up from the bottom and allowing the narrow ends to overlap, pin and cut to shape, then lightly stitch.

The turnings should be nicked around the neck-line and snipped on the outer edge. The turnings of the stole after being turned over on to the interlining are catch-stitched—working upwards from the bottom (then if it does not set it is possible to adjust the seam of the interlining).

The lining is cut out and joined to fit (for a baptismal stole the white may be lined with purple). The seam is pressed open and after the usual preparation it is slip-stitched along the edges, starting each side at the centre back and working downwards. Where a contrasting colour is used the edge should be kept just inside. Any fringe or tassels can be attached to the interlining, being neatened by the lining, but if the heading is to show it is sewn on the right side. Often plain, well-proportioned ends lend added dignity.

THE MANIPLE

This matches the shape of the stole and is at least 3 feet long, usually 4 feet or more. The Roman rite requires one cross each on the stole and maniple (Church of England none). Three crosses is peculiar to the City of Rome itself (e.g. to a local rite).

The maniple is made up in the same way as the stole, but it is a straight strip, sometimes widening slightly towards the ends. A band of elastic may be sewn to the lining to keep it in position on the wrist; this is about 13 inches long. But the edges of the maniple must be caught together at the right point, i.e., to catch the width of the cassock sleeve plus the thickness of the alb and so hold it firmly in position on the arm.

In the pattern of a full chasuble (98a), which is to scale, no turnings are allowed, the seam is at the shoulder. For better draping extend the shoulder-line by 8 to 12 inches and re-shape hem curve.

Fig. 98b shows the cone shape, with modifications. Generous turnings and a 2-inch hem have been allowed. The seam is down the centre back and centre front. The line of the yoke represents the position for a Y-shape orphrey. A join in the material is taken across the bottom on the front.

Fig. 99b: a Gothic chasuble which drapes beautifully. There is a centre back and centre front seam, generous turnings and hem have been allowed. The position for a Y-shape orphrey is indicated. The material is joined diagonally across each side at the base of the front. (Here too the shoulder-line could be extended and hem curve re-shaped.)

A Spanish shape is also given.

It is possible to make a pattern for a full cone shape by cutting a complete half-circle with a radius equal to the centre back measurement. It is folded at the

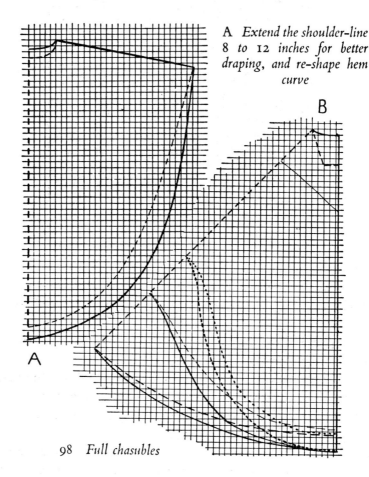

A *Extend the shoulder-line 8 to 12 inches for better draping, and re-shape hem curve*

B

98   *Full chasubles*

centre back, then the hem-line is shaped, making it shorter in the front and at the sides. The neck-line is shaped.

Usually two whole and two part widths of material are put together with a seam down the centre back. It is cut to shape then folded at the centre back so that the straight edges come together at the front, this is seamed, leaving the required measurement for the neck opening.

228

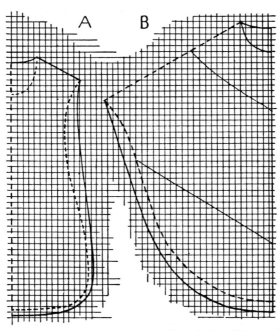

99   *Spanish and Gothic shaped chasubles*

THE DALMATIC AND TUNICLE

These garments are alike in shape; they are generally worn rather longer in the English Church, and when they form a set with a Gothic chasuble are more graceful in shape.

The making-up follows the general principles; the nature of the fabric determines whether a soft interlining is required or not.

If there is to be a fringe, either round the sleeves or down the open sides and along the hems, then this may be sewn on to the back or front and neatened with the edge of the lining. But many more recent dalmatics and tunicles gain in appearance by being left plain at the edges.

It will be seen from fig. *100* that the shape is simple; in this more traditional form the under-arm of the sleeve and the sides down to within 17 to 24 inches of the bottom can either be seamed together, laced with cord or even tied at intervals of 3 or 4 inches; when this is done the sleeve seams are left open underneath.

At the neck, which is curved or rectangular, the shoulder may be open for a few inches and laced through rings sewn to the edges. (Originally the shoulders were laced together.) The cords may terminate in rich tassels. Sometimes these cords are simply sewn on at random in the vicinity of the shoulders, which is pointless.

When not identical the tunicle may be a little shorter and rather less elaborate than the dalmatic, but with longer slightly tighter sleeves.

Fig. *100a* and *b* shows a dalmatic which accords well with the more contemporary approach towards simplicity of shape and decoration. B shows the slightly longer sleeve of the shorter tunic. There can, of course, be variations of

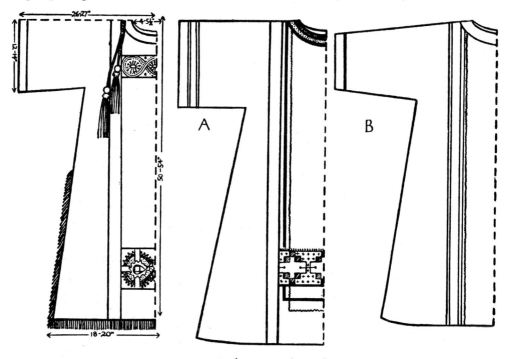

100   *Dalmatics and tunicle*

decoration which retain the characteristics associated with both, and in keeping with the chasuble.

Fig. *101* gives a basic shape for a dalmatic and tunicle, no turnings are allowed and the total length and length of sleeve should be adjusted to the wearer. The detail shows the inset triangular pieces which give shaping at the shoulders.

THE COPE

In practice, when drafting the pattern for a cope, the centre of the semicircle is taken 3 or 4 inches above the straight edge of the orphrey (*102a*). It is advisable to take the wearer's measurements from the shoulder for the front length required and down the centre back and to calculate the radius according to this.

Although the orphrey was sometimes as much as 8 inches wide, it is now usually narrower. Worked separately it would be attached to the cope whilst the latter is in the frame, or it may have to be specially mounted for the purpose.

Generally the backing would have to be cut away, as it is essential that a cope shall fall in good folds.

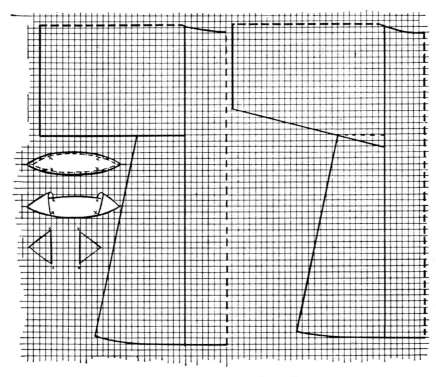

101   *Dalmatic and tunicle*

The addition of a soft interlining is seldom required, unless the fabric seems to need more substance, in which case the right choice of lining may compensate.

Cut the cope with ¾- to 1-inch turnings, nick about 1 inch apart, and turn up the edge, tack, being careful not to stretch it, then catch-stitch into the back of the material so that no stitches show at the front, lightly press.

Next, cut, interline, prepare and complete the morse; this is a strip 6 or 8 inches long and may be richly embroidered and jewelled. But its length must be adjusted so that the cope does not poke at the back of the neck, and the bottom fronts hang parallel and do not overlap. Sew on firmly three large eyes to the end, and slip-stitch the lining to neaten the back. Strongly stitch the completed morse to the edge of the orphrey on the wearer's right-hand side, about 12

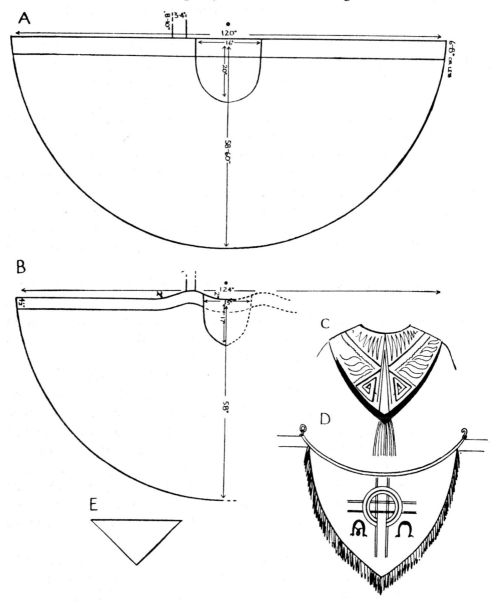

102   *The cope and hood*

inches down from the centre. (It is sometimes attached to the left-hand side.) Then sew three large hooks in the corresponding position on the left-hand side.

Make up the lining, pressing out the seams. It is most important to select a material which is firm and not "floppy" as this would drop. Mark in the centre, snip round the edges, which are sometimes turned up and tacked, whilst other workers prefer to leave this until later.

Stretch the cope out flatly face downwards, place the lining in position, matching up the centres, smooth it out, down and across, keeping to the grain of the material. With the aid of small lead weights and pins where necessary to keep it in place, tack down the centre and all round, about 3 or 4 inches in from the edge; if this has already been prepared it can be slip-stitched, keeping just within. Otherwise turn it up, so that the edge is slightly inside that of the cope, and pin with the points towards the centre, slip-stitch and lightly press.

The lining can be attached to the seams of the cope invisibly, with tiny stitches on the surface and through to the turning, with very long connecting ones between the two fabrics, or the cope may hang for a short time and when on the wearer the position for tie tacks may be marked, followed by little tie stitches, catching the lining and fabric together at the seams, but this is not generally necessary.

The hood can be shaped in various ways, and generally measures from about 17 to 22 inches long by about 15 to 18 inches wide, but these proportions require careful consideration in relation to the vestment as a whole. It is made up over an interlining and separate, being attached by strong press studs or loops and buttons to the upper edge of the orphrey, generally, in England.

The cope can become an ungainly vestment when it is too stiff and the unsatisfactory proportions are caused by an over-large hood and an orphrey which is too wide. There is a reaction towards the gracefully falling medieval cope (*102b*) with its slightly shaped and narrower orphrey (the measurements given are necessarily very approximate); the neck can be curved in to as much as 4 inches; with it can be worn the types of shaped hood given in fig. *102c* and *d*. The former, when it is set on to a straight orphrey, is shaped as at E or the draped cowl hood, which may be ornamented on the lining and have a tassel at the point. But this would have to be modelled on a stand and a pattern made from this *toile*.

There is also the cope with shaping at the shoulders; this would have to be fitted on the wearer and the shaping marked out before being stitched, then the orphrey attached over it. With this either the shaped or cowl hood would be worn. Sometimes the decoration is planned to suggest a hood, but not in any sense to be an imitation. With these more softly falling copes a handsome clasp frequently replaces the embroidered morse. When the material is suitable sometimes the cope is unlined, but where there is a lining it is shaped in the same way at the front or on the shoulders.

THE MITRE

Method I

The pattern for a simple shape can be prepared by constructing a rectangle, the long sides of which are determined by the head measurement of the individual wearer, and the shorter sides by the measurement of the height required; in this instance the points are right angles, and the mitre might be made up without stiffening (if this were required) and all in one piece (*103a*). The rectangle would be divided in half and half again. From the centre front draw a line at an angle of 45°, extend a similar line from the centre back point, the two will meet at point O which should be about 3 or 4 inches up from the head-line, and repeat for the other side.

Mark this out on the material, apply any orphreys and complete decoration but leave the centre back orphrey attached on one side only. Cut out, leaving ¾-inch turnings all round the rectangle, and make a little slit of ⅓ inch at points O. Join up the centre back seam, and sew the orphrey over it. Then turn the mitre on to its wrong side and match up balance—mark X with the similar mark on the other side and then the centre front to the centre back, snip the turnings. Stitch along from X to X and press the seams open. Fold up the turnings at the head-line and catch-stitch, not allowing the stitches to penetrate right through. Turn the mitre out to the right side again.

Make up the two lappets or infulae and attach about 1 inch either side of the centre back. Then make the lining just a fraction smaller and slip-stitch to the lower edge and put a few tiny stitches through from the points to keep it in place.

Putting point to point, fold the mitre flat and mark the edges of the folds with colour or gold.

Method II

The pattern is made in the same way, but the height may be increased, though it must be remembered that a mitre appears much higher when worn than it does in the hand. Therefore the angle will be more acute and the line to O increased. The difference is in the fact that this is cut out leaving turnings (*103b*) and a separate diamond shape cut with sides equalling the measurement from the point to O. When cutting in material turnings should be added, and it may be of a contrasting colour. This part is not interlined but it is completed with a lining.

234

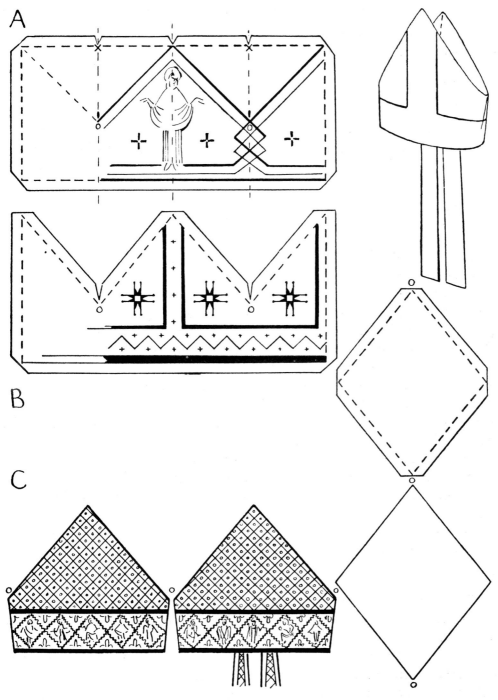

103 *The mitre*

235

Round the mitre there may be a band of stiffening about 4 inches wide, of leather, buckram, sparterie or tailor's canvas or the whole may be interlined. This would be put in after completing the centre back join. The turnings would be finished in the usual way, the lappets sewn in place and lining attached.

Next match up the balance marks O on the mitre and the diamond-shaped piece, likewise the points, and overcast the edges together. Neaten by some suitable means.

Method III

The pattern is made and two pieces cut out, a front and a back, also a diamond-shaped gusset (*103c*) (the seams are at the sides). When a taller or more bulbous mitre is required the shape should be altered accordingly and the gusset adjusted to fit. Though still in common use this shape is unbecoming to the wearer, and is rather decadent.

Two pieces of interlining are cut to the exact size, the turnings and lining of each being finished as before, the lappets attached, also the diamond shape completed. Put the sides of the front and back together and oversew, and matching points O to O stitch the diamond into place, neatening the edges of the mitre either in colour or gold.

THE BURSE

Method I

Have four 9-inch squares of cardboard cut, or they can be purchased already prepared. (The two for the lining may be thinner.) Mark the centres each way.

1. Tack round the front and back squares on the fabric, cut leaving about 1-inch turnings except on one side of the back where a 2-inch turning should be left. Do not cut away the backing from the embroidery, as it helps to lessen the rub upon the material at the edges.

2. Place the embroidery face down, put the board in position, matching up the centres, then bend over the edge of the fabric, cut across for the corners and pin all round, top and bottom first then the sides. Lace across the back with strong thread downwards first then across (*104a*). Sticking is quicker but a poor substitute, as it is not possible to get the material really taut.

3. The two squares for the lining are covered in the same way, using washed white linen.

4. These can be oversewn along one edge. But a better hinge is produced by making a narrow fold of linen less than $\frac{1}{4}$ inch wide and 9 inches long and

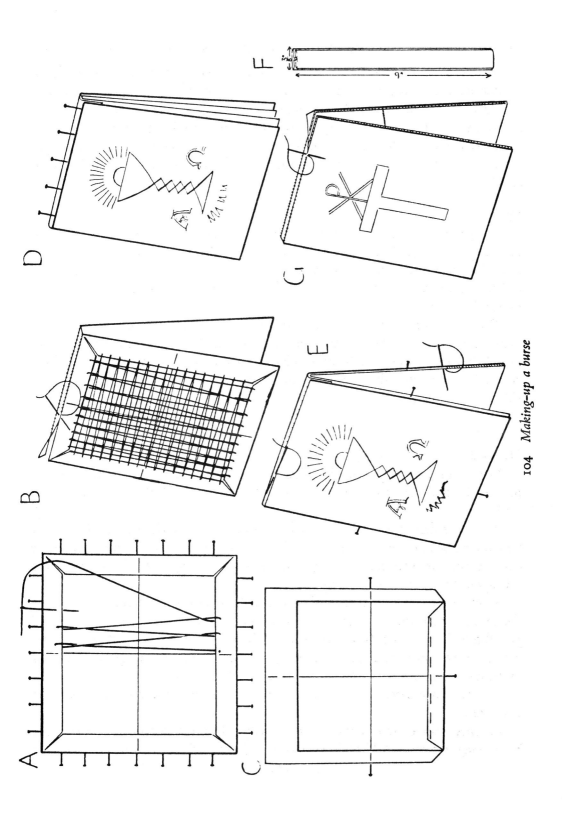

104 *Making-up a burse*

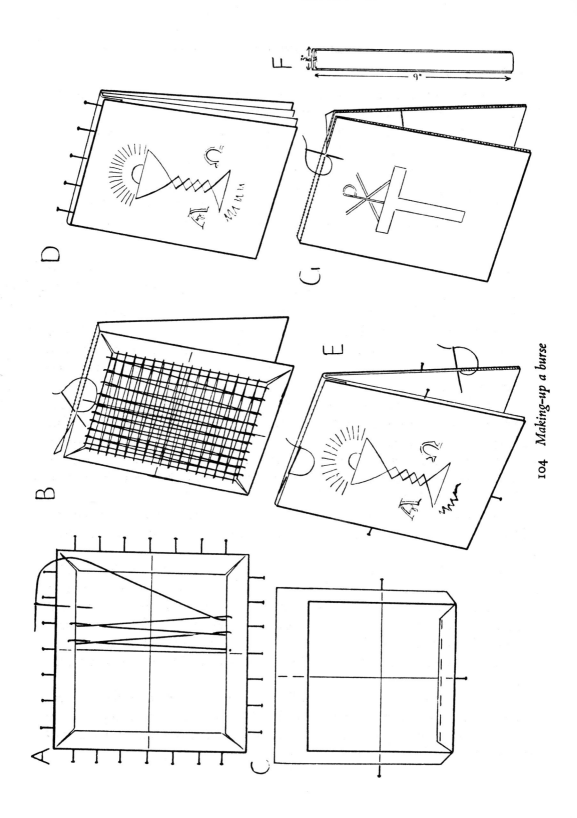

The Chalice Veil

This is a square of from 20 to 24 inches or even 30 inches. But in the English Church it is generally the smaller measurement.

Any backing should be cut away close to the embroidery. If there is an interlining it is very thin and soft, such as butter muslin.

The edges are turned over and very lightly catch-stitched so that no stitching will come through to the front and the corners are arranged in the usual way.

As the chalice veil hangs in soft folds the lining must not be stiff. For some softer linings it may be found necessary to attach it as shown in fig. *96f* before slip-stitching it round the edge.

The Frontal

The dimensions depend upon the height and width of the altar.

Almost invariably the backing is retained, unless the background fabric is badly puckered, and if the frontal has been worked in sections these are joined together, and the seams pressed open, and any lines of embroidery which cross the seams are completed. Then put a tack down the centre, and cut leaving $\frac{3}{4}$-inch turnings.

If a wide sailcloth can be obtained, this may obviate the necessity for joins. Other suitable materials for the interlining are cotton duck and deck-chair canvas; if they are used with the grain running across then the long narrow strip to be joined is put at the bottom. Any creases must be removed, and the interlining cut to the exact size, unless there is to be a 2-inch hem at the bottom which should be allowed for. Mark the centre.

Spread the frontal, face down, on a clean surface, put the interlining in place, matching up the centre line; if it is too stiff to tack down the centre and at intervals in lines, then rely upon small lead weights.

Turn over the edges (where the super-frontal is to be attached the top edge is cut without a turning and is stitched to the interlining). Some workers prefer to start stitching at the top and work downwards, pinning the bottom in place, and holding the frontal up (if this is possible) to see that it is flat before catch-stitching the bottom edge. Others, however, work from the bottom upwards.

There are several ways in which the frontal may be kept in position on the altar.

1. It can be attached to a length of linen which goes right over the altar and hangs down behind, at the bottom of which there is a hem wide enough to take the heavy rod which is put through to weight it. In this way there is less risk of uneven hanging, dropping or crookedness.

2. Rings can be sewn along the top, to correspond with hooks placed at similar intervals beneath the edge of the altar (with this method some slight adjustment may have to be made to the overall measurement of the frontal when calculating the size).

3. There are practical methods for hanging the frontal, such as that consisting of a lightweight metal bar attached to the front edge of the altar table; brass clips are sewn to the frontals and these clip over the bar. But it does not seem reverent to drive hooks, etc., into or have fixtures attached to the altar.

4. The frontal can be mounted upon a wooden stretcher, to which it is nailed all round. This is slotted in beneath the altar. It is a way not now often used.

THE SUPER-FRONTAL OR FRONTLET

This is made up in the usual way and is from 5 to 7 inches deep.

In some instances it is attached to the top of the frontal, but this is impracticable when it is desirable to use one frontlet with several frontals.

Otherwise it is sewn to a linen cloth which fits over the top of the altar; the advantage of this lies in the fact that it can stay in position when the frontal is changed (if the method of hanging makes this possible) according to the season, and so saves stripping the altar each time.

Both the super-frontal and frontal can be attached to a lathe.

THE LAUDIAN OR THROW-OVER FRONTAL

When this is a simple rectangle, the dimensions will be calculated from the size of the altar top, with the depth of the overhang added all round, plus the allowance for a hem.

Whether the seams in the fabric run parallel with the length or across the width must depend upon the fabric, and if it has a pattern with an up and down or not. Bearing in mind that where there is a design to match up more material is needed. The corners may be slightly rounded if required. There is seldom a lining or interlining. If there is some large embroidered symbol or monogram it is usually worked on linen and applied. The method of turning up the hem varies with the fabric; for a thick one herringbone-stitch, taking each stitch into the back only and not right through to the front of the material. Or another method is to cut and stitch the fabric to fit the altar, but having the two front corner seams open; into these, two squares of fabric are inset, the sides measuring the height of the altar. The other two sides of each are turned up as a part of the hem.

(a) *Red Choir Banner, embroidered by Sister M. Theodata, Über Saulgau, Germany*

(b) *Cross for a Stole-end (the Needlework Development Scheme)*

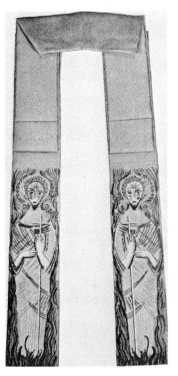

(c) (left) *Red Stole, designed by Susan Riley*

(d) *Stole, white embroidered in silver with a little gold, by Ethel M. Stevens*

Altar Frontal, embroidered by Sister M. Regina, Kloster St. Ursula, Augsburg

Alternatively, there may be a rectangle of material cut to fit the top of the altar, plus turnings. The sides may be composed of a long strip, measuring that of the four sides with the amount required for the fullness at the corners added; the selvedge grain should run down, therefore several widths have to be joined, care being taken to avoid a join being placed in the centre of the front. The fullness would extend from the corner for about 2 feet or more on the long side and less on the shorter (105a). To make up, mark the centres of the sides of the rectangle, and halve and quarter the long strip, run in a gathering thread at each corner, commencing at the required distance from the centre mark, and draw each up to fit. Put the right sides of the fabric together and stitch round. Neither A nor B is advocated.

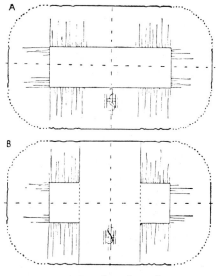

105   *Laudian frontals*

When one width of fabric runs right across from back to front, the pieces to be joined on either side to form the rectangle are joined before the sides are sewn on (105b). This method is preferred when the embroidery is worked directly on to the material. By whichever method the Laudian is constructed it may need to be weighted.

AUMBRY VEIL

There can be no given measurements, but this veil must be detachable; if the method of attaching is through a slot, a hem is required or rings can be sewn to the top edge, the lining should be soft and thin. It should be remembered that aumbries are generally on the north wall of the sanctuary and that the curtain is therefore seen by the congregation from the side and not from the front. In view of the smallness of the curtain itself care must be taken to find a method of hanging which is not clumsy as seen from this angle.

TABERNACLE VEIL

The actual measurements and construction must depend upon each individual tabernacle, as the fitting will vary according to the shape. The veil may be made to cover the tabernacle completely, the top as well as the sides, with the detachable top going above it. This should be graceful, avoiding any stiffness, with a division in the centre. Or the curtains, which should be full enough to hang well, are attached so that the detachable top fits over, and the valance conceals the method of hanging (106a and b). The material selected should be supple and not too thick and should be cut sufficiently full; it may even measure twice the perimeter. At the bottom there may be some form of decorative finish which should not obstruct the fall of the veil.

An alternative method is to cut the veil circular, with a division down the centre (106c). Here the hem should be prepared with care or it will stretch; a narrow cross-cut facing applied and invisibly hemmed up may give a better result; anyway the edge must first be nicked round. There can be some narrow, very flexible finish to the edge; the hole at the top may be treated in the same way. As far as the making-up is concerned, for this shape a more satisfactory result would be achieved by cutting a similarly shaped lining in really very soft thin material such as jap silk, and putting the right sides together, stitching from the centre back round and up the opening to the point and down and round, but instead of joining the stitching, leave a few inches open. Nick round and turn the whole thing out through the space left in the stitching; after tacking round, slip-stitch the open space at the hem and press, then finish the top.

THE VEILS OF CIBORIUM AND MONSTRANCE

The ciborium is covered with a white veil, which may be cut circular with a hole at the top; the material should be supple and generally unlined (106d). It is with hesitancy that the method of lining with very thin soft fabric, suggested for the tabernacle, be employed for this veil too, as it recalls examples made of satin embroidered and stiffly lined and standing out like a circular skirt! But this is not the result when the right materials are used. The hole at the top should be finished in the same way as the hem, avoiding little loops which may become entangled with the arms of the cross. A stiff cover, made in four shaped sections and elaborately decorated, should be avoided.

The monstrance veil measures in length nearly twice the height of the monstrance, and is a strip of soft white silk without lining and with hemmed edges (106e).

THE HUMERAL VEIL

The measurements are about 3 yards long by 24 to 30 inches wide; it is usually unlined, and as it must drape well, any treatment of the edges which will not

244

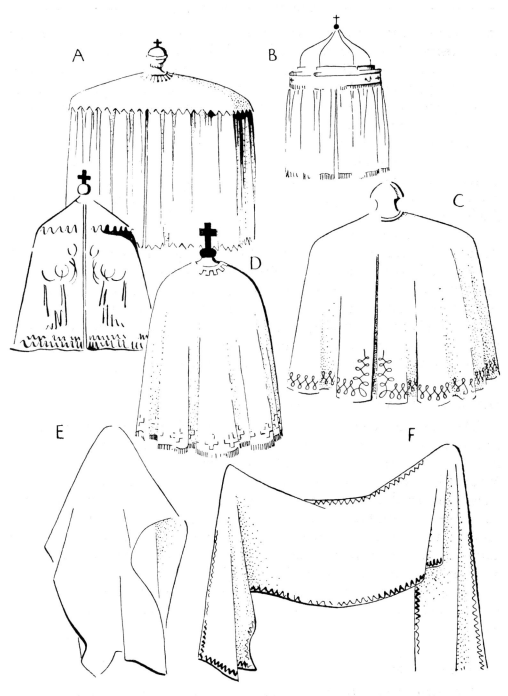

106   *Veils*

prevent the draping can be used (*106f*). It can be fastened with a little chain and hook to keep it in place during wear.

FUNERAL PALL

This is usually a rectangle of material, with a soft interlining and also lined. The corners may be rounded, or a square cut away from each as in the earlier examples. Many heavy materials are suitable, but unrelieved black is seldom used. A thick cord can be sewn on, and if a fringe is added its depth is subtracted from the overall measurements—an average coffin is about 6 feet by 19 inches, depth 15 inches. The size of the pall varies according to its purpose, but seldom exceeds 4 yards by 3 yards.

ALTAR CUSHION AND MISSAL STAND COVER

When a cushion is used instead of a book-rest, it usually has a board inside to stiffen it for carrying the Book of the Gospels; this is padded above and to a lesser extent underneath; horsehair and feathers or kapok are generally used. The cushion is usually rectangular and made of velvet or silk and can have a finishing cord and tassels. If an embroidered cross is added it should not be of a metal thread as this would scratch the binding.

There is no specific method of making up the missal stand cover as the size must depend upon that of the stand; the material, which may be slightly stiffened, should be soft in texture and it may have some means whereby it can be clipped to the stand, such as pieces of braid across the corners. A metal or wood missal stand is a later substitute for the much more traditional and now often reintroduced altar cushion.

ALMS BAGS

These are usually made in the form of a bag with an extended top, by which they are held. The material must be strong and a darker colour is more practical, and as they need to be renewed fairly frequently, very elaborate embroidery is unsuitable. When planning the shape it is more interesting to think out something a little unusual yet suited to its purpose. There are wooden and metal handles procurable to which the bag may be attached, but these are usually very dull in design.

The general rules for making up apply, except that:

1. Two pieces of silk fabric are cut (plus turnings) for the back part and one of interlining, which is cut very slightly smaller than the actual size (*107a*).

2. The pocket part (with the embroidery) may be cut a little wider across the pocket mouth. There is an interlining and a lining which may be a darker-

coloured sateen or chamois leather. Sometimes the inside back piece is lined for part of the way up with chamois also. This may be sewn in such a way that it is easily removed for washing, after which it is replaced.

The edges of the outside of the back piece are turned over the interlining and catch-stitched down, and the edges of the inside back piece snipped and

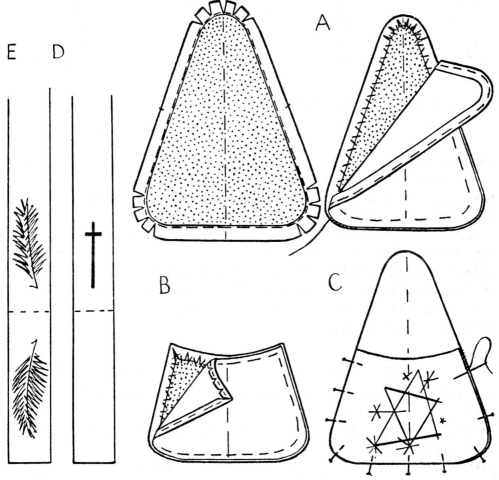

107 *Making-up an alms bag*

turned in and lightly pressed, then matching up the centre lines the edges are caught together with oversewing or slip-stitching.

The front pocket piece is finished in the same way, but here the lining is hemmed in and its edge is just inside that of the front (*107b*).

247

Matching up the centre of the back portion and that of the front pocket piece, pin round the edge and oversew (*107c*). Some form of neatening round the edge is inevitable; a cord is too clumsy and ordinary; a bunch of threads couched or some very narrow braid or a fine metal or handmade cord can be used. To sew a cord on, tuck the end down inside at the side of the pocket, stitch it on all round, tucking it in again for the finish, securing it with stitches. When the cord is to be taken across the top of the pocket piece too, do this first, then go round the base of the bag and up and around the top, tucking in the end and securing it.

When the bag is to be attached to any type of mount, the two pieces are completed separately, then oversewn together to form the bag, the sides being left open for a short distance down to allow the wooden handles to be inserted. In other forms of alms bag, after making-up eyelets are worked and it is attached by lacing.

DESK HANGINGS

Pulpit and reading-desk falls are made to harmonise in colour and design with the frontal. These hangings are often made much too small; a long narrow hanging can look dignified and rich. The completed embroidery is made up in the same way as a banner and mounted to the required size; this is judged in relation to the width, as the covered boards to which it is to be attached must completely cover the top of the desk or book-rest; they are kept in position by a wide elastic sewn at each side. There are other devices with which the hangings can be attached.

BOOK-MARKERS

Ribbon is usually used, but it must be soft, to avoid damaging the leaves; the finished length is determined by the dimensions of the binding, plus a projection at the top and more at the bottom. It is cut to allow a length sufficient to be turned over and hemmed in place to neaten the back of the embroidery (*107d*). This decoration should not extend above the bottom of the page and when it is to be worked on both sides is arranged as in fig. *107e*. Additional weight may be added by a tassel or fringe. When one length of ribbon is used and bent over at the top, care must be taken that the embroidery for both ends is not on the same side of the material. Near the top, the markers must be sewn to or round a little roll of material or a little piece of stick covered. This acts as a stop and keeps it in position. Alternatively little attachments can be procured to which the markers may be sewn.

BOOKBINDINGS

In the past, but less frequently now, bindings for books have been embroidered; there are several most interesting examples in the British Museum. Gold threads, rough purl, small jewels and pearls have been used in various ways. A binding has to withstand very hard wear and this determines the materials and type of embroidery employed. It is recommended that the book should first be sewn by the binder, and prepared so that the exact size is known before the design is started. When the embroidery has been finished the actual binding must be undertaken by one who understands the nature of embroidery and so prevents it being flattened in the process of binding.

Each aspect has been covered in this introduction to a vast subject: design, materials, embroidery and making-up of furnishings and vestments, from the cope to bookbindings. May it have helped towards the production of creative embroideries for the Church, especially for the younger people, whose instruction in design at school will have laid a foundation from which to develop this approach, giving them the courage to be true to the age in which they live. We may be stimulated to think afresh, allowing tradition to enrich rather than to restrict. The need to respect the tenets of the Church leads to individual decisions as to the extent to which the limitations of the craft shall influence the intention. To some only complete freedom will enable them to give of their very best, whilst there will always be others who welcome a release from the responsibility of independent thought and action; their contribution of patient skilled work is also required.

What is important to one generation on being realised, becomes stale and another aspect receives perhaps undue emphasis. At present the need is for an increasingly vital approach through design; we have a heritage of excellent craftsmanship. When a balance has been struck, along which lines will embroidery, as a minor sacred art, develop in the future?

BIBLIOGRAPHY

Anson, Peter F., *Churches, their Plan and Furnishing*, Bruce Publishing Co., *c.* 1928.

Addleshaw, G. W. O., and Etchells, Frederick, *The Architectural Setting of Anglican Worship*, Faber & Faber Ltd., 1950.

Book of Scripts, King Penguin Books Ltd., 1952.

Caudwell, Irene, *The Care of God's House*, Faith Press Ltd., 1943.

Christie, A. H., *English Medieval Embroidery*, Oxford University Press, 1938.

Dean, Beryl, *Church Needlework*, B. T. Batsford Ltd., 1961.

Dearmer, Percy, *Linen Ornaments of the Church*, A. R. Mowbray & Co. Ltd., 1950.

★De Farcy, Louis, *La Broderie du XIe Siècle jusqu' à Nos Jours*, 1890.

Henze, Anton, and Filthaut, Theodor, *Contemporary Church Art,*, Sheed and Ward, New York, 1956.

★Hope, St. John, *Grammar of English Heraldry*, Cambridge University Press, 1913.

★Hope, St. John, *Heraldry for Craftsmen and Designers*, Sir Isaac Pitman & Sons., *c.* 1930.

Jenkins, Graham, *The Making of Church Vestments*, Challoner Publications, 1957.

★Kendrick, A. F., *English Needlework*, A. & C. Black Ltd., *c.* 1932.

★Kendrick, A. F., *English Embroidery*, George Newnes, 1904.

Milburn, R. L. P., *Saints and Their Emblems in English Churches*, Blackwell Ltd., 1957.

★Millet, Gabriel, *Broderies Religieuses de Style Byzantin* , Presses Universitaires de France, 1947.

Molesworth, H. D., *Sculpture in England, Medieval*, The British Council, Longmans Green & Co. Ltd., 1951.

★Molesworth, H. D., *Sculpture in England, Renaissance to Early XIX Century*, The British Council, Longmans Green & Co. Ltd., 1951.

Norris, Herbert, *Church Vestments, Origin and Development*, J. M. Dent & Sons Ltd., 1949.

O'Connell, J., *Church Building and Furnishing, The Church's Way*, Burns, Oates & Washbourne Ltd., 1956.

Roeder, Helen, *Saints and Their Attributes*, Longmans Green & Co. Ltd., 1955.

★Roulin, E. A., *Vestments and Vesture*, The Newman Press, Westminster, Maryland.

★Symonds, Mary, and Preece, Louisa, *Needlework through the Ages*, Hodder and Stoughton, 1928.

Victoria and Albert Museum, *Early Christian and Byzantine Art*, H.M.S.O., 1951.

Victoria and Albert Museum, *Early Medieval Art in the North*, H.M.S.O., 1950.

Victoria and Albert Museum, *Romanesque Art*, H.M.S.O., 1951.

Victoria and Albert Museum, *Fifty Masterpieces of Textiles*, H.M.S.O., 1957.

Wagner, Anthony, *Heraldry in England*, King Penguin, Penguin Books Ltd., 1953.

★Warner, Ed., *Facsimile of Saint Mary's Psalter*, 1912.

White, T. H. *The Book of Beasts*, Jonathan Cape Ltd., 1955.

Journals

   L'Art d'Église, L'Abbaye de Sainte André, Bruges, Belgium (quarterly).

   Liturgical Arts, The Liturgical Art Society Inc., New York, U.S.A. (quarterly).

★ Now out of print.

INDEX

The numerals set in *italic type* denote the *figure numbers* of the line illustrations in the text; those in **bold type** denote the **plate numbers** of the photographic illustrations